The Church
and the
Racial Divide

The Church
and the
Racial Divide

Reflections of an
African American
Catholic Bishop

BISHOP EDWARD K. BRAXTON

ORBIS BOOKS
Maryknoll, New York 10545

ORBIS BOOKS
Maryknoll, New York 10545

Fathers and Brothers
ARYKNOLL™

Founded in 1970, Orbis Books endeavors to publish works that enlighten the mind, nourish the spirit, and challenge the conscience. The publishing arm of the Maryknoll Fathers and Brothers, Orbis seeks to explore the global dimensions of the Christian faith and mission, to invite dialogue with diverse cultures and religious traditions, and to serve the cause of reconciliation and peace. The books published reflect the views of their authors and do not represent the official position of the Maryknoll Society. To learn more about Maryknoll and Orbis Books, please visit our website at www.orbisbooks.com.

Library of Congress Cataloging-in-Publication Data

Names: Braxton, Edward K, author.
Title: The church and the racial divide : reflections of an African American
    Catholic Bishop / Bishop Edward K Braxton.
Description: Maryknoll, NY : Orbis Books, [2021] | Includes bibliographical
    references and index. | Summary: "Reflections from an African American
    Catholic Bishop on the racial divide in the United States"—Provided by
    publisher.
Identifiers: LCCN 2020036336 (print) | LCCN 2020036337 (ebook) | ISBN
    9781626984066 (trade paperback) | ISBN 9781608338702 (epub)
Subjects: LCSH: African American Catholics. | Race relations—Religious
    aspects—Catholic Church. | Racism—Religious aspects—Catholic Church.
Classification: LCC BX1407.N4 B73 2021 (print) | LCC BX1407.N4 (ebook) |
    DDC 261.8/3208996073—dc23
LC record available at https://lccn.loc.gov/2020036336
LC ebook record available at https://lccn.loc.gov/2020036337

In Memory of my beloved parents,
Evelyn Kathryn Gardner Braxton
(1920–2008)
and
Cullen Lawrence Braxton Sr.
(1915–1995)
who were the greatest influence for all that is good in my life.

And dedicated to
African American Catholics, who, remarkably, have remained steadfast
in their commitment to the Catholic Church, even though the racial divide
continues to manifest itself within the church in many ways to this day.

And to Congressman John Robert Lewis (1940–2020),
the conscience of the United States Congress
and the prophetic maker of "good trouble"
for the good of the Beloved Community.

"God is not God the way we would be God, if we were God."

Contents

Are We Finally Woke?

Not everything that is faced can be changed, but nothing can be changed until it is faced.

—James Baldwin

Two hundred fifty years of slavery. Ninety years of Jim Crow. Sixty years of separate but equal. Thirty-five years of racist housing policy. Until we reckon with our compounding moral debts, America will never be whole.

—Ta-Nehisi Coates

The arc of the moral universe is long, but it bends towards justice.

—The Reverend Dr. Martin Luther King Jr.

I can't breathe! I can't breathe! Mama! Mama!

—George Floyd

I am writing this preface on June 19, 2020, or, more to the point, on Juneteenth, 155 years after the enslaved free human beings[1] in Texas learned that President Abraham Lincoln had

---

[1] I avoid the use of the words "slave" or "slaves" in my writings. Instead, I speak of "enslaved free human beings." The substantive "slaves" can be read to imply that there is a group of human beings in the world, namely slaves, who can be bought, sold, and owned. Obviously, this is not true. As a Catholic priest and theologian, I hold firmly to the position that, from the perspective of sound philosophy, anthropology,

signed the Emancipation Proclamation two and a half years earlier. I am writing this Preface on the day that the president of the United States was scheduled to have a huge reelection rally, where he expected at least 20,000 people (and thousands more in an overflow area) in Tulsa, Oklahoma, ninety-nine years after the Tulsa Race Massacre in the Greenwood District, during which over 300 African American people were murdered. As I write, I am wondering, are we finally "woke"?

When I wrote the pastoral letter *The Racial Divide in the United States* in 2015, the expression "Black Lives Matter" was widely perceived as the radical slogan of a small, fringe, in-your-face extremist movement, which many, if not most, Americans looked upon with anxiety and suspicion, associating the phrase with mob violence and militant extremist ideologies. I now write five years later, in the summer of 2020, a month after the murder of Mr. George Floyd (arrested for attempting to use a counterfeit $20 bill) in Minneapolis, Minnesota. Former police officer Derek Chauvin ended Mr. Floyd's life on Memorial Day, May 25. Mr. Chauvin casually knelt on George's neck for 8 minutes 46 seconds with his hands in his pockets, while George's hands were cuffed behind him. Mr. Floyd, who had been arrested a number of times, may have been intoxicated, but his family and friends described him as "a Christian, a good man, who loved to help people." Many Americans still feel uncomfortable with and threatened by the phrase "Black Lives Matter," but surveys indicate that more and more find the expression acceptable. The expression is ever in the news, analyzed in serious journals, and shouted at peaceful demonstrations by people of different races, ages, religions, and economic, political, and social backgrounds. Heads of corporate

---

and authentic Catholic theology, no one can "own" another human being despite the political, social, and economic reality of human bondage. In my view, they were free human beings who, even when "enslaved" by others, remained ontologically free. This is also true of victims of human trafficking in our own day. (The word "slave" is derived from "Slav." In the late Middle Ages, Slavic people were forced into labor so often that they gave their name to human bondage. See also Old French *sclave*, from Medieval Latin *sclāvus*.)

America have joined athletes, entertainers, and some political and religious leaders in affirming boldly in newspaper ads and television announcements that they not only believe that Black Lives Matter but, they say, they intend to put their financial resources and their considerable influence behind their new affirmation.

The death of Mr. Floyd, 46, was not the first time an African American man or woman died in a questionable altercation with a white representative of law enforcement. It was simply the next incident in a painfully long list. But precisely because the list is so long, because the horrific details of the killing were made visible for all to see through widespread social media, because so many people staying home due to the coronavirus pandemic had time to talk and think about what they had seen and heard, this single death triggered a tsunami reaction not only in this country but also worldwide. Huge throngs of people protested in cities around the country and beyond shouting, "Black Lives Matter!," "No Justice, No Peace!," "Say His Name, George Floyd!," "Stop Killing Us!," and "Defund the Police!" In Washington, DC, a section of 16th Street leading to the White House was renamed Black Lives Matter Plaza and the words were painted on the street in huge yellow letters. Demands for the arrest and charging of all four police officers involved in the death of Mr. Floyd were eventually met. His funeral services, meanwhile, were must-see television events for millions of Americans. The phrase "Get your knee off our necks!" became a metaphor for centuries of racial oppression, police brutality, and systemic racism.

Nonviolent protests, which many Americans seemed to think were understandable, became, in some cases, violent and destructive social upheavals. People were killed. Buildings and police cars were burned, and shops were vandalized and plundered. In some cases, these stores were the livelihoods of poor People of Color. Terms like "rioters" and "looters" were frequently used. While most commentators acknowledged that the destruction was the work of a few (perhaps organized outsiders bent on destruction and turning the tide of public opinion against the peaceful demonstrators), the damage was done. The demand for "law and order" became the primary message from the White House. Other voices argued that African Americans were taking a posture of "victimhood" expecting others, including the government, to solve problems that they should solve themselves.

"Looters," "looting," and "loot" are oddly used words. In today's context, "looters" are often presumed to be African Americans, even though white people also steal during social disturbances. "Loot" usually refers to the "physical things" stolen during social unrest. However, the word has a far deeper connotation, largely ignored today. The United States was established by "looting." The lands of Indigenous people were "looted," along with the labors of African people brought here during the Middle Passage. The bodies of enslaved free human beings (especially the women taken and cruelly used and abused by their so-called masters) and the wealth they produced on plantations were "looted." During the race massacres of 1917 (East St. Louis, Illinois), 1921 (Tulsa, Oklahoma), and 1923 (Rosewood, Florida), African American people were murdered by white people, who, with little objection from the police, burned and "looted" the homes of many.

Civil rights advocates and some in the media regularly remind the country and the world of a near endless litany of deaths of African Americans who, like George Floyd, lost their lives in conflicts with white police officers or civilians.

- Eric Garner, 44, died July 17, 2014, in Staten Island, NY, when former New York policeman Daniel Pantaleo used a banned chokehold while arresting him for selling unlicensed cigarettes. He cried out eleven times, "I can't breathe." Mr. Garner's death was ruled a homicide. The grand jury did not indict the officer. On June 8, 2020, the New York State Assembly passed the Eric Garner Anti-Chokehold Act.
- Laquan McDonald, 17, was shot to death in Chicago by former Chicago police officer Jason Van Dyke on October 20, 2014. At first, police said Mr. McDonald refused to drop his knife and was walking and acting erratically. The police reports ruled the shooting justified and the officer was not

charged in the fatal shooting. Thirteen months later, the police were ordered by the courts to release a dashcam video of the shooting. The video showed Mr. McDonald being shot as he walked away from the police. Officer Van Dyke was charged with first-degree murder and later found guilty of second-degree murder.

- Freddie Gray, 25, who died on April 19, 2015, was arrested April 12, 2015, by the Baltimore Police Department. He was charged with possessing a knife. Mr. Gray became comatose after being tossed around while traveling in a police van without restraints. His death in the hospital was attributed to injuries to his spinal cord. Six Baltimore police officers were suspended and faced criminal charges. But in 2017, the US Department of Justice decided not to bring federal charges against the police officers involved in the in-custody death of Freddie Gray.
- Sandra Bland, 28, was stopped for a minor traffic violation on July 10, 2015, by Texas State Trooper Brian Encinia. There was an altercation between Ms. Bland and the trooper and Ms. Bland was arrested and charged with assaulting a police officer. Trooper Encinia's dashcam, Ms. Bland's cell phone, and a witness recorded part of the encounter. The trooper was placed on administrative leave because he did not follow correct procedures for a traffic stop. On July 13, 2015, three days after her arrest, Sandra Bland was found hanged in a jail cell. It was ruled that she had committed suicide. The FBI determined that the jail did not do time checks on inmates. Nor did they ensure that employees had the necessary mental health training. Many protested her arrest, arguing that she was the victim of racial bias and questioning the ruling of suicide. A grand jury did not indict the county sheriff or the jail staff for a felony relating to Ms. Bland's death. Trooper Encinia was fired by the Texas Department of Public Safety for making false statements about the circumstances surrounding Ms. Bland's arrest.
- Ahmaud Marquez Arbery, 25, was fatally shot on February

23, 2020, near Brunswick, Georgia, where he was jogging. Two armed white men, Travis McMichael and his father, Gregory, pursued and confronted Mr. Arbery in their truck. William Bryan, who was following Mr. Arbery in his truck, videoed the shooting. The video went viral and on May 7, 74 days after the shooting, the Georgia Bureau of Investigation arrested the father and son, charging them with felony murder and aggravated assault. Later, William Bryan was arrested and charged with felony murder and attempted false imprisonment. William Bryan said Travis McMichael called Mr. Arbery a "fucking nigger" while standing over his dead body, leading to possible hate crime charges. The incident was widely condemned as an example of racial profiling in America. All three men have been charged with multiple counts of murder.

- Breonna Taylor, 26, an emergency medical technician, was shot to death in Louisville, Kentucky, by Louisville Metro Police Department officers on March 13, 2020. Carrying out a no-knock search warrant, plainclothes officers entered her apartment. Her boyfriend thought someone was breaking in and began to shoot in self-defense. Ms. Taylor was shot eight times by the officers who were actually looking for two men suspected of selling drugs from a drug house ten miles away. Ms. Taylor's apartment was included in the search warrant because they thought one of the drug dealers received drugs at Ms. Taylor's apartment. However, no drugs were found there. The incident report filed by the police said that Ms. Taylor had not been wounded when, in fact, she died from gunshot wounds. The report said forced entry had not been used. But the police had actually used a battering ram. The three officers were placed on administrative reassignment awaiting the results of the investigation. Later, Officer Brett Hankison was fired by the city's police department because he violated procedures by showing "extreme indifference to the value of human life" when he "wantonly and blindly" shot ten rounds of gunfire into Ms. Taylor's apartment.

No one has been charged in her death. In September 2020, the city of Louisville paid a $12 million wrongful death settlement to her family. On September 23, 2020, a grand jury ruled that the two officers who shot Ms. Taylor six times would not be charged, leading to national protest.

And now, since the death of George Floyd, Mr. Rayshard Brooks, 27, was shot and killed in Atlanta by Garrett Rolfe, an Atlanta police officer, on June 12, 2020. Mr. Brooks was asleep in his car, which was blocking the drive-through lane at a Wendy's restaurant. Officer Devin Brosnan responded to a complaint, and Officer Rolfe arrived after Officer Brosnan radioed for assistance. They found Mr. Brooks's blood-alcohol content to be above the legal limit for driving. Mr. Brooks offered to walk to his nearby sister's house. Instead, as the officers began to handcuff him, Mr. Brooks wrestled with the police. He took an officer's taser and began to run away, turning to point the taser, which is not considered a weapon, at them. Officer Rolfe shot Mr. Brooks twice in the back. He died a short time later. Various videos of the incident spread rapidly on social media. Prosecutors argued from these videos that after Mr. Brooks was shot, Officer Rolfe said, "I got him" and kicked him while Officer Brosnan stood on Mr. Brooks's shoulder. Officer Rolfe was charged with felony murder and other offenses on June 17.

By the time these pages are published, many more names will surely be added to this list.

***

I share the view that the majority of police officers are committed to serve all members of the community with justice and fairness. I also agree that the work of law enforcement is very difficult, requiring split-second decisions that can be a matter of life and death, especially when they encounter individuals suspected of wrongdoings that endanger the lives of the officers or others. It is a fact that some African Americans commit serious crimes for which they should be arrested, charged, convicted, and punished. However, when they are suspected of minor offenses, the police have no right to impose a death sentence on the streets. Good and fair police deserve our respect and admiration and, in most cases, they deserve the benefit of the doubt. Nevertheless, the cumulative evidence of many years makes it almost impossible to argue that we are dealing with only "a few bad apples."

The evidence suggests that there are some serious issues of bias in the culture and internal attitudes of at least some police forces, where systemic racism may be present. It is in the face of this culture of uneven treatment of People of Color that the calls to "Defund the Police" or even "Do Away with the Police" have emerged. Some individuals and groups may wish to do away with all forms of police forces and replace them with new forms of community policing. However, I share the view of those like Mr. Jacob Frey, mayor of Minneapolis, who argue strongly for major structural, attitudinal, and policy reforms in police departments (including reevaluating "qualified police immunity") that will create an environment within which police and members of diverse communities will see themselves as working together for the safety, well-being, and harmony of everyone. Have we reached a tipping point where such radical reform can be undertaken not only in our police departments but also in our places of government, education, employment, worship, and in our hearts and consciousnesses?

Commentators and demonstrators, observers and critics alike are saying that the ongoing protests born from the death of George Floyd might actually be the start of not only an era of change but actually a change of eras in the United States equal to and even surpassing the Civil Rights Movement of the Reverend Dr. Martin Luther King Jr., who had a dream. Have a critical mass of Americans come to a willingness to look at a most shameful aspect of its history with open-eyed honesty and set out on a self-examination and commitment to real and lasting change that uproots systemic racial bias and prejudice spawned from human slavery and the near destruction of the Indigenous peoples, the original sins of the country? Have we initiated an urgent, long-overdue nationwide conversation about racism that can yield lasting results? In these dystopian times, are we finally "woke," or are we just in a moment that will pass? We have been sleeping for so long, perhaps since the murder of the dreamer. Are we really and truly "woke"? Has our social consciousness been roused and raised? Are American people ready to "#staywoke"?

"Woke" is used here in the sense of what is sometimes called the African American Vernacular English meaning of the word, where being or staying woke refers to those who are alert, self-aware, and committed to change for as long as it takes. To be "woke" requires a willingness to question prevailing paradigms and consider paradigm shifts that will forge social orders that are new and better. Does the willingness of large numbers of people to at least think about the meaning of "Black Lives Matter" for the first time suggest that the consciousness of the nation has been raised to a level of awareness of racial injustice that will lead to dedicated actions for reform? Are we experiencing a sea change?

This much we know is true. The coronavirus pandemic kept large numbers of Americans home from work and school for long periods of time. They used this new "free time" in different ways. There is some evidence that many have read more, studied more, watched the news more, Googled more, spent more time on Facebook, written letters to the editor, and engaged in Zoom conversations with relatives and friends with whom they do not often speak. Because they had the time, many people who had never done so before participated in protest marches. At least for some, this has led to conversations of substance. George Floyd has often been the starting point of these new dialogues.

Conversations have moved from topic to topic. White people have been fired from their jobs for making cruel jokes about Mr. Floyd's murder on social media. The House and Senate bills and President Trump's executive order contributed to debates about new ways for police forces to operate, about practices such as chokeholds and warrantless arrests that might be reconsidered, and the ways that some of their funds might be used in other community services. There have been fierce arguments about the value and long-term effectiveness of massive peaceful protests. Doctors and social scientists have offered opinions about why the pandemic is killing more African American people than others. Many conversations have focused on the expanding dialogue about race in American culture. The Curatorial Department of New York's Guggenheim Museum wrote to the museum's leadership insisting on immediate changes in "an inequitable work environment that enables racism, white supremacy, and other discriminatory practices." Major newspapers, which often in the past carried mainly negative stories about People of Color, began to feature numerous positive stories about various aspects of the African American experience, which opened the eyes of many. Books addressing racial bias like Ibram X. Kendi's *How to Be an Antiracist* and Robin Di Angelo's *White Fragility: Why It's So Hard for White People to Talk about Racism* have soared to the top of best-seller lists.

HBO Max temporarily removed David O. Selznick's classic popular film *Gone with the Wind* from view and returned it with an introduction and panel discussion on the true dehumanizing nature of plantation slavery in contrast to the romanticized depiction in Margaret Mitchell's novel. Meanwhile, the National Aeronautics and Space Administration (NASA) announced it would name its Washington, DC, headquarters after "Hidden Figure" Mary W. Jackson, NASA's first African American woman engineer. Hopefully, more than a few Catholics were reading "Open Wide Our Hearts: The Enduring Call to Love," the new pastoral letter of the American Bishops acknowledging and challenging the enduring presence of racial hatred in our church and our country.

Quaker Oats announced that it would rebrand Aunt Jemima pancake syrup, because the character is based on a racial stereotype. Mars, which owns Uncle Ben's Rice, announced plans to change the rice maker's "brand identity," which has long been criticized for perpetuating a harmful racial stereotype. Meanwhile, the popular trading card game *Magic: The Gathering* removed seven cards with racist imagery, including the Invoke Prejudice card, which depicts figures in pointed hoods suggestive of the Ku Klux Klan. Then, pressed by their only African American driver, Darrell "Bubba" Wallace Jr., NASCAR, the Talladega, Alabama, Superspeedway decided to ban all displays of the Confederate flag from its grounds.

On June 22, 2020, Governor Gina Raimondo issued an executive order that the State of Rhode Island and Providence Plantations will eliminate "Providence Plantations" from its official name on state documents. She said, "We can acknowledge our history without elevating a phrase that's so deeply associated with the ugliest time in our state and in our country's history." In November voters will decide whether to change the state's official name.

On June 26, 2020, the Board of Trustees of Princeton University voted to remove the name Woodrow Wilson from its famous School of Public and International Affairs, judging that President Wilson's racist thinking and policies make him an inappropriate namesake. As Princeton President Christopher Eisgruber said, "Wilson's racism was significant and consequential. He segregated the federal civil service after it had been racially integrated for decades, thereby taking America backward in its pursuit of justice." Wilson called racial segregation "a benefit" and enslaved people "were happy and well-cared for."

On June 28, 2020, legislators in Mississippi voted to abolish the state's 126-year-old flag, which bears the Confederate battle emblem as its centerpiece. This long-opposed action is a key moment in the long history of efforts to remove offensive relics of the Confederacy from the South. Though many white Mississippians had claimed the flag as a proud expression of their Old South heritage, Philip Gunn, the Republican House Speaker said, "People's hearts have changed. We are better today than we were yesterday."

At the same time, the impetus to remove the most offensive monuments of Confederate leaders, who fought against the United States to preserve the "lost cause" of enslaving free human beings, gained momentum, along with moves to change the names of federal military bases in the South, named after Confederate generals, both of these over the objections of the president and many of his supporters.

All these things were happening as the country quietly noted the fifth anniversary of the "slaughter of the innocent," the terrible Charleston, South Carolina, church massacre on June 17, 2015, when nine African American people were brutally murdered as they prayed over the Word of God at the Emanuel African Methodist Episcopal Church by a man whose sole purpose was to start a race war. But their heartbroken relatives forgave him despite his heinous crime.

Do these and many other signs of change give us reason to think we really are "woke"?

***

One of the significant reasons to think that more Americans were finally "woke" after George Floyd's murder was the renewed awareness of Juneteenth and the Tulsa Race Massacre after President Trump announced that he was planning a major political rally in Tulsa on June 19, 2020, even as the coronavirus pandemic was spreading in Oklahoma. When there was an outcry about having this political event on the historic Juneteenth holiday, he did not seem to understand the reason for the outcry. He was criticized for being insensitive to the racial crisis the country was going through and indifferent to the sensibilities of African American people about the date and the city. People wondered out loud if he would address the convergence of Juneteenth with the events in Tulsa in 1921 and the murders of African Americans by white people. He did not. In response, the rally was rescheduled for the following day, June 20. In a *Wall Street Journal* interview, the president said he learned about the importance of Juneteenth from an African American Secret Service agent. He said that he had done something good by making the unknown unofficial holiday "very famous." "It's actually an important event. But nobody had ever heard of it."

Actually, many people have heard of it. Juneteenth has been well known for a long time, not only in the African American community but also to many others. In recent years it has been commemorated in more and more cities, and there are serious efforts to make it a national holiday. Still, the president's insensitivity paradoxically may have brought Juneteenth into the consciousness of many white people for the first time.

Juneteenth celebrates June 19, 1865, when Major General Gordon Granger went to Galveston, Texas, and announced that the War Between the States had ended. He read an order informing enslaved free human beings there that President Lincoln's January 1, 1863, Emancipation Proclamation had declared that all persons held as slaves within the rebellious states are, and henceforward, shall be "free." But slavery was not abolished until later that year when the 13th Amendment was ratified. There were more than 250,000 enslaved free human beings in Texas at that time. When this joyful news finally reached Texas, the president was already dead, assassinated on April 15, 1865.

The jubilation over the news that they were "free at last" led to annual celebrations in many African American communities in Texas, and the tradition of Juneteenth, also known as Freedom Day or Emancipation Day, continued. Juneteenth festivities usually included prayers, readings, songs, picnic meals, fishing, horseback riding, and remembrances of beloved dead enslaved ancestors. Juneteenth, the oldest known celebration commemorating the end of slavery, became an official state holiday in Texas in 1980.

Contemporary celebrations of Juneteenth often include public readings of the Emancipation Proclamation, singing African American songs like "Lift Every Voice and Sing" as well as the reading of works by noted African American writers such as Ralph Ellison, Maya Angelou, Toni Morrison, Alice Walker, and Ta-Nehisi Coates. Billie Holiday's "Strange Fruit" and Nina Simone's "You Know How I Feel" might be playing in the background.

Opal Lee, a 93-year-old activist from Texas, has been working tirelessly for years to make Juneteenth a national holiday. Many others are campaigning for Congress to recognize Juneteenth as a national holiday. Forty-seven states recognize Juneteenth in some way. Only Hawai'i, North Dakota, and South Dakota do not recognize it. Texas, Virginia, New York, and Pennsylvania are the only states that recognize it as an official paid holiday for its employees.

During this year's celebrations of Juneteenth, many white Americans who were interviewed said they felt embarrassed that they never celebrated or thought about Juneteenth until this year. They asked, "How is it possible that we didn't know about it? Why weren't we taught about it in school? Was it deliberately left out of our history books? All Americans should know about a holiday that is such a critical moment in our history." Perhaps they are now "woke."

When President Trump announced that he was going to Tulsa, Oklahoma, for a political rally on June 19, many in the media and the city wondered why he was going to Oklahoma, a state he is favored to win by a large margin and a state where instances of Covid-19 infection were on the rise. Some African American people wondered if he was going to use this historic location of the Tulsa Race Massacre ninety-nine years ago to announce specific proposals of his administration to address the urgent concerns of African Americans, to express his awareness of increasing racial tensions in the country, and suggest actions that might help bridge the racial divide.

However, on June 20, he did not speak about the racial divide of the past or the present. He referred to those peacefully protesting in the name of George Floyd outside the Bank of Oklahoma Center as "bad people," "trouble-makers," "thugs," and "anarchists." Nevertheless, his very presence in the city and his silence raised awareness of the tragic events of nearly a century ago that still influence Tulsa today. If we are to be truly "woke," there is wisdom in refreshing our memories about the terrible days, beginning May 30, 1921. Those who ignore the sins of the past run the risk of repeating them.

The massacre was one of the most destructive episodes of racial terrorism in American history. On May 30, 1921, a young African American man was arrested. No one seems to know exactly what happened. He was accused of attempting to assault a white teenage girl in an elevator of an office building in Tulsa's thriving African American Greenwood District. Greenwood at the time had a business district that was known as the Negro Wall Street. It was the proud center of African American affluence in the Southwest, with some of the finest Black-owned businesses in the country. The story of the alleged assault attempt appeared in a newspaper the next day. The white press lit the match for the destruction of Greenwood by labeling the community as "Niggertown," full of "jazz clubs" and places of vice. An armed mob of angry white people formed, bent on vengeance. Things escalated quickly into mob violence. The goal was "to run the Negroes out of Tulsa."

White vigilantes systematically burned nearly forty square blocks, destroying more than 1,000 homes, a dozen churches, five hotels, thirty-one restaurants, four drugstores, eight doctors' offices, the public library, and the local hospital. Ten thousand were left homeless. It is estimated that 300 African Americans were slain.

At the beginning of the twentieth century, lynch mobs commonly hanged, shot, or burned African Americans alive. They also roped men of color to cars and dragged them to death. The killers in Tulsa reenacted this barbaric ritual. One helpless elderly African American blind man, whose legs had been amputated, was shredded alive behind a fast-moving car. This "good old colored man" was tied to a convertible that sped down the street for all to see. The bodies of the dead were stacked up on street corners, carried out of town on city-owned trucks, burned in an incinerator or dumped into a river. Photographs survive showing the bewildered survivors as they were led at gunpoint to what could only be called concentration camps. No one was arrested, charged, or convicted for these horrid deeds. No restitution was made.

This deeply disturbing episode was long hidden from view. This episode was often referred to as "the Tulsa Race Riots," which suggested that African Americans were the agents of horror, since "riot" has been given racial overtones. In 2001, serious research into the events was undertaken and historians rightly began to speak of the "Tulsa Race Massacre." In 2019, HBO's highly praised series *Watchmen* brought the story of the Tulsa Massacre back into the consciousness of many Americans, as did *Greenwood,* the 2019 Dance Theater ballet choreographed by Donald Byrd, continuing the Alvin Ailey legacy of challenging social injustice through dance.

This year Juneteenth was celebrated in Tulsa with greater exuberance than ever. The community celebrated the moment in history when the news of Abraham Lincoln's bold, pragmatic action reached their ancestors; they celebrated the resilience of African Americans today, in the face of a pandemic that is disproportionately affecting our communities, resilience in the face of police brutality against People of Color, and in the face of a president who boasts of how much he has done to strengthen African American communities in spite of stark evidence to the contrary. They ask what does "Make America Great Again" mean. At what point in the country's history was America great for all Americans? Since no such date exists in the past, that greatness must lie in the future.

The people of Tulsa fully understand the country's renewed anxiety ignited by George Floyd's senseless death because they lived through such senseless death at the hands of white supremacists intent on maintaining white privilege a century ago. Many Tulsa residents of all races are "woke." They believe their journey can be a model for the rest of the nation. Hannibal Johnson, a Tulsa historian and a professor of African American history, argues that the way forward is a three-step journey of *"acknowledgment, apology, and atonement."*

Is this country now on that journey? Is there a critical mass of the American people who are ready to acknowledge the truth of the nation's long history of racial injustice? Is the country ready and willing to express its remorse and apologize from the highest levels of government? Are there grounds for hoping that rank-and-file citizens are ready for atonement? Or, as Nikole Hannah-Jones asks, is there a willingness to move toward atonement and even reparations?

I am fearful that for all of the momentum that suggests the country might be "woke," the long, sharp eye of history may look back at the present ferment as our Prague Spring—that period of political liberalization and mass protest in Czechoslovakia under reformist Alexander Dubček, that began January 5, 1968, that ended August 21, 1968, when the country was invaded and the reforms were suppressed by the Soviet Union and other Warsaw Pact members.

My hope is that we are at a crossroad, a moment in history of "kairos" in the Christian sense of "the appointed time in the purpose of God," an opportune moment, a time when the grace of God will prevail. Theologian Paul Tillich spoke of *kairoi* as crisis moments in history which seem to demand that human beings make existential decisions. He considered the emergence of Jesus Christ in human history to be the supreme example. Liberation theology and Nelson Mandela's confrontation with South Africa's oppressive, racist apartheid regime was a smaller example. *Kairoi* constitute "the crucial time" when individuals and communities must make life-altering decisions.

I have several concerns that temper my hope.

My first concern is this. Will the current relatively large number of white people who have either participated in the protests or said they sympathize with the cause of racial justice be sustained? The outcry over Mr. Floyd's death seems to have moved many white Americans to acknowledge that, to some degree, they have contributed to the racism that is ingrained in much of American society. A wellspring of awareness has prompted many, especially younger people, to concede their own culpability for the racial divide. Growing numbers of white people feel that they cannot and should not collectively ignore the ordeals experienced daily by many African American people.

Many white Americans of different nationalities say they have attended demonstrations for racial justice for the first time. They have bought books on race in America and even made a conscious effort to protect their children from the poison of racial prejudice. Talk show panelists, thinking out loud, have asked: Does being white give me advantages to which I simply presume to be entitled? Is that "white privilege"? What part can I play in creating a more level playing field for People of Color?

Will this new awareness continue to be a motivating force in their lives for years to come? Or will it dissipate? Real change will not come about without a multiracial coalition. Are these white people who today are sincerely concerned truly "woke"?

I remember well the enthusiastic talk about a "post-racial America" after President Barack Obama was elected. Those who were hopeful that this historic event was a "kairos" moment in American history were proven wrong. Are the positive developments that seem to signal a change in consciousness causing us to ignore the evidence right before our eyes that the attitudes of the past are simply festering just below the surface?

I began writing the essays in this book five years ago. Each chapter, in its own way, addresses different aspects of being "woke" to the challenges caused by the racial divide in this country. The events of this past year make them timelier and more relevant than when I wrote them. I have written from the "moving viewpoint" of my experiences as a human being, a person of color, a Catholic priest for fifty years, and a Catholic bishop for twenty-five years. I have lived in many different parts of the country from Chicago to Cambridge, from Cleveland to Washington, DC, from New York to South Bend, from St. Louis to Lake Charles to Belleville. I have not only seen but also have personally experienced the impact of the racial divide on my life in society and in the Catholic Church.

And through these many years with their negative and positive experiences, I now realize that I personally have become more and more "woke." I have no fear of what James Baldwin and Toni Morrison have called "the master's narrative" and "the white gaze." I have found my own voice.

Are the people of the United States ready for atonement? Are more of us finally "woke"?

I hope so!

Bishop Edward K. Braxton
JUNETEENTH 2020

Introduction

The Journey
of an African American
Catholic Bishop

This book, compiled from a number of my writings on the Catholic Church and the racial divide in the United States, is written from the moving viewpoint of my life, beginning with my childhood with my parents and continuing with my adult life as a Catholic priest and bishop of the church. In my family history, I have experienced the racial divide. I have lived this divide, in a certain way, in my own person. I have also experienced the happiness born of close enriching friendships with people of different races. You may better understand the meaning behind the words in the pages that follow if I share some vantage points of the moving viewpoint of my life with you.

My dear father, Cullen Lawrence Braxton Sr. (April 21, 1915–May 23, 1995) and my "Mother Dear," Evelyn Kathryn Gardner Braxton (March 11, 1920–February 10, 2008) were both born when Woodrow Wilson was the twenty-eighth president of the United States (March 4, 1913–March 4, 1921).

Historians debate the successes and failures of his time in office, which included World War I. However, almost all commentators acknowledge that he perpetuated and reinforced the racial divide that prevailed in his day. Many, especially in more recent years, argue that evidence supports that his policies were those of a racist and a segregationist. He was the first president elected from the

South in sixty-five years, and he promptly appointed segregationists to cabinet positions. He favored segregation in the military.

President Wilson expanded the racial bias, discrimination, and segregation practiced by his predecessors President Theodore Roosevelt and President William Taft when it came to filling offices. He insisted on the re-segregation of multiple agencies of the federal government. When he took office, he personally appointed white supervisors to replace fifteen out of seventeen African American supervisors in the federal service whom he had dismissed. He also accepted the practice of segregating the workers in the offices of members of his cabinet. By the end of his first year in office, the navy and other government offices maintained segregated dining rooms, bathrooms, and offices. W. E. B. Du Bois, who, in 1895, was the first African American to earn a PhD from Harvard University, noted that one "colored" clerk, who could not actually be segregated, because of his particular work, had a cage-like structure built around him to keep him separate from white co-workers. These policies, the president argued, eliminated tensions and conflicts between workers of different races. To facilitate racial discrimination, beginning in 1914, the federal government required all applicants for employment to attach a photograph to their application.

In February 1915, two months before my father was born, the president had a screening in the White House of *The Birth of a Nation*, D. W. Griffith's pioneering, controversial epic film about the Civil War and Reconstruction. The film, based on the book *The Clansman*, written by the president's classmate Thomas Dixon Jr., depicted the Ku Klux Klan as deliverers of the post–Civil War South from dangerous former enslaved free human beings and unscrupulous carpetbaggers from the North.

The Birth of a Nation, which celebrated the frightful mythology of the so-called Lost Cause view of the Civil War, argued that Reconstruction was a disastrous failure, and it condemned extremist Republicans for seeking minimally fair treatment of former enslaved free human beings. The People of Color in the movie are a reinforcement of common, degrading stereotypes:

ignorant and almost subhuman characters. Still, most moviegoers of the day embraced the film, uncritically accepting its blatant racial bias.

After seeing *The Birth of a Nation*, it was widely reported that President Wilson said, "It's like writing history with lightning. My only regret is that it is all so terribly true." Scholars debate the authenticity of these words. Did the president actually utter them? Whether he did or not, there is no evidence that he condemned or rejected the premises of a film based on the book written by his friend and considered one of the most racist major motion pictures in American history.

In November 2015, when there was a renewed awareness of Wilson's documented history of racial bias, a group of Princeton University students demanded that his name be removed from all programs and buildings at the university. This would include the Woodrow Wilson School of Public and International Affairs, which honored Wilson who, from 1902 to 1910, was the president of Princeton. (In 2020, in the context of new awareness and protests surrounding systemic racism, the university agreed to this change.)

The Princeton protest happened when my father would have been one hundred years old. Many aspects of the racial divide maintained by President Wilson when my parents were born have been effectively challenged and dismantled in the past century. One cannot deny the extraordinary progress that has been made in bridging the racial divide. Yet, paradoxically, in significant ways and in critical areas, rather than narrowing, the racial divide is growing wider.

In 1941, my parents moved from Mississippi to Chicago, where I was born. They were part of "the Great Migration" of African American people fleeing the economic, political, social, and cultural oppression of the Jim Crow South. They settled, inevitably, on the south side of the city in neighborhoods which came to be known as the "Black Belt." My father worked for the railroad. My mother maintained a small beauty shop, where African American women had their hair "straightened" and "curled" with smoking hot straightening and curling irons because the European American culture taught them to believe that their natural hair was "nappy" and unattractive. My parents were surprised to find that, even though in Chicago where there was a degree of improvement in economic and social conditions, the racial divide was as real as in the South. At times, they struggled against what Rev. Dr. Martin Luther King Jr. called "the degenerating sense of nobodiness" due to the forces of absolute racial segregation. The city, unbeknown to my father and mother, was still struggling to recover from one of the country's worst eruptions of racial conflict just twenty years earlier. These disturbing events of 100 years ago, which came to be known as "the race riots of 1919," took place during the final years of the presidency of Woodrow Wilson. However, his personal views on race relations prevented him from offering significant leadership during this crisis.

The great social upheaval in Chicago in 1919 was sparked by a match placed on the dry wood of intense racial prejudice and the fears of many recently arrived immigrants to the city from Europe. They feared that "the Negroes" would fill unskilled labor jobs in factories and steel mills which they themselves needed. The "colored people" were also willing to work for lower wages, leading to a conflict with the unions. The match may have been a conflict that occurred on a beach when a crowd of angry white youths stoned an African American teenager who allegedly had been swimming in an area reserved for white people. The boy drowned.

The subsequent riot began on July 27 and lasted several days. By the time it ended thirty-eight people were dead, more than five hundred were injured, and many African American families were left homeless due to arson. In the downtown area, people riding public transportation were pulled to the ground and beaten violently by angry white mobs. Military personnel wearing their uniforms attacked them with bricks and anything they could find. A number of deaths and many injuries resulted from the mayhem. Parts of Chicago had become the scenes of a horrific race war. Stormy weather and the reserve guardsmen ended the chaos. *The Negro in Chicago*, a study of the riot published in 1922, said, "The relation of whites and Negroes in the United States is our most grave and perplexing domestic problem." It might be argued that it remains so to this day.

Henry Louis Gates Jr.'s book *Stony the Road: Reconstruction, White Supremacy, and the Rise of Jim Crow* describes and explores the racial divide as it existed in the decades before my parents were born and as it endured for more than half of their lifetimes. My parents and their parents certainly experienced the racial divide in the United States as it was perpetuated from the post–Civil War era in various evolving forms of white supremacy and white privilege to the present. *Stony the Road* is a detailed roadmap that provides a historic overview with words and pictures cataloguing the persistence of the racial divide in social, political, educational, and economic realities deep within the structures and practices of American society and at different levels of American politics.

Stony the Road guides readers of all backgrounds through the life experiences of my parents and their parents before them. Only by facing and coming to terms with this history can we grasp the challenges of the present and commit to changing the future. It is a past filled with terrifying and degrading experiences that I heard firsthand from my parents, my grandparents, and my aunts and uncles.

In 2018, I made my way to Montgomery, Alabama, to visit the Legacy Museum: From Enslavement to Mass Incarceration, shortly after it opened, and the National Memorial for Peace and Justice. The Legacy Museum is built in a location where enslaved free human beings were warehoused as if they were hogs or cows in pens awaiting slaughter. I found myself in conversation with my parents and grandparents as I viewed the sober exhibits. One startling exhibit consists of large jars of soil of different colors collected from the places where African American men were lynched. I imagined my grandfather Daniel Braxton saying, "I truly hope what is shown here will finally educate Americans about the humiliating hardships our people endured. Maybe this knowledge can help bridge the racial divide through reconciliation between the races today."

The nearby National Memorial for Peace and Justice is a stark memorial commemorating the experiences of African American men who were routinely presumed guilty of minor offenses and publicly lynched in the Jim Crow South, almost as a form of entertainment, commemorated with postcards. The central focus of the memorial is more than 800 six-foot steel monuments, representing the different counties where lynching occurred. The steel slabs, which evoke giant grave markers, are engraved with the names of those who were tortured to death before crowds of eager onlookers.

If my mother and father were walking at my side reading the faceless names of the murdered, I am sure they would urge me to try to forgive but never to forget these horrors. They would tell me to ignore those who would prefer to dismiss this history as exaggerated or as "simply the past" with no relevance to the present. My father, especially, would remind me of the memorials and museums in Europe and around the world that document the suffering of Jewish people in the Nazi Holocaust. He would insist that the Montgomery museums preserve the record of the African American Holocaust, which took place on American soil. Both of my parents would be deeply distressed to look at our country today and see the evidence that the root system of our painful past is not dead. It is springing to life again in new and different ways with the resurgence of militant white nationalism, neo-Nazism, devotees of *The Turner Diaries*, the Ku Klux Klan, xenophobia, talk of "the great replacement," latent racial prejudice, and the hurtful language of President Donald Trump, who recently described the impeachment inquiry by the House of Representatives as a "lynching."

Stony the Road takes its title from a visionary poem well known to my parents and their contemporaries, who knew many of the stanzas by heart. "Lift Every Voice and Sing" was written by James Weldon Johnson (1871–1938), a leader of the National Association for the Advancement of Colored People, in 1900, fifteen years before my father was born and twenty years before my mother was born. Five years later, in 1905, James Weldon's brother, John

Rosamond Johnson (1873–1954), immortalized the masterful poem by setting it to rousing, powerful music.

The song gradually came to be known as "the Negro (later 'Black' and later still 'African American') National Anthem." It has never been thought of as in any way a replacement of the traditional American National Anthem. But this hymn gives voice to experiences *not* expressed in Francis Scott Key's poem "The Star-Spangled Banner," written September 14, 1814, and set to a popular British melody written by John Stafford Smith in 1773, with various lyrics that were well known in the United States. "The Star-Spangled Banner" was recognized for official use by the United States Navy in 1889, and by President Woodrow Wilson in 1916, when my father was one year old and three years before the Chicago race riots. Congress made it the national anthem in 1931. The anthem's soaring lyrics from Key's "Defence of Fort M'Henry" are well known:

> *Oh, say can you see,*
> *by the dawn's early light,*
> *What so proudly we hailed*
> *at the twilight's last gleaming?*
> *Whose broad stripes and bright stars,*
> *through the perilous fight,*
> *O'er the ramparts we watched,*
> *were so gallantly streaming?*
> *And the rockets' red glare,*
> *the bombs bursting in air,*
> *Gave proof through the night*
> *that our flag was still there.*
> *O say, does that star-spangled*
> *banner yet wave*
> *O'er the land of the free*
> *and the home of the brave?*

It is an extraordinary anthem which the majority of Americans of all backgrounds sing proudly. These heroic words were written after the author saw the bombardment of Fort McHenry by British ships during the War of 1812. He was moved by the sight of the flag of the United States with fifteen stars and fifteen stripes waving above the fort for all to see at the hour of victory. When my sisters and brother and I learned this anthem as Catholic school students, we were not taught that these lyrics were written by an evangelical Episcopalian who owned enslaved free human beings who were the source of his considerable wealth. The lyrics are silent about the great tragedy of the Middle Passage and the nation's original sin of enslaving of free human beings. Though he is said to have given some legal advice to enslaved free human beings struggling to be free, Key used his expertise as an attorney to aid slave owners in their efforts to "recapture" their "slaves" who had "escaped." Sadly, Key's faith in Jesus Christ did not move him to a fierce opposition of human oppression and enslavement.

When he wrote of this country as "the land of the free," Key, like Thomas Jefferson, the owner of enslaved African people who wrote "all men are created equal," held racist views concerning the intrinsic inferiority of African people. Key called them "a distinct and inferior race of people, which all experience proves to be the greatest evil that afflicts a community." His Christian faith did not open his eyes to the equality and dignity of all human beings. When Key was writing "O'er the land of the free," it is probable that enslaved African people were desperately attempting to reach British ships in the harbor at Baltimore thinking they had a greater chance of gaining freedom under the British flag than under the "Star-Spangled Banner."

The misery and horror my ancestors were seeking to escape is captured by the second stanza of "Lift Every Voice."

> *Stony the road we trod,*
> *Bitter the chastening rod,*
> *Felt in the days when hope unborn had died;*
> *Yet with a steady beat,*
> *Have not our weary feet*
> *Come to the place for which our fathers sighed?*

We have come over a way that with tears has been watered,
We have come, treading our path through the blood
  of the slaughtered,
Out from the gloomy past,
'Til now we stand at last
Where the white gleam of our bright star is cast.

I have asked that, when the flickering light of my brief earthly existence is extinguished, this mighty anthem would be sung with full force during the recessional at the end of the Liturgy of Christian Burial. This will express the link between me, my parents, and my parents' parents, to the Middle Passage and the "old neighborhood" of my life.

When my parents arrived to Chicago in 1941, they were not members of the Catholic Church. They, like many others in the Great Migration, were from a long tradition of Baptists. Both of my parents were well aware of the virtual exclusion of African Americans from the Catholic Church in the South. They had never thought of becoming Catholics. My mother, however, knew of the reputation of Catholic schools for providing excellent education, moral formation, and discipline. She was determined to send me and my sisters and brother to a Catholic school. She was very appreciative of the education we were receiving, and she gradually took an interest in becoming a Catholic. Once she was received into the church, her faith, which she viewed as a flower born of a Baptist seed, grew, and she was eager to have her children baptized. My father, who did not become a Catholic until many years later, supported her decision.

My sisters, Gwendolyn and Patricia, and my brother, Lawrence, and I attended the neighborhood Catholic elementary school together. We were taught by the Sisters of Charity in a tentatively integrated school, where the majority of the students were white. Next to our parents, the Irish nuns and the Irish monsignor, who was pastor, may have had the greatest impact on our early intellectual and religious formation. They urged us to take our studies seriously and introduced us to a wide range of topics beyond the ordinary textbook lessons. We all benefited tremendously from the dedication and commitment of the sisters, and our horizons were broadened by their comprehensive and holistic approach to education. "Education is the key!" the pastor often said.

But when we studied American history and covered the Civil War, the full, brutal story of enslaved free human beings at the foundation of that war was only mentioned in passing, as if it had been a minor part of the story. Nor was the history of Reconstruction, the Jim Crow South, and the racial divide examined with a focus on their very real impact on the contemporary African American community, including the students in our class. In a similar way, our survey courses on American presidents made no mention of the impact of President Wilson's deep-seated racial prejudice on the life of the nation. There was no mention of just how stony was the road we trod. My father eventually became a Catholic during these years. I still recall his bitter tears in 1955 when he was informed in the bluntest terms that there was no room for him in the Knights of Columbus. He later discovered and joined the much smaller and all-African American Knights of Peter Claver. He often wondered out loud why these groups were segregated. As a bishop, my experience of the Knights has been generally positive and supportive of my ministry. I am aware of the subsequent modestly successful efforts made by the Knights of Columbus to be more inclusive. I know well the generosity of the Knights in supporting and funding many worthy causes doing much good for the church.

Later that same year, the murder of fourteen-year-old Emmett Till by white racists on August 28, 1955, in Money, Mississippi, deeply disturbed my father. Emmet's grief-stricken mother, Mamie, brought him home to Chicago. My father and my uncle Ellis took me and my brother to the wake. After viewing the bloated, unrecognizable body of this little boy, only three years older than I was, my father told us, "Don't go south! They will kill without giving it a thought."

Our Catholic school music appreciation classes were quite

Eurocentric. We were all taught to sing "When Irish Eyes Are Smiling." When my brother brought our well-worn copy of "Lift Every Voice and Sing" as an example of music he liked, he was told that this "type" of music was not considered to be of "high quality." Similarly, when I told my teacher that, at home, my family enjoyed the music of Billie Holiday, Duke Ellington, Louis Armstrong, Mahalia Jackson, and Nat "King" Cole, I was told that these artists were not considered "great" musicians. Later, when I was in the seminary, the film of George and Ira Gershwin's opera *Porgy and Bess*, starring Sydney Poitier, Dorothy Dandridge, Pearl Bailey, and Sammy Davis Jr., was shown on television. I have a vivid memory of a fellow seminarian informing me that Gershwin's use of "Black music styles" was the reason why the work could not be really considered opera in the same way that Puccini's *Madame Butterfly* or Bizet's *Carmen* are called operas! (Significantly, the Metropolitan Opera of New York opened its 2019 grand opera season with *Porgy and Bess*.)

This brings me to my seminary years and the slow and complex process involved in my discernment to become a priest. Though I went to Mass daily and helped the parish sacristan, I always thought I would be an attorney, a heart surgeon, or an actor, marry, and have many children. Rather than going to St. Ignatius College Preparatory High School, the monsignor at my parish persuaded me to consider Quigley Preparatory Seminary. The decision to persevere in the seminary was not an easy one. I was one of a very small number of African American students.

The seminary was certainly welcoming in many ways, and I developed genuine friendships there. But the culture was not marked by diversity and inclusion. Still, I found I liked studying philosophy and theology, so I continued my discernment. My parents only wanted me to be happy. They never pressured me to become a priest. They both, especially my father, spoke openly with me about what we already knew about the long history of racial prejudice in the Catholic Church. I can still hear my father saying, "The Catholic Church did not oppose the evil of slavery!" I was honest with them about my positive and negative seminary experiences. I told them I heard the word "nigger" more than a few times.

In 1962 when a group of seminarians went to see *To Kill a Mockingbird* based on Harper Lee's Pulitzer Prize–winning novel. I was deeply moved by the story of Tom Robinson, played by Brock Peters, who is killed after being falsely accused of sexually assaulting a white woman. He was defended by the upright Atticus Finch, played by Gregory Peck. To my surprise my classmates did not know who Brock Peters was. And one of them observed that the moral of the story was that "birds of a feather should flock together." One faculty member, noticing my aptitude for scholarship, cautioned me against having any hopes of academic ministry as a priest. "You should prepare yourself to be appointed to one of the Black parishes. This is what the church needs and this is God's will for you."

During my seminary high school years (1958–1962), I became aware of a certain dualism. I regularly read *Life*, *Time*, and *Look* magazines, *Readers Digest* as well as *National Geographic*, with interest. But, at the same time, I anxiously read the influential John H. Johnson publications, *Ebony* and *Jet*, which were filled with positive stories about hard-working, successful African Americans (as well as gossip!), *Negro Digest*, and the *Chicago Defender*, the city's must-read African American newspaper. It gradually dawned on me that I was living in and knowledgeable of two distinct worlds, the "White World" as well as the "Black World." I could easily talk with my seminary classmates about events in the "White World." However, most of them were ignorant of or indifferent to the "Black World." This made me reluctant to bring up topics from *Ebony* or the *Defender*. I was inescapably saturated with the world of Eurocentric culture. However, there was no need for my seminary classmates to know or care about the world of Afrocentric culture.

In later years, I discovered a vocabulary for these experiences in W. E. B. Du Bois's pioneering 1903 study, *The Souls of Black Folk*.

Du Bois described my experience and the experience of my parents before me as "double consciousness." He argued, correctly, I think, that African Americans almost always see the world around them through two rather distinct lenses. There is the lens shaped by the unique history of descendants of enslaved free human beings, that is, their self-consciousness, their self-understanding. But there is also the lens of consciousness through which the larger white world views them. These two consciousnesses are, at times, almost contradictory. This is not unlike what James Baldwin, Toni Morrison, and others have called "the white gaze." They spoke of their struggle to write in their own voice without a constraining regard for what white critics or readers thought of their work. This freed them to speak in their own authentic voice with no heed to the "white gaze" looking over their shoulder.

The Souls of Black Folk also speaks about a metaphorical "veil" within which People of Color live. They are capable of venturing outside of the veil when they enter the world of white people. To some degree, they are able to raise the veil so that white people can partially see the passions, sorrows, and struggles of the African American soul. Some readers, from 1903 to the present, find Du Bois's distinctions to be artificial, unnecessarily complex, and difficult to understand and accept. But they are, at least to some degree, consistent with my personal experiences.

My early reading of W. E. B. Du Bois's landmark study provided me with insights that were a great help to me throughout all of my years of study. I understood why when I read texts of seminal philosophers such as Aristotle; Plato; Kant; Hegel; Kierkegaard; Camus; Sartre; Heidegger; Otto; Ricœur; Wittgenstein; and Derrida and influential theologians such as St. Augustine of Hippo; St. Thomas Aquinas; Bernard Häring, CSsR; Fr. Hans Urs von Balthasar; Henri de Lubac, SJ; Pierre Teilhard de Chardin, SJ; Karl Rahner, SJ; Bernard J. F. Lonergan, SJ; Paul Tillich; and Karl Barth—their works are all written from a Eurocentric perspective, which is perceived by many to be a universal perspective.

As a result, when liberation theology, Black theology, and feminist theology emerged, many commentators dismissed these works as transient fads, of interest, perhaps, because of their detailed angst-laden theological insights and concerns about the life experiences of particular so-called minority groups, with little or no universal or lasting value. They are "period pieces" and not "classics." Other critics have dismissed these theological developments as a type of victimization that takes the paradigm of God calling Moses to deliver the children of Israel from the pharaoh's oppression in Egypt and analyzes the experience of African American oppression, for example, through the social conflict lens of Karl Marx. Still others commentators judged all such "political" and "subjective" approaches to theology to be incompatible with the biblical foundations and objective truth of Christian theology which cannot be appropriated and used to advance social and political objectives, no matter how worthy they may be.

When I was ordained a priest for the Archdiocese of Chicago on May 13, 1970, I somewhat boldly chose to deliver the homily at my First Mass, something that was uncommon at that time. In my homily I said, "The primeval meaning of priest as mediator at the altar is unchanged. All the more today must he be a man of deep personal faith, conformed to Jesus Christ. All the more grave is his responsibility to know Scripture and to know the community in whose name he offers sacrifice. All the more must he be a servant of the whole Church. While supporting a healthy pluralism, he must avoid fragmentation. Instead, he must call the People of God to a greater love for one another and to unity in action. To do all of this, he must be a man of professional competence making every use of his natural talents. By his life of faith in Christ, by his fidelity to the *magisterium*, by his sacramental ministry, by his proclamation of the Gospel, by his tireless work for justice and peace, and by his unconditional affection for his people, the priest must be the mediator of meaning. His life and work must be a clarion call announcing the intelligibility hidden in the riddle of life" (May 17, 1970, Pentecost Sunday, the Church of St. Philip Neri, Chicago).

Fifty years have passed since that day, and I am convinced that my words ring with a greater truth today than they did when I first spoke them. After my ordination, the moving viewpoint of my life and ministry led me down unexpected paths, from associate pastor at Holy Name Cathedral and Sacred Heart Parish in Winnetka, Illinois, to doctoral studies at the Catholic University of Louvain, to postdoctoral studies at the University of Chicago Divinity School (while also serving as associate pastor of St. Felicitas Parish on the south side and as campus minister at Chicago State University), to the faculty of Harvard Divinity School and the University of Notre Dame, to the personal theologian to James Cardinal Hickey of Washington, DC, to scholar in residence at the North American College in Rome, to director of Calvert House, the Catholic Student Center at the University of Chicago, to official theological consultant to William H. Sadlier, Inc., in New York, to pastor of St. Catherine of Siena Parish in Oak Park, Illinois. I was serving as pastor when I was appointed auxiliary bishop of St. Louis and later as Bishop of Lake Charles, Louisiana, and ultimately as Bishop of Belleville, Illinois. In each of these positions I had the opportunity to observe and experience the racial divide in the United States and in the Catholic Church from very different perspectives.

Since the happy day of my First Mass, the Catholic Church and the priesthood have endured great turmoil caused by the greatest crisis in the history of the church in the United States: the sin, the moral crime, and the terrible scandal of members of the clergy sexually abusing children. The church has also suffered because of a reticence to speak up in the public square about systemic racial bias in society and in the practices of the church. At other times, the church has spoken with a prophetic voice but has remained hesitant to act with equal prophetic urgency to remedy vestiges of racial inequality which are visible in the life and practices of the church. In the course of this long history, there have been days when I have been profoundly unhappy as a priest and as a bishop. However, I can honestly say that since the day of my ordination by John Cardinal Cody, I have not experienced even one day that I was unhappy that I was priest. This is true even of those days when I was discouraged, manipulated, and denied opportunities by leaders in the church explicitly because of my race.

In the years immediately following my ordination, African American or Black theology began to emerge with great prominence through the writings of influential African American Protestant thinkers. Among them were forceful new theological works, including Albert G. Cleage Jr.'s *The Black Messiah,* J. Deotis Roberts's *Liberation and Reconciliation* and *Black Theology in Dialogue,* Joseph Washington's *Is God a White Racist?*, and James Cone's *Black Theology and Black Power, A Black Theology of Liberation,* and *God of the Oppressed.* I had the opportunity to meet Dr. Cone, who is often called the founder of Black theology. Speaking with him, reading his books, examining his methodology, and experiencing his passionate commitment opened my eyes! His works along with others made me aware of a more existential approach to theology that was quite different from traditional European and American academic theology.

My training in classical Catholic theology and methodology made it clear to me that there was a necessary tension between Black theology and the traditional theology of the Catholic Church. This tension is rooted, in part, in the fact that Catholic theological thought is necessarily linked to the *magisterium*, the formal, normative teaching authority of the Catholic Church as expressed by the Holy Father, the Bishop of Rome, along with the bishops of the world in communion with him as pope, the primary teacher of Catholics on matters of faith and morals.

Having published writings concerning African American Catholics and commentaries on Black theology, at a certain point I was encouraged by James Cone to become one of the Catholic voices of Black theology. Though I was very sympathetic to many of the themes and concerns of Black theology, I was not fully at ease with the confrontational and in-your-face style of some proponents of Black theology. Nor did I want to oppose or contradict the teachings of the church. I sensed that there were other Catholic scholars who might more effectively explore Black theology through the lens of the Catholic tradition and the social teaching of the church since the Second Vatican Council.

My careful study of Black theology led me to think of theology as a discipline that can have three distinct contexts or conversation partners. There is theology in the world of the church, theology in the world of a divinity school at a secular university, and theology in the world of sociocultural and political situations. Black theology, like liberation theology and feminist theology, is primarily in conversation with the concrete reality of social, cultural, political, and economic situations. It is less concerned about fidelity to traditional teachings, doctrines, and beliefs of a specific faith community or with rigorous scholarly methodology and internal coherence of the academy and more concerned about the relevance and power of religious symbols, iconography, and narratives to address situations of exclusion, oppression, and disenfranchisement with the result of promoting change and improvement in the everyday lives of marginalized people. Theology expressed in this manner may be better equipped than classical academic theology to address the racial divide in the United States with the urgency it deserves.

I am writing this introduction while at the Chautauqua Institution, a summer educational, recreational, and spiritual renewal center that attracts a large, dedicated following to its nine-week sessions in a beautiful, bucolic setting outside of Buffalo, New York. It lends itself to reflection and introspection. Week Nine focused on ways to explore the question of race and culture in America. During these days the great trumpeter, Wynton Marsalis, and his Jazz at the Lincoln Center Orchestra performed his brilliant "The Ever Funky Lowdown," a dazzling theater piece for narrator, orchestra, chorus, and a dance trio that celebrates, among other things, the work of Fannie Lou Hamer and other civil rights activists. The work confronts the racial divide in the United States in a subversively entertaining fashion.

I met an especially interesting group of people of different racial backgrounds at Chautauqua's new African American Heritage House. We watched the exceptional documentary on the life of Toni Morrison, *The Pieces I Am*, just days after her death. We had dinner together on the porch of the one-hundred-and-forty-year-old Athenaeum Hotel on the shore of Lake Chautauqua. The evening's informal, spontaneous, and far-ranging conversation seemed to bind us together like old friends. We began to share some of our most personal thoughts and feelings as our discussion ranged from Colson Whitehead's novel *The Underground Railroad*, to Ta-Nehisi Coates's *We Were Eight Years in Power: An American Tragedy,* and recent commentaries on Ralph Ellison's classic *Invisible Man,* and the disturbing manner in which divisive words and deeds of President Donald Trump seemed to be exacerbating the racial divide.

The most intense parts of the conversation occurred when the topic turned to our views on the question of various forms of possible reparations for African Americans in response to the reality of slavery. We started with House of Representatives Bill 40 which proposes the establishment of a Commission to Study and Develop Reparation Proposals for African Americans; to examine slavery and discrimination in the colonies and the United States from 1619 to the present and recommend appropriate remedies. According to the bill, this commission should identify the role of federal and state governments in supporting the institution of slavery; identify forms of discrimination in the public and private sectors against freed slaves and their descendants; and identify lingering negative effects of slavery on living African Americans and society.

Two of the participants argued forcefully that this is a completely unrealistic proposal with no hope of succeeding as a piece of government legislation. What would be "appropriate remedies"? Money? How much money? Paid to whom? Only to poor African Americans? How poor must they be? Who would decide? Whose money? Other participants asserted that these are the very questions the proposed bill has asked the government to study.

When most of us in the conversation realized we did not have a clear idea of what most Americans think about reparations, we did some investigating. We learned that most Americans do not support reparations. Less than 40 percent of Americans believed that former enslaved free human beings should have received money as compensation once slavery ended. Barely 15 percent think living African Americans are entitled to financial payments because of slavery in the past. While 59 percent of African Americans support cash payments to those whose ancestors were enslaved, only 6 percent of white Americans hold that opinion. Whereas 63 percent of African Americans are in favor of educational and job training opportunities for those whose ancestors were enslaved, only 19 percent of white people share that position.

Opponents of any form of reparation argue that no single group was enriched by slavery. And no single group should bear the responsibility for slavery. The number of white people who owned slaves was small. Many more white people died in the Civil War that opposed slavery. Today's multiracial, multiethnic, pluralistic society should not be arbitrarily blamed for misdeeds of the past. Let the past bury the past.

But someone in the group asked about the government's response to the Japanese after their incarceration. In 1988, President Reagan signed the Civil Liberties Act. This act compensated more than 100,000 people of Japanese descent who were imprisoned in internment camps during World War II. The government formally apologized and gave $20,000 in compensation to each survivor of this ordeal. It took the Japanese American community only ten years to persuade the Congress to approve this legislation. Could this be a model for African American reparations? I pointed out a key difference. Unlike the Japanese, there are no survivors of African American enslavement alive to receive compensation.

One of the week's Chautauqua speakers, Maryland Episcopal Bishop Eugene T. Sutton, who testified before Congress in support of House Bill 40, said reparations should not be thought of simply as white people giving money to individual African American people out of feelings of guilt. It requires us to acknowledge the racial divide among us. Reparations will help mend the brokenness. None of us caused this brokenness, but all of us have a moral responsibility to mend it. For generations the bodies of African Americans did not belong to themselves, but were bred, used, and sold for the purpose of attaining wealth. A structure with a broken foundation cannot hope to stand unless it is repaired.

Reparations, quite simply, are meant to repair that which has been broken, an attempt to make whole again, to offer atonement; to make amends; to reconcile for a wrong or injury. Reparations, Bishop Sutton said, should be a work of healing the country. He then proposed $500 billion for reparations, which he contrasted with the $6 trillion our government has spent on wars since 2001. And the money should not be given to individuals but to schools, job training, housing, environmental sustainability, and nursing homes that benefit needy People of Color. Our group could not agree that this was the best approach. All agreed that the federal government would never support such a proposal.

In the course of conversation, I was forced to realize that I had not really given serious thought to an issue which is of great concern to many people. But our extraordinary discussion caused me to think more deeply about the full implications of this difficult question. In an introspective mood, I thought particularly of my father and mother, my grandparents and my great-grandparents whose life stories go back to the era of President Wilson and beyond. Recalling stories they told me, I thought that my parents, especially my father, would probably not be so quick to dismiss the topic of reparations. He might well argue that some form of remuneration for what he and his parents endured was a topic worthy of serious examination. My great-grandparents, who lived closer to the era of the enslavement of African people in America, might well have dismissed the idea of reparations as a kind of cruel joke put forth not out of serious concern for the suffering they experienced but as a way of adding salt to old wounds. I do not think the Catholic Church has given any attention to this controversial topic at the national level.

Still, there are some indications that religious institutions may be among the first to take modest steps toward some forms of reparations. In September 2019, more than one hundred years after the last enslaved free human beings ceased their work building the school, Virginia Theological Seminary took a step toward reparations for its practice of slave labor. The seminary became one of the first American institutions to set aside money for the direct purpose of benefiting current family members of those who built the seminary. A $1.7 million reparations fund has been established. Part of the money will be used to cover the tuition of African American students.

This comes after the Sisters of the Society of the Sacred Heart established a reparations fund to create scholarships for African American students in Grand Coteau, Louisiana, where 150 enslaved free African people were once "owned" by the religious order. This comes after the vote by students at Georgetown University to establish a fund with student fees. This money would assist descendants of the 272 enslaved free human beings once "owned" by the Jesuits and sold in 1838 to maintain the school. The university also offered a formal apology to the descendants and offered preferential admission to them. At the same time, some of these descendants have asked for a $1 billion foundation to fund some of their educational, health, and housing needs. Such a fund has not been established. These unexpected modest steps may indicate that the issue of reparations has the potential of being more than a topic hesitantly discussed by the Democrats contending for the 2020 presidential nomination.

My experiences at Chautauqua, especially this long conversation about the reparations debate, were very significant to me. They were the catalyst for writing this introductory essay in a style unlike anything I have ever written before. It is more personal and revelatory about my family and my personal experiences. Thinking and praying at Chautauqua about the new and deepening racial divide and recalling W. E. B. Du Bois's "double consciousness" pushed me to be more transparent, with less need for concealment.

Finally, this book is clearly not an exercise in Black theology. But, looking back, I now see the influence of Black theology in compelling me to write what is now the first chapter in this book, "The Racial Divide in the United States: A Reflection for the World Day of Peace 2015" (January 1, 2015). The immediate impetus for writing this reflection was the shooting death of Mr. Michael Brown Jr., 18, in Ferguson, Missouri, on August 9, 2014. The widespread interest in this pastoral letter led to chapter 2, "The

Catholic Church and the Black Lives Matter Movement: The Racial Divide Revisited" (February 26, 2016). The subsequent related essays and addresses make up the remaining chapters. Each piece was written at a distinct moment and in unique circumstances. Although I have edited these chapters, I have not rewritten them in order to create an artificial continuity. Each piece is a self-contained examination of some aspect of the Catholic Church and the racial divide. Though distinct, the chapters are internally related. Like my life they reflect a moving viewpoint.

I hope these reflections from my moving viewpoint give you a helpful key to the pages that follow. May these writings assist you in determining the things you can do, great or small, to help bridge the racial divide in the United States, so acute in our time. These pages can provide a useful resource for the study of *Brothers and Sisters to Us: US Catholic Bishops' Pastoral Letter on Racism* (1979), *What We Have Seen and Heard: A Pastoral Letter on Evangelization from the Black Bishops of the United States* (1984), and *Open Wide Our Hearts: The Enduring Call to Love: A Pastoral Letter against Racism* (2018).

The remarkable St. Teresa of Calcutta, when faced with the enormous suffering and poverty in Calcutta, was often told that she and her sisters were having no impact on the social, economic, and political structures in India that were the root cause of the suffering that moved her so deeply. She quickly conceded that she and her sisters could not possibly have a major impact on such unspeakable pain and suffering. They could not overcome the caste system, end political corruption, and provide food, housing, health care, education, and employment for the vast numbers starving and dying on the streets each day. Then she said, "We may not be able to do a great deal to change the world around us. But, everyone can do something, no matter how seemingly insignificant. Every one of us should feel compelled to do what we can!"

Listen! Learn! Think! Pray! Act!

The Racial Divide
in the United States

A Reflection for the World Day of Peace

JANUARY 1, 2015

When I read No Longer Slaves, But Brothers and Sisters, *the 2015 World Day of Peace statement of Pope Francis, I had been reading, thinking, praying, and talking about the controversy surrounding the number of instances of violent encounters between young African American men and white representatives of law enforcement. The media accounts of these often deadly encounters underscored the differences that often exist among the ways that people of different racial, economic, educational, and social backgrounds perceive these events. In many poor African American communities, it is widely believed that white police officers have a bias against People of Color, suspecting them of criminal activities and assuming them to be dangerous. In the larger white community, people of diverse backgrounds generally have a different perception of white police officers. These officers, who risk their lives every day for the safety of the community, are doing the best they can to enforce the law, in difficult and rapidly changing situations.*

The dramatic difference in perceptions was painfully evident in the aftermath of the sad event of August 9, 2014, when 18-year-old Michael Brown Jr. was fatally shot by the 28-year-old white Ferguson, Missouri, police officer Darren Wilson. Ferguson is a part of the Archdiocese of St. Louis, where I served as Auxiliary Bishop from 1995 to 2000. I am the Bishop of Belleville, Illinois, which lies directly across the Mississippi River from St. Louis. As I was following the intense emotions and conflicts, pain, and suffering experienced by all of the people of Ferguson, I found myself wishing that there was something that I could do, at least in a small way, that might help the people of my Diocese to bring open-mindedness and compassion to their conversations about a story that had become national news. When I spoke infrequently about these volatile events, I urged the People of God in my Diocese not to make rash judgments. I invited them to Listen, Learn, Think, Pray, and Act in ways that might help to bridge the racial divide.

As I became quite preoccupied with this tragic story I began to feel strongly that the perspective of an African American Catholic Bishop might be a small contribution to a much needed dialogue. This is how "The Racial Divide in the United States: A Reflection for the World Day of Peace 2015" came about. Now that I have decided to include it in this book, along with some of my subsequent writings on the racial divide, I have not attempted to rewrite it or update it. I think that it continues to have relevance in the format in which it was originally written, even though the events that prompted it have continued to change and develop.

Dear Sisters and Brothers in Christ:

May the grace of the Lord Jesus Christ, the Prince of Peace, fill your hearts throughout the New Year!

As the Catholic Church celebrates the World Day of Peace today, I am pleased to share this Reflection with you. Please be generous with your time so that you can read it carefully. I invite you to reflect on its contents, pray about its concerns, and discuss its challenges with your sisters and brothers in Christ.

This Reflection has a moving viewpoint in six parts.

Prologue

(This is an invitation to imagine the country and the church from a different perspective.)

A New Awareness of the Racial Divide and a Call to Christian Dialogue

(Our Christian faith emboldens us to enter this conversation.)

Trayvon Martin, Oscar Grant, John Crawford III, Michael Brown Jr., Eric Garner, and Tamir Rice

(This is a summary of the known facts about the deaths of six African American males and the international protests that followed.)

What We Have Seen and Heard
(This is an invitation to reflect on these events within the context of the church's teachings and actions concerning the racial divide in America.)

Conclusion: Pray, Listen, Learn, Think, and Act
(This section provides specific suggestions of activities that may help bridge the racial divide.)

Prologue

I would like to begin by asking you to do something rather unusual. It requires you to use your imagination in order to enter into the role reversal presented in the narrative that follows. The narrative portrays an imagined Catholic Church in the United States in which most American Catholics are People of Color and white Catholics are members of a very small "minority group."

Imagine yourself as a white American teenager living in a poor urban area with few opportunities for you to get a good education and find meaningful employment. Imagine that some of your friends are troublemakers and when the African American police come around they often intimidate them. This frightens you because another white friend of yours was shot and killed by African American police when he reached into his pocket for his wallet which they thought was a gun. Since you were very young, your parents have cautioned you to avoid contact with the police because they may suspect you of wrongdoing.

You and your friends, whose families are struggling to make ends meet, live near the neighborhood Catholic Church. You have never been inside the church. You and your family are not members of the Catholic Church, which some of your relatives call a "Black racist institution" which traditionally has not shown much interest in inviting white people to join the parish. You and your friends feel that a church that promises the joy of eternal life after you die while offering little to help in your daily struggles is not very meaningful. You feel you need a church that will be at your side, engaged in the struggle, helping you find a God of the oppressed and an angel of freedom and justice. You need a church that embraces, celebrates, and is informed by the "white experience." If God is to really be God for you, he must be God the liberator, who uproots injustice and oppression by his mighty power. A God of the status quo is dead.

Now imagine that an African American acquaintance, sensing that you are discouraged, persuades you to go with him to this very church, St. Charles Lwanga, for Mass. You enter the church and all images of the sacred are in Afrocentric art. All images of Jesus, Mary, Joseph, and all the saints are as People of Color (African, Hispanic, Asian, or Native American). God the Father Himself is painted on the ceiling of the church as a distinguished older Black gentleman. You think to yourself, "God the Father is absolute spirit. He has no race or nationality, or anatomical gender. Scripture never describes Him as an elderly, African-looking, brown-skinned man." You wonder if the Catholic Church believes that only people of African ancestry are in heaven.

You notice that even the angels in the church have African features. If angels have no bodies and no gender, if they are pure spirits, why are they not represented in all races? Just think of the impact it would have on unchurched white people, like you, if they encountered the image of a magnificent white angel with blond hair and blue eyes when they entered a Catholic church. You also notice that in the Catholic Church "Black" symbolizes everything that is "good" and "holy" whereas "white" symbolizes evil and sin. The images of Satan, the devil, and demons in the church are all white. Later, you search art books and cannot find one image of Satan painted in dark hues. He is always depicted in light, pale colors.

You ask your African American acquaintance, "Wouldn't the Catholic Church be more truly universal and welcoming of all if the holy men and women of the Bible were pictured as people of different ethnic and racial backgrounds? After all, though we know they were Jewish, no one knows what they actually looked like. All Semitic people do not look like Western Europeans."

He responds, "That question has been asked before, and the response has usually been people who are white should realize that the Afrocentric art represents them as well. Afrocentric art is universal. The all-Black religious art is there for historical reasons. Even though a few churches have added a white saint here and there, for the most part the few white Catholics we have in the church have simply accepted the fact that the majority of churches have few or no images of the citizens of Heaven who look like them."

You ask your acquaintance, "Does the Catholic Church intend to perpetuate this all-Black image of heaven in the churches of the future?"

Your African American acquaintance replies, "There are a few churches in big cities with a large number of 'minorities' where they have painted white angels and saints. But some of the older white people don't like it. They say they do not believe God looks like them. In many countries where all of the people are European, the people almost never complain about the all-African religious art."

"But," you ask, "what about here in the racially diverse United States? What a powerful statement the church would make if it mandated all future churches to have racially diverse images of God, Jesus, Mary, saints, and angels? Wouldn't it convey a more authentically universal image of heaven?"

He answers, "I really don't think that is ever going to happen."

"Why not?" you ask. "Why not?"

A New Awareness of the Racial Divide
and a Call to Christian Dialogue

Our Holy Father Pope Francis has selected the theme *No Longer Slaves, But Brothers and Sisters* for the 2015 World Day of Peace celebration. Human slavery can take many forms, including the literal enslavement of human beings by other human beings, which, sadly, continues to exist in our world today. There are also forms of social, emotional, and psychological slavery: slavery to prejudice, racism, bias, anger, frustration, rage, violence, and bitterness in the face of systemic injustices. Regrettably, these forms of slavery endure in the United States, and they are born from the tragedy of the European "slave trade" that captured innocent human beings from West Africa and brought them to the United States to be "sold," "bought," and "owned" in bondage to work on the lucrative plantations in southern states. Long after the cruel evil of slavery was ended, its consequences continued to cast a shadow over our nation as a racial divide. Recent dramatic eruptions of racial conflict have made this shadow more apparent. Painful "breaking news" accounts call all Americans to rededicate themselves to the work of peace and reconciliation among our citizens of different races, ethnic origins, and social, cultural, educational, economic, and religious backgrounds. As Catholics, as members of the Body of Christ, the church, this is more than a call; it is our vocation, born of baptism.

Our World Day of Peace celebration always comes during the season of joy, between Christmas and the Epiphany, the showing forth of the glory of Christ to the nations. The radical source of this joy is the tremendous mystery that the Word of God is made flesh in Christ Jesus. Christ, the Prince of Peace, announces the dignity and worth of every man, woman, and child. In a number of communities in the United States, the spirit of community fellowship, goodwill, and optimism that accompany Christmas and the New Year have been overshadowed by dramatic and disturbing events that have reminded the nation and the world of the racial divide that endures in our country. While many African American people live in southern Illinois, most of them are not members of the Catholic Church. When I am on parish pastoral visitations, I occasionally see a small number of African Americans and a smaller number of African people in the congregations. The only predominantly African American parish in the diocese is St. Augustine of Hippo in East St. Louis. This should not be surprising since of the roughly 78,000,000 Catholics in this country, only about 3,500,000 are African Americans. Many members of the church may have only infrequent and somewhat superficial contact with Catholics of a different racial background.

During the past few months, Catholics, like the rest of the country, have pondered distressing events in cities around the country. These events include the deaths of young Men of Color during confrontations with local white police officers or a neighborhood watch person; the public expressions of grief by family members; the reactions to grand jury decisions to indict or not to indict the persons who shot these men; unprecedented unrest (including not only peaceful demonstrations, but also the taunting of the police, violence, the senseless destruction of property, and heinous "revenge" murders) in cities across the country; statements by President Obama, governors, and mayors about the current racial crisis; investigations of possible civil rights violations initiated by Attorney General Eric H. Holder Jr.; and published surveys and media commentaries suggesting that a great gulf exists between the way many Black Americans and many white Americans view these events. This gulf is, in fact, a racial divide.

It is my hope that this World Day of Peace Reflection will help families, parishioners, neighbors, support groups for priests, ecumenical ministerial groups, chancery staff members, and school faculties to engage in fruitful conversations about the events that are unfolding in the United States. It would be particularly valuable if people of different racial backgrounds could partake in the same conversations. There are surely some Catholics who would rather not have these conversations. But our Christmas faith in Christ, the redeemer of all people, urges us to overcome our hesitation. Now that the busy Christmas season has passed, this reflection could serve as a resource for discussions marking January 15, the eighty-sixth anniversary of the birth of Dr. Martin Luther King Jr. In the New Year, Lent, which begins early, on February 18, 2015, would be a very appropriate opportunity to give time and serious consideration to the topics addressed here.

Let's begin with ten observations about which I hope there will be some degree of agreement.

1.   Each of the accounts of encounters between white police (or a neighborhood watch person) and young Men of Color
ending in death is a unique event. While there are some obvious
similarities, they are completely distinct and the people involved
are all unique individuals about whom we should not generalize
or stereotype.

2.   We each realize that our views about these complex events
are influenced by our age, education, family background, personal
experiences, religious beliefs, and the media, which may make
difficult situations worse if their reporting is sensational and/or
biased.

3.   The deaths of the individuals who lost their lives in these
incidents are sad events: a source of grief and sorrow for their
families. It is also true that the experiences of the men who caused
these deaths are a source of sorrow for them and for their families.

4.   None of us knows, with certainty, exactly what happened
in these and other incidents because we were not there. None of
us has a full and complete knowledge of all grand jury proceed-
ings. Even when grand jury documents have been released, it is
not the same as experiencing the manner in which the cases were
presented. Perhaps only God and the people involved know exactly
what happened. Unfortunately, in each case, a key participant is
dead. Most of our information is derived from various forms of
media, which have their distinct points of view.

5.   The work of police officers is very difficult and very dangerous. Because of the violence in American society, they leave
their homes each day not knowing if they will return unharmed.
They deserve our respect and gratitude. They are forced to make
split-second, life-and-death decisions on which their lives and the
lives of others depend. In some communities, many police officers
are faithful Christians, who strive to live by the Gospel. Every
community needs dedicated police officers to keep order and to
protect the citizens and their property. Most police are fair-minded
and respect the human dignity and worth of all citizens. Some,
however, are not. There is credible evidence that bias and prejudice
influence the attitudes and actions of some police officers, no matter what their race or nationality may be. Significantly, 57 percent

of African American police believe Black offenders are treated with far less respect by white officers than white offenders. However, only 5 percent of white officers agree that this is true. It is a fact that some young Black men commit crimes requiring their arrest by the police. However, this should not lead to the demonization of all Black men as dangerous, violent criminals. It is a fact that some white police officers use excessive force and display racial prejudice when they interact with Black men suspected of crimes. However, this should not lead to the demonization of all white police officers as racists ready to kill Black men at the slightest provocation.

6.   Some individuals firmly believe that it is completely inappropriate for religious leaders to make any comments about these events beyond generalized statements about working for peace and justice, while others firmly believe that the Gospel compels religious leaders to address such issues forthrightly despite their complexity in a constructive spirit of mutual respect and reconciliation.

7.   In some communities, African American males are taking the lives of other African American males in alarming numbers. Several investigations suggest that 93 percent of African Americans who are murdered are murdered by other African Americans and 84 percent of white Americans who are murdered are murdered by other white Americans.

8.   All American citizens have the right to protest peacefully and demonstrate when they believe that they are faced with unjust laws, unresponsive government officials, and morally unacceptable social structures that do not respect the dignity and worth of every human person.

9.   No one has the right to break the law by expressing frustration by violence, arson, looting, destruction of property, and endangering the lives of fellow citizens. These inexcusable crimes only undermine the efforts of those with legitimate grievances.

10.   Most American neighborhoods are made up of people of similar racial, economic, and cultural backgrounds. This is also true of most American church congregations. Most American Catholic parishes have very few or no African American members.

Significantly, more and more Americans of different races work, socialize, and recreate together, and the number of biracial marriages continues to increase. However, the majority of Americans do not have significant numbers of intimate friends of different races whose homes they visit, with whom they vacation, and with whom they share their most personal feelings.

Catholic people, like other Americans, have reacted in a variety of ways to these deaths, court decisions, and protests. For some, the events are simply another fleeting news item that has no direct impact on them. The participants are not their friends or family members. It is not their neighborhood. For others, these are disturbing events, and they are concerned about their impact on the nation; but they do not dwell on them. For still others, there are feelings of anger and frustration about the cries of "white racism," the criticism of the police, the attack on the judicial system, the disruption of normal life by protesters, and the destruction of property by vandals. As one Catholic expressed it to me, "Slavery and racism are things of the past. The protesters should stop complaining, obey the law, follow the orders of the police, get a job, and get on with their lives." But there are still other Catholics who are profoundly distressed. They feel that they were naïve in thinking the era of racial conflict was behind us. They are upset by the attitudes and comments of some of their Catholic neighbors. Some of these individuals, concluding that there is systemic racial prejudice in American society that is morally wrong, have taken to the streets taking part in the mass nationwide peaceful protests while condemning the acts of vandalism.

Before we continue, let me add a personal note. I am not a completely impartial outside observer in the face of these events. I have had two personal experiences with law enforcement officers that made me very conscious of the fact that simply by being me, I could be the cause of suspicion and concern without doing anything wrong. The first experience was when I was a young priest. The second was when I was already a bishop. In both cases I was not in clerical attire. I was dressed informally.

In the first experience, I was simply walking down a street in an apparently all-white neighborhood. A police car drove up beside me, and the officer asked, "What are you doing in this area? Do you live around here? Where is your car? You should not be wandering around neighborhoods where you do not live." I never told him I was a Catholic priest, but I wondered what it was I was doing to attract the attention of the officer. This was long before I heard the expression, "walking while Black."

In the second experience, I was driving in my car in an apparently all-white neighborhood with two small chairs in the back seat and a table in the partially open trunk tied with a rope. A police car with flashing lights pulled me over. The officer asked, "Where are you going with that table and those chairs? Before I could answer, he asked, "Where did you get them?" Then he said, "We had a call about a suspicious person driving through the area with possibly stolen furniture in his trunk." I wondered what I was doing to make someone suspicious. Many years would pass before I would hear the expression "racial profiling."

As we examine the racial divide, we may be tempted to yield to the seeming pessimism of Reinhold Niebuhr. He suggested in *Moral Man and Immoral Society* that while some individuals (Moral Man) might frequently strive for and sometime attain the ability to perform altruistic acts of compassion and love; larger communities (Immoral Society) are generally slow to be moved to generous acts of love, compassion, and reconciliation. Our Christmas faith in the mystery of Incarnation emboldens us to believe that we, as individuals and as communities, can and should cross the racial divide.

Trayvon Martin, Oscar Grant III, John Crawford III, Michael Brown Jr., Eric Garner, and Tamir Rice

> God gave Noah the rainbow sign.
> No more water, but the fire next time!
> —from a slave song

Undercurrents of the racial divide in the United States have been apparent to all serious observers of events from the time of the civil rights movement, spearheaded by the prophetic, nonviolent work of the murdered Rev. Dr. Martin Luther King Jr., to the present. There have been a number of commentators who, at least until recently, have erroneously suggested that the election of a biracial American, Barack Obama, as president ushered in a postracial era in America. Born to Stanley Ann Dunham (of English and German heritage) and her husband Baraka—later Barack—Obama Sr. (of Kenyan heritage), the president, at times, seems to embody the racial divide in his own person. Because he embodies the reality of Harvard pioneer W. E. B. Du Bois's *The Souls of Black Folk* to some African Americans, Mr. Obama does not speak forthrightly enough about racial prejudice in America. To some white Americans, Mr. Obama sees racism everywhere and never stops talking about it. The president is presiding over events in which the misperception of a postracial era has been shattered by a series of events dealing with encounters between young African American males, white representatives of law enforcement, the judicial system, and the responses of the larger Black and white communities. It is important for you to have the main points of these events before you to facilitate your conversations. While the accounts that follow are drawn completely from public records, it is impossible for them to be complete and absolutely balanced accounts. They are not provided to provoke argument about who was right and who was wrong. They are provided to give common narratives and to provide the context for discussions, since the issues before us cannot be fruitfully discussed in the abstract. They are provided to help us learn and move forward. (The list is now much longer.)

On February 26, 2012, Mr. Trayvon Martin was shot and killed in Sanford, Florida, by George Zimmerman, a white neighborhood watch volunteer (NOT a police officer), who told the police he looked suspicious. The police told him not to pursue Mr. Martin on foot. However, he did. There was an altercation between the two men, and Mr. Martin, who did not have a gun, was shot to death by Mr. Zimmerman. No charges were filed against Mr. Zimmerman by the police who stated they found no evidence to refute Mr. Zimmerman's claim that since Mr. Martin was attacking him, he shot in self-defense. The "stand your ground law" in Florida does not allow the police to arrest or charge someone in these circumstances. There were no eyewitnesses. Later, Mr. Zimmerman was formally charged with second-degree murder in a hearsay affidavit filed by special prosecutor Ms. Angela Corey. Many commentators argued that the prosecution would have had a better chance of succeeding if the case had been presented to a grand jury considering a lesser charge. In July 2013, he was acquitted on grounds of self-defense in a jury trial.

After the death of Mr. Martin, there were protest marches and rallies across the nation. The 2012 presidential campaign was eclipsed by the media coverage surrounding these events, which were followed by a short-lived national debate concerning "stand your ground laws" and "racial profiling."

During the same year of Mr. Zimmerman's acquittal (2013), the film *Fruitvale Station*, documenting the case of Mr. Oscar Grant III, was released to critical acclaim. On New Year's Day 2009, Mr. Grant, who was unarmed, was shot and killed by Johannes Mehserle, a Bay Area Rapid Transit officer in Oakland, California. Mr. Grant, along with a number of other passengers, was detained by police at the train's Fruitvale Station when they responded to a call saying there was a fight on one of the rapid transit trains. Mr. Grant, who was resisting arrest and lying face down, was being restrained by Officer Mehserle. The officer stood and said: "Get back, I'm gonna Tase him." The officer drew his pistol and shot Mr. Grant once in the back. Mr. Grant shouted, "You shot me!" Mr. Grant died the next morning. This episode was recorded by several bystanders on cell phone cameras and millions of people viewed the digital videos, which spread quickly via websites and social media.

In 2010, the county prosecutors charged Officer Mehserle with murder for the shooting. He resigned his position and pleaded not guilty. Mr. Mehserle's criminal defense attorney argued that Mr. Mehserle shot Mr. Grant with his pistol by mistake. When he saw Mr. Grant reach for his waistband, he intended to use his

Taser. The jury found Mr. Mehserle guilty of involuntary man-slaughter and not guilty of second-degree murder and voluntary manslaughter. At first, there were peaceful protests against the ruling. By nightfall, nearly eighty people had been arrested because of violent protests, arson, destruction of property, and looting.

On November 5, 2010, Mr. Mehserle was sentenced to two years, minus time served. He was released on May 3, 2011, and is now on parole. In 2010, the US Justice Department opened a civil rights investigation against Mr. Mehserle. However, so far, no charges have been filed. In 2011, the Bay Area Rapid Transit settled a wrongful death claim with Mr. Grant's family for $2.8 million.

Most recently, there have been the cases of John Crawford III, Michael Brown Jr., Eric Garner, and Tamir Rice, among others.

On August 5, 2014, Mr. John Crawford III, a 22-year-old African American, was shopping in a Walmart store near Dayton, Ohio. He picked up a toy gun, an unpackaged BB/pellet air rifle in the toy section of the store. Another shopper who saw him walking through the store with the gun called 911 saying "a Black man" was carrying a rifle in the store. The caller later conceded that "At no point did he (Mr. Crawford) shoulder the rifle and point it at somebody."

The two white officers of the Beavercreek Police who arrived at the store said Mr. Crawford did not respond to their directives to put the gun down and lie on the floor. Instead, he seemed to try to escape. Officer Sean Williams thought the toy was a real gun. He shot Mr. Crawford twice, and he died on the scene. The security camera recorded the incident. When he was shot, Mr. Crawford was talking on his phone. The gun was in his left hand. When the police questioned his girlfriend, they did not believe her when she stated that Mr. Crawford did not bring the toy gun into the store with him. Officer Williams was placed on desk duty. A grand jury decided not to indict the officers involved.

Mr. Crawford's family has filed a wrongful death lawsuit against Walmart and the Beavercreek Police Department. In order to prevent future catastrophic events, Alicia Reece, an Ohio state representative, has proposed a "John Crawford's Law," which would require toy guns to look like toy guns.

On August 9, 2014, Mr. Michael Brown Jr., 18, who was unarmed, was shot and killed in Ferguson, Missouri, by Ferguson Police Officer Darren Wilson, who said he did so to save his own life from the threat of Mr. Brown who was moving aggressively toward him. Mr. Brown's body lay in the street for hours after the shooting. On the night of November 24, after months of deliberation, St. Louis County prosecutor, Mr. Robert McCulloch, announced that the grand jury, having reviewed all of the evidence, decided "not to indict Officer Wilson."

Officer Wilson, in his patrol car, saw Mr. Brown and a friend walking down the middle of the street. He directed them to move off the street to the sidewalk. They did not comply. As Officer Wilson drove past them, he noticed that Mr. Brown looked like the person suspected of stealing cigars from a convenience store and assaulting the salesperson. A struggle took place between Officer Wilson and Mr. Brown through the police car window. In the course of the conflict, the officer's gun was fired twice. Mr. Brown was wounded in the arm. When the officer testified before the grand jury, he said that when he (6 foot 4 inches, 210 pounds) was trying to restrain Mr. Brown (6 foot 4 inches, 292 pounds) during this altercation, he "felt like a 5-year-old holding onto Hulk Hogan."

The officer pursued Mr. Brown on foot. The analysis of blood stains on the street indicates that Mr. Brown, who had been shot a number of times, continued to move toward Officer Wilson. The policeman fired at least six shots. The fatal shot was a head wound. Officer Wilson said the race of Mr. Brown did not matter. He only shot him because he had to. Some witnesses said this was not true. This entire encounter between the officer and the unarmed teenager lasted less than ninety seconds. Feeling that some Ferguson residents and the media were judging Officer Wilson prematurely, a number of white residents organized expressions of support, raising funds for his defense.

There is no video of the event. A number of witnesses stated that Mr. Brown had his hands up in a position of surrender, resulting in the later mantra, "Hands up! Don't shoot!" After months of deliberation, the grand jury announced that Officer

Wilson would not be indicted. Several examinations of the secret grand jury documents, which were made public, concluded that there were many problems in the witnesses' testimonies. There were statements that were "inconsistent, fabricated, or provably wrong." Some witnesses even admitted that they changed their testimony for various reasons. Commentators noted that the jury's refusal to indict Officer Wilson marked the fifth time that Mr. McCulloch had presented evidence to a grand jury in prosecuting a policeman involved in a shooting. In all five cases, there was no indictment. A number of observers said Mr. McCulloch should have been replaced by a special prosecutor because of his close relationship with police and because his father, a policeman, was killed in the line of duty.

Once the grand jury decision was made public, protests and demonstrations erupted in Ferguson and more than 150 other cities, including St. Louis, Philadelphia, Seattle, Albuquerque, New York, Cleveland, Los Angeles, Oakland, Minneapolis, Atlanta, Portland, Chicago, and Boston. In Ferguson, some demonstrations turned violent and destructive. Businesses were destroyed by arsonists, cars were burned, and merchandise was stolen from shops. There were indications that much of the violence and destruction was instigated by outside agitators. Governor Jay Nixon declared a state of emergency and called out the National Guard. President Obama said that he understood the disappointment and anger of those who staged peaceful protests. However, he had no sympathy for those who destroyed property because these were criminal acts.

Archbishop Robert J. Carlson of St. Louis was a visible presence in Ferguson, participating in a prayer service for peace and reconciliation along with other clergy on the night of the grand jury's decision. He stated, "With the grand jury decision not to indict Officer Darren Wilson, I know that many feel hurt, betrayed, forgotten, and powerless. I know anger, disappointment, resentment, and fear abound in our community. But we must accept this decision as the proper functioning of our justice system. In our collective desire for justice, we can be blinded by the poisonous desire for vengeance, which can be contagious and bring a desire for violence. We all want justice, so we should respect the integrity of our system of justice as something that aims for the common good."

Father Robert Rosebrough, pastor of Blessed Teresa of Calcutta Parish, moved about the community after the violence and destruction visiting with employees now out of work. People lamented the fact that the lack of economic opportunity in poor communities had been a major concern after Mr. Brown's death.

Mr. Holder, the attorney general, was critical of Mr. McCulloch's presentation of the grand jury's findings. He expressed concern about the wisdom of the late-at-night announcement, which could have contributed to the unrest that followed. The director of the Harvard Criminal Justice Institute at Harvard University, Ronald S. Sullivan Jr., said the case was "the most unusual marshaling of a grand jury's resources I've seen in my 25 years as a lawyer and scholar." However, Mr. Rudy Giuliani, former US Attorney for the Southern District of New York, said that the prosecution could have never convicted Officer Wilson at a trial, and that the grand jury made the right decision not to indict him. He said, "If you can't prove probable cause, how are you going to prove it beyond a reasonable doubt when the witnesses are contradicting themselves?"

Obviously, all instances in which a white police officer shoots an African American male are not marked by questions and ambiguities that may warrant peaceful protests. On December 23, an unnamed white Berkley, Missouri, police officer shot and killed Antonio Martin, 18, an African American male. The video of the event and eyewitness testimony indicate that police arrived at a gas station where there had been a report of shoplifting. The officers recognized two men who fit the description of the alleged shoplifters. The officers exited their police car and engaged them in conversation. The surveillance video of the event shows Mr. Martin walking away from the officers several times. Then Mr. Martin pulls a gun from his pocket and points it toward the officer. The officer fires several shots and appears to stumble as he backs away. Mr. Martin died shortly afterward.

This is certainly a sad event because a young man's life has been ended, and his family is in mourning. However, in this case, there seems to be no evidence to suggest questionable or possibly overly aggressive conduct by the officer. He did what he was compelled to do, namely to defend his life and the lives of others in the face of a person pointing a gun directly at him. A small number of protesters gathered shortly after this incident comparing the death of Mr. Martin to the death of Mr. Brown in nearby Ferguson. A physical fight broke out, and some of those involved were arrested. Unfortunately, instances in which members of the community have a credible reason for peacefully protesting what may be inappropriate conduct by the police will be significantly undermined if protests take place even when the police are acting properly in difficult circumstances with regrettable deadly results.

On July 17, 2014, Mr. Eric Garner, 44, who did not have a weapon, died in Staten Island, New York, after Police Officer Daniel Pantaleo put him in what has been described as a chokehold, a tactic banned by the New York Police Department. The event was recorded on cell phones and spread rapidly via the internet. The police suspected Mr. Garner was selling single cigarettes from packs without tax stamps, called "loosies." He had multiple prior arrests for this and other violations including assault and grand larceny. He was out on bail. Mr. Garner said that he was not selling cigarettes and told the police they should stop harassing him. When the officers were attempting to arrest him, Mr. Garner backed away. Officer Pantaleo approached him from behind and put his arms around Mr. Garner's neck, applying what has been widely regarded as a chokehold by those who have viewed the video recording. The officers subdued him on the sidewalk with his face down. Mr. Garner, a married man with six children, said over and over again, "I can't breathe." He was taken to a local hospital where he was pronounced dead. Though he had been accused of selling loose cigarettes in the past, none were found at the scene.

The city medical examiners determined that the cause of Mr. Garner's death was neck compression from the apparent chokehold, along with "the compression of his chest and prone positioning during physical restraint by police." His asthma, heart disease, and obesity contributed to his death, according to the medical examiner. After this incident, Officer Pantaleo and another policeman were transferred to desk duty and Officer Pantaleo was required to turn over his badge and his service revolver. He was the subject of two civil rights lawsuits in 2013 in which plaintiffs accused him of falsely arresting them and abusing them. In one of the cases, Officer Pantaleo and other officers ordered two African American men to strip naked on a public street in order to be searched. The charges against both men were dismissed.

Many people thought the video was self-evident. This led to a widespread expectation in some parts of the New York community and beyond that Officer Pantaleo would be indicted by the grand jury. However, on December 3, 2014, the Staten Island grand jury announced its decision not to indict him. This announcement resulted in large demonstrations (including die-ins), rallies, and protests in different parts of New York as well as in Boston, Washington, DC, Chicago, Oakland, Atlanta, and in Europe. These protests were organized quickly via social media. Many of the participants were young Americans of noticeably different races and different social and cultural backgrounds. They condemned racial bias and police brutality chanting "Black lives matter!" "Hands up! Don't shoot!" and "I can't breathe!"

The protests were largely nonviolent. Nevertheless, many arrests were made of those who would not disperse. At the University of California in Berkeley, protests turned violent. There was extensive damage to businesses, and many were arrested. Some of these demonstrations have now been going on for weeks, and they have been covered by media from around the world. The attorney general announced that the Justice Department would conduct a civil rights investigation that would be "independent, thorough, fair, and expeditious." Officer Pantaleo later spoke about the incident saying that his action was not a "chokehold." It was a standard "takedown maneuver" for someone noncompliant that he learned in the police academy. He did not intend to harm Mr. Garner. Nor did he put pressure on his throat or windpipe. Skeptics rejected his statement, indicating that the medical examiner's report, which ruled the death a homicide, was clear.

On November 22, 2014, just days before the December 3 grand jury ruling in the case of Mr. Garner, Tamir Rice, 12, was shot in Cleveland, Ohio, by Police Officer Timothy Loehmann after a report that he had been seen brandishing a gun in a local park. The gun was, in fact, a toy airsoft (plastic pellet) gun that resembled a real gun. The boy died the next day. The 911 caller said the gun was "probably fake." Apparently, Officer Loehmann and Officer Frank Garmback, who responded to the call, did not receive this information. According to the officers, there was a very brief encounter during which Tamir reached toward his waistband. However, within two seconds of arriving on the scene, Officer Loehmann fired two shots. One report stated that Tamir did not threaten or point the airsoft gun at the policemen. Yet another report states that he was asked to put down the gun and he did not. How it happened that the officers were not given the information that the gun was "probably fake" has not been explained.

After this incident, reports surfaced that Officer Loehmann had been deemed an emotionally unstable recruit and unfit for duty in his previous position as a member of the Independence, Ohio, police force. Again, a very sad story became national and international news.

A grainy surveillance video of the shooting, without audio, shows Mr. Rice pacing around the park, occasionally holding up a gun in his hand, talking on his cell phone, and sitting at a table in a gazebo. The video shows the officers' patrol car pulling up beside the gazebo. Mr. Rice then appears to move his right hand toward his waist. According to published reports, Officer Loehmann exited his car and shot him immediately.

On November 24, Cleveland officials announced that a grand jury would hear the case and determine whether charges will be filed against either policeman. Meanwhile, the officers are on administrative leave. Tamir's family urged those who have mounted demonstrations and protests to do so peacefully. "Again, we ask for the community to remain calm. Please protest peacefully and responsibly." They have since filed a wrongful death lawsuit. On December 12, 2014, the Cuyahoga County Medical Examiner ruled the death was a homicide.

By mid-December, growing national and international protests intensified. On Thursday, December 11, 2014, members of Congress, staffers, and other Capitol Hill employees stood silently on the House steps and raised their hands in the air to protest the killing of unarmed African American men by police. Athletes demonstrated their solidarity in a variety of ways. On Friday, December 12, 2014, the church commemorated the apparition of the Mother of Jesus to St. Juan Diego, an Aztec. Her features were like those of the natives, brown skin and dark hair. She is patroness of the Americas as Our Lady of Guadalupe. Significantly, on that same day, people engaged in nonviolent protests by the thousands in major cities in a national day of resistance. In New York, more than 25,000 marched, expressing outrage that the grand jury did not indict any officers in the death of Mr. Eric Garner. In Washington, DC, more than 5,000 marched down the Capitol Mall calling for an end to the use of deadly force by white police in dealing with unarmed Black men. The cases cited here and many others like them are unique. But many people have begun to view them collectively because of similar elements: unarmed African American males killed by white police (with the exception of Mr. Zimmerman), no judgment of guilt and no punishment (with the exception of former officer Mehserle), and the perception that racial bias contributed to the deaths of these African American males.

Near the end of December, a tragic situation was made far worse. On December 20, Mr. Ismaaiyl Brinsley, 28, a troubled, mentally unstable African American, with a criminal record, shot his former girlfriend in Baltimore and then traveled to New York City armed with a gun and harboring intentions to attack police officers. He walked up to a marked squad car on a Brooklyn street and opened fire at the two police officers inside, Officer Wenjian Liu, 32, and his partner, Officer Rafael Ramos, 40. One witness said Mr. Brinsley "took a shooting stance on the passenger side and fired his weapon several times through the front passenger window, striking both officers in the head." He then killed himself. Officer Liu, who had been married for only two months, was Chinese American, and Officer Ramos, who was married with two children, was Hispanic American. Mr. Brinsley reportedly made "very anti-police" statements and expressed the desire to revenge the deaths of Mr. Michael Brown Jr. and Mr. Eric Garner. Through a spokesperson, Mr. Garner's family expressed outrage on hearing of the murders of the two officers. "Any use of the names of Eric Garner and Michael Brown, in connection with any violence or killing of police, is reprehensible and against the pursuit of justice in both cases." This horrific, senseless crime has resulted in unspeakable suffering for the families involved and heightened the growing tensions in New York, especially when some protesters rejected Mayor William de Blasio's request to discontinue their demonstrations until after the funerals for the slain police officers.

A growing awareness seems to be emerging that renewed efforts must be made to reestablish bonds of trust and respect between law enforcement, the judicial system, and local communities. There has been a call for greater racial diversity in local police departments. Body cameras have been proposed to provide more accurate records of deadly encounters. Law enforcement personnel have acknowledged the need for better training in responding to situations which can escalate quickly to violence and death. Some young men may be becoming more aware of the importance of complying promptly with police instructions, even if they seem unfair or unjust. Religious leaders are appreciating the urgent need for them to take a more active role in bridging the racial divide especially between young African American men and white representatives of the law.

What We Have Seen and Heard

What happens to a dream deferred?
Does it dry up
like a raisin in the sun?
Or fester like a sore—
And then run?
Does it stink like rotten meat?
Or crust and sugar over—
like a syrupy sweet?
Maybe it just sags
like a heavy load.
Or does it explode?

—Langston Hughes

In the face of the racial tensions that have emerged in the wake of these deaths and other events, Catholic bishops such as Archbishop Robert Carlson of St. Louis have called for renewed efforts to overcome racial injustice, while urging those who exercise their right to protest to do so in a manner that respects the safety of other citizens and the rule of law.

On this World Day of Peace 2015, as we ponder the Bishop of Rome's reminder that we are no longer slaves but brothers and sisters, we are forced to acknowledge that by its own admission, the Catholic Church in the United States has a flawed history in the area of racial equality. Many young students of history are surprised, even shocked, to learn that Catholic institutions and religious communities "owned" human beings from West Africa as enslaved workers on their plantations. They are amazed that the Catholic bishops did not forcefully condemn human bondage as contrary to the Gospel of Jesus Christ. It is difficult for them to believe that some Catholic authors wrote tracts in defense of the slave trade and that the church did not vigorously oppose apartheid-like Jim Crow laws in the South.

It is news to them that Men and Women of Color were excluded from seminaries and convents and generally could not become priests or sisters, except in orders designated for "colored people." It is a revelation to them to learn that when Bishop Joseph A. Francis, SVD, late auxiliary bishop of Newark, New Jersey, was asked why there were so few African American Catholics, his response was, "If you had seen and heard what I have seen and heard, you would not be amazed that there are so few, you would be amazed that there are so many."

Young students are often equally surprised at the efforts that many in the church have made to move beyond this painful, flawed legacy. A number of Catholic priests and sisters were active in the civil rights movement working and marching for racial integration in the North and South. Catholic schools in urban communities have made important educational contributions to the intellectual and moral formation of African American youths, many of whom were not Catholic. The church has also been at the forefront of programs that confront the sources of poverty, which is a fact of life for many African American families. In 1958, the American bishops published *Discrimination and Christian Conscience* and in 1968 they published *National Race Crisis*. But most honest students of history would acknowledge that these documents, though well intended, were not widely disseminated or implemented. Catholic parishes and schools, North and South, remained largely segregated. And many church practices that reinforced racial bias remained largely unchanged.

Eleven years later in 1979 and then in 1984 two landmark pastoral letters of seminal importance appeared. The first was the United States Conference of Catholic Bishops' document *Brothers and Sisters to Us*, which bluntly condemned racism as a sin and heresy present in the church. The second was *What We Have Seen and Heard*, the 1984 pastoral statement of the then ten African American Catholic bishops, who were all auxiliary bishops at the time. (Both documents are available online and from the Bishops' Conference.) These pivotal texts made a significant impact in certain parts of the country. However, there are parishes and dioceses where they were all but ignored. Many American Catholics today do not even know these documents exist. Reading (or rereading) these historic texts would be an excellent resource for entering the current urgently needed conversation. Here are several key excerpts.

While the statistics in *Brothers and Sisters to Us* (1979) are no longer current, much of the content is as current as this morning's news. Important passages from this historic document are presented below.

Racism is an evil which endures in our society and in our Church. Despite apparent advances and even significant changes in the last two decades, the reality of racism remains. In large part, it is only external appearances which have changed. In 1958, we spoke out against the blatant forms of racism that divided people through discriminatory laws and enforced segregation. We pointed out the moral evil that denied human persons their dignity as children of God and their God-given rights. A decade later in a second pastoral letter we again underscored the continuing scandal of racism and called for decisive action to eradicate it from our society. We recognize and applaud the readiness of many Americans to make new strides forward in reducing and eliminating prejudice against minorities [*sic*]. We are convinced that the majority of Americans realize that racial discrimination is both unjust and unworthy of this nation. . . .

With respect to family life, we recognize that decades of denied access to opportunities have been for minority [*sic*] families a crushing burden. Racial discrimination has only exacerbated the harmful relationship between poverty and family instability.

Racism is only too apparent in housing patterns in our major cities and suburbs. Witness the deterioration of inner cities and the segregation of many suburban areas by means of unjust practices of social steering and blockbusting. . . .

Today in our country men, women, and children are being

denied opportunities for full participation and advancement in our society because of their race. The educational, legal, and financial systems, along with other structures and sectors of our society, impede people's progress and narrow their access because they are Black, Hispanic, Native American or Asian.

The structures of our society are subtly racist, for these structures reflect the values which society upholds. They are geared to the success of the majority and the failure of the minority [*sic*]. Members of both groups give unwitting approval by accepting things as they are. Perhaps no single individual is to blame. The sinfulness is often anonymous but nonetheless real. The sin is social in nature in that each of us, in varying degrees, is responsible. All of us in some measure are accomplices. . . .

Discrimination belies both our civil and religious traditions. The United States of America rests on a constitutional heritage that recognizes the equality, dignity, and inalienable rights of all its citizens. Further, we are heirs of a religious teaching which proclaims that all men and women, as children of God, are brothers and sisters. Every form of discrimination against individuals and groups—whether because of race, ethnicity, religion, gender, economic status, or national or cultural origin—is a serious injustice, which has severely weakened our social fabric and deprived our country of the unique contributions of many of our citizens. While cognizant of these broader concerns, we wish to draw attention here to the particular form of discrimination that is based on race.

Racism is a sin: a sin that divides the human family, blots out the image of God among specific members of that family, and violates the fundamental human dignity of those called to be children of the same Father. Racism is the sin that says some human beings are inherently superior and others essentially inferior because of race. It is the sin that makes racial characteristics the determining factor for the exercise of human rights. It mocks the words of Jesus: "Treat others the way you would have them treat you." Indeed, racism is more than a disregard for the words of Jesus; it is a denial of the truth of the dignity of each human being revealed by the mystery of the Incarnation.

What We Have Seen and Heard (1984) is a one-of-a-kind document in which African American Catholics spoke for the first time with a common voice when the bishops declared:

Central to any discussion of the Black family today is the question of the Black man as husband, father, co-provider and co-protector. For many historical reasons, the Black man has been forced to bear the crushing blows of racial hate and economic repression. Too often barred from access to decent employment, too often stripped of his dignity and manhood, and too often forced into a stereotype that was a caricature of his manhood, the Black male finds himself depreciated and relegated to the margins of family life and influence. . . .

Black people know what freedom is because we remember the dehumanizing force of slavery, racist prejudice and oppression. No one can understand so well the meaning of the proclamation that Christ has set us free than those who have experienced the denial of freedom. For us, therefore, freedom is a cherished gift. For its preservation, no sacrifice is too great.

Hence, freedom brings responsibility. It must never be abused, equated with license nor taken for granted. Freedom is God's gift, and we are accountable to Him for our loss of it. And we are accountable for the gift of freedom in the lives of others. We oppose all oppression and all injustice, for unless *all* are free *none* are free. Moreover, oppression by some means freedom's destruction for both the oppressor and the oppressed, and liberation liberates the oppressor and the oppressed.

Our African American ancestors knew the liberating hand of God. Even before emancipation they knew the inner spiritual freedom that comes from Jesus. Even under slavery they found ways to celebrate that spiritual freedom which God alone can give. They left us the lesson that without spiritual freedom we cannot fight for that broader freedom which is the right of all who are brothers and sisters in Christ. This is the gift we have to share with the whole Church. This is the responsibility that freedom brings: to teach others its value and work to see that its benefits are denied to none. . . .

On the other hand, we are in a position to counter the assumption which many have advanced that to become a Catholic is to abandon one's racial heritage and one's people! The Catholic Church is not a "white Church" or a "Euro-American Church." It is essentially universal and, hence, Catholic. The Black presence within the Catholic Church in America is a precious witness to the universal character of Catholicism. . . .

The historical roots of Black America and those of Catholic America are intimately intertwined. Now is the time for us who are Black Americans and Black Catholics to reclaim our roots and to shoulder the responsibilities of being both Black and Catholic. The responsibility is both to our own people and to our own Church. To the former, we owe the witness of our Faith in Christ and in His Body, the Church. To the latter, we owe this witness of faith as well as the unstinting labor to denounce racism.

Hopefully, your conversations about the church's past actions and statements will help you put the current challenges we are facing in a larger historical context of Catholic teaching and actions addressing the racial divide in our land. Perhaps there is no urgent need for the church to make more statements. The urgent need may be to live by the statements the church has already made. Personally appropriating and acting on these clear teachings of the pastors of the church will assist you in changing "World Day of Peace" from a slogan into a reality.

Pray, Listen, Learn, Think, and Act

In this New Year's Day Reflection on Peace, I have deliberately placed the headline-grabbing events just across the Mississippi River in Ferguson, Missouri, and in cities around the United States in the larger context of the racial divide in our country and in our church. I have invited you to enter into dialogue and prayer about complex and difficult issues without passing premature judgment on those with whom you might disagree. Many of you may well already be actively engaged in this much-needed dialogue and prayer. If you are, I encourage you to continue and to expand and deepen your conversations.

You are surely aware that there is usually a degree of tension in conversations concerning the racial divide. In schools, at places of work, in restaurants, in bars, and in homes, people are talking. If they are not, then there may be a deafening silence when the topic of racial differences is raised. The tone of these conversations is usually influenced by the age and the cultural, economic, educational, and racial backgrounds of the participants. Because people have such different experiences and vantage points, some may have withdrawn from the conversation, believing that reconciling different worldviews is all but impossible. It may be best not to try and avoid pain and conflict. Many people, Black and white, believe that since the issue of race is so volatile, it is best not to think about it, talk about it, or even hear about it. They simply strive to do the best they can to be fair and just in the world immediately around them without getting involved with the larger conversation.

In his message for this World Day of Peace, His Holiness, Pope Francis reminds us that in today's world, slavery comes about when we treat our fellow human beings not as persons but as objects. Then our brothers and sisters are no longer considered of equal dignity to ourselves, sharing our common humanity. They are simply the means to an end. Concerning contemporary causes of human enslavement, the pontiff says, "I think in the first place of poverty, underdevelopment and exclusion, especially when combined with a lack of access to education or scarce, even non-existent, employment opportunities." These concerns of the pope speak directly to the impact of the great divide discussed in this reflection.

We know that it is almost impossible for a family, a parish, or even a diocese to transform nationwide social structures that reinforce the racial divide. The place for us to begin is with ourselves, praying that the Holy Spirit will open our hearts to live by the words of St. Paul to the Thessalonians (5, 18–19). "Do not quench the Spirit. Do not despise prophetic utterances. Test everything; retain what is good. Refrain from every kind of evil." Dietrich Bonhoeffer, the German Lutheran pastor and theologian, murdered by the Nazis for his opposition to Adolf Hitler's slaughter of the Jewish people, reminded us that the "cost" of true discipleship of Jesus Christ requires us to reject the "cheap grace" we think we can obtain by going through religious rituals in which our hearts and souls are not involved. God's redeeming grace requires our obedience to his law of love and our concrete actions on behalf of others.

Therefore, I will conclude this reflection with suggestions for your consideration. Listen, Learn, Think, Pray, and Act.

1. Go to Mass and Communion at least one weekday a week and pray specifically for guidance concerning ways in which you can bridge the racial divide.

2. Read the Sacred Scriptures regularly, focusing on the four Gospels, the Acts of the Apostles, and the Epistles of St. Paul. Meditate on passages that remind you that in Christ, God reveals his love for every human being.

3. Pray the Rosary once a week with your family on the same day at the same time for the intention of the end to racial conflict and prejudice in the United States. Listen to the voice of the Holy Spirit within you and the voices of others around you.

4. Examine your conscience at least once a month acknowledging any acts or omissions (thoughts, words, or deeds) that re-

inforce the racial divide. Receive the Sacrament of Reconciliation.

5.   Participate in serious discussions about this World Day of Peace 2015 Reflection with your parish staff. Place the document on your parish website. Urge the chancery staff, school faculty, and small groups of parishioners to discuss it before, during, or after Lent.

6.   Take up *Brothers and Sisters to Us* (1979) and *What We Have Seen and Heard* (1984). Study these key documents and learn about important examples in the church's teaching on the racial divide in America. There are valuable, unheeded suggestions in each letter that are relevant for today. Examine the expression "white privilege." What does it mean to you? Does consideration of this idea diminish or increase the racial divide?

7.   Contact St. Augustine of Hippo Parish and Sister Thea Bowman Catholic School in East St. Louis. Learn about the ministry of the church in the African American community. Create opportunities for your parishioners to visit these communities. Make new friends.

8.   Initiate an effort to get to know the police officers who serve your communities. Thank them for their important service. Help the young people in the community to appreciate the role of the police, to get to know and respect them. Help the police to get to know and respect the young people.

9.   Work to establish or improve constructive, worthwhile activities for teenagers in your community. Is your parish doing all it can in this area?

10.   Become involved with any community activities that support and strengthen families. Direct your children to proper role models who will help them lead mature, responsible, Christ-centered lives.

11.   If you live near or work with individuals whose racial background is different from your own with whom you have never discussed the issues raised by this reflection, break the ice, start the conversation.

12.   Take note of the way in which the racial divide has been portrayed in films old and new. A viewing of such recent influential

motion pictures as Tate Taylor's *The Help*, Lee Daniels's *The Butler*, Steven Spielberg's *Lincoln*, and Ava DuVernay's *Selma* could prompt fruitful discussions, especially with people of diverse backgrounds.

13. This year is the 75th anniversary of David O. Selznick's 1939 film of Margaret Mitchell's *Gone with the Wind*, the Academy Award–winning epitome of old Hollywood moviemaking, with Hattie McDaniel's exceptional Oscar-winning performance as the house "slave," "Mammy," in a completely romanticized presentation of what the evil of slavery was actually like.

Steve McQueen's 2013 Oscar-winning film of Solomon Northup's 1853 slave narrative, *Twelve Years a Slave*, recounts the true story of a New York State–born free African American man who was kidnapped in Washington, DC, in 1841 and "sold" into slavery. Chiwetel Ejiofor's exceptional Oscar-nominated performance as Mr. Northup provides a far more realistic account of human bondage than *Gone with the Wind*. A discussion comparing these films would almost certainly shed light on the contemporary experience of the racial divide.

14. You, your parishioners, your friends, and neighbors may well have far better and more relevant ideas than these suggestions. Obviously, you should make use of them. These suggestions are simply to stimulate your conversations. If you think that I, as your bishop and as one who lives in the midst of the divide, can contribute to your conversations, I will gladly join you.

Racism is a sin: a sin that divides the human family, blots out the image of God among specific members of that family, and violates the fundamental human dignity of those called to be children of the same Father. What I have written here is incomplete and imperfect. You may very well have agreed with one point and then completely disagreed with another. This is to be expected. These reflections are not in any sense definitive. The primary objective has been to assist you in thinking, talking, and praying about how Americans of different racial backgrounds relate to one another at this critical juncture. A number of people directly involved in the conflicts that have caused us all to stop and think have given voice to hope that we are living through an important moment that has the power to transform our nation. Do you share that hope? Are there things you can do, as a faithful Christian, that can bridge the different experiences and attitudes that cause the racial divide?

New Year's Day is often associated with resolutions. We look back on the past year and give thanks to God for the progress we have made in our Christian life during our journey around the sun. We look ahead to the New Year, another journey around the sun, and pray for the grace we need to make even more progress in our life in Christ in the year ahead. On Christmas Day, we commemorated the coming of Christ in long-ago history. Now we must resolve to do whatever we can in the year ahead to prepare a place for the Lord Jesus Christ to be born in the cold stable of our hearts and our world, since there is still no room in the inn.

That saving birth confronts and comforts each of us with the life-giving, sin-shattering truth. Before God there is no racial divide because the life, teachings, wondrous signs, suffering, death, resurrection, and ascension of Christ and his Pentecost gift of the Holy Spirit have redeemed us all. Get Jesus out of the manger and into the world.

2

The Catholic Church and the Black Lives Matter Movement

The Racial Divide in the United States Revisited

The Fourth Anniversary of the Death
of Trayvon Martin, 17, in Sanford, Florida
African American History Month

FEBRUARY 26, 2016

When we hear the expression "Black Lives Matter" we tend to think of the tragic death of Michael Brown Jr. in Ferguson, Missouri, on August 9, 2014. But long before that painful incident, Malcolm X (1925–1965), the Reverend Dr. Martin Luther King Jr. (1929–1968), Jesse Jackson, and others had been proclaiming and defending the intrinsic worth and value of African American lives in their own words and idioms. Perhaps the most eloquent voice was that of Frederick Douglass (1818–1895).

As David W. Blight documents in Frederick Douglass: Prophet of Freedom, *Mr. Douglass's entire life of suffering, writing, lecturing, traveling, and confronting may rightly be called a continuous, unrelenting plea to the conscience of slaveholding America that the lives of every enslaved free human being captured and "sold" from West Africa matters as much as the life of any other human being. Reflecting on the widespread practice of lynching in Mr. Douglass's time, Blight writes that even after emancipation a slaveholding mentality shaped the thinking of many white Southerners. He quotes the prophet of freedom, "Their institutions have taught them no respect for human life, and especially the life of the Negro." The author argues that more than one hundred years ago Mr. Douglass forcefully voiced a Black Lives Matter argument against extralegal slaying of African Americans.*

Despite his monumental accomplishments, many Americans do not have a full appreciation of Frederick Douglass. In February 2017, at the start of African American History Month, President Donald Trump said, "I am very proud now that we have a museum on the National Mall where people can learn about Reverend King, so many other things. Frederick Douglass is an example of somebody who's done an amazing job and is being recognized more and more, I notice." Commentators criticized the president for referring to Mr. Douglass in the present tense as if he thought he was a contemporary civil rights leader. Some said, "Trump has raised the dead!" "Does he even know who Frederick Douglass was?" "Someone should tell him that Douglass, renowned as one of the most influential figures in American history, died in 1895."

Whatever explanation might be given for the president's comment, it highlights the fact that many Americans are ignorant of Mr. Douglass's singular life. Though he was born into the quagmire of slavery, he taught himself to read and write, managed to escape his so-called owners, and became one of America's most eloquent spokesmen.

With the skill of a scholar, he sought to demolish racial oppression using the US Constitution itself as his weapon, arguing that this foundational document grounds a guarantee for individual human rights for all Americans, including African Americans.

In his lectures, he often spoke of "Self-Made Men," saying: "If they have traveled far, they have made the road on which they have travelled. If they have ascended high, they have built their own ladder." "There is no Negro problem. The problem is whether the American people have honesty enough, loyalty enough, honor enough, patriotism enough, to live up to their own Constitution."

When I wrote "The Catholic Church and the Black Lives Matter Movement: The Racial Divide in the United States Revisited," I was very aware of the importance of Frederick Douglass as a major prophetic voice in the Black Lives Matter movement, before it was so named. I considered using his writings as an organizing structure for the essay. My main reason for not doing so was the fact that you can find in his writings an intense anti-Catholic bias. He belittles Catholic liturgy, culture, and art. Reflecting the anti-Catholic views of some Protestants of his time, he implied that the devotions of the church were "superstitions." While admiring the baroque beauty of the Vatican, his, perhaps uninformed, view of the church was largely negative. During a visit to Rome, he wrote, "The sight of these things only increases my sense of the hollowness of the vast structure of the Romish Church and my conviction that Science must in the end do for that church what time has done for the vast structures of kingly pride and power."

Keeping this caveat in mind, I think the Catholic reader of this chapter would come to a more profound understanding of the roots of the Black Lives Matter movement and the challenges this confrontational youth-centered phenomenon presents to the church.

Dear Sisters and Brothers in Christ:

May the grace of the Lord Jesus Christ, the Prince of Peace, fill your hearts throughout the remainder of Lent and in the coming Easter Season! As the Catholic Church celebrates the suffering, death, and resurrection of Jesus Christ during this Jubilee Year of Mercy proclaimed by His Holiness, Pope Francis, I am pleased to share with you this pastoral letter, "The Catholic Church and the Black Lives Matter Movement: The Racial Divide in the United States Revisited."

This pastoral letter has a moving viewpoint in eight parts.

Introduction
  (Birds of a feather flock together)

All Lives Matter
  (Love your neighbor as you love yourself)

The Black Lives Matter Movement
  (A protest becomes an international movement)

The Catholic Church and Black Lives Matter
  (Do we live in different worlds?)

The Teachings of the Church
  (The need for ongoing personal and social transformation)

Abortion and Black Lives
 (The right to life versus the "right" to end life)

Crime and Black Lives
 (Let's stop killing each other)

Concluding Dialogue
 (Christ is our hope)

Introduction

Incident

> Once riding in old Baltimore,
> Heart-filled, head-filled with glee,
> I saw a Baltimorean
> Keep looking straight at me.
> Now I was eight and very small,
> And he was no whit bigger,
> And so I smiled, but he poked out
> His tongue, and called me, 'Nigger.'
> I saw the whole of Baltimore
> From May until December;
> Of all the things that happened there
> That's all that I remember.
>
> —Countee Cullen

When I was a senior at Quigley Preparatory Seminary studying to be a priest for the Archdiocese of Chicago, I was the only Person of Color in my class of several hundred seminarians. A group of us saw the film version of the late Harper Lee's brilliant, Pulitzer Prize–winning novel, *To Kill a Mockingbird*. It is the story of Tom Robinson set in Maycomb, Alabama, during the Great Depression. Tom, an upright and honest, innocent Black man is falsely accused of sexually assaulting a white woman. He is defended by an equally upright and honest white attorney, Atticus Finch. Predictably, the all-white jury finds Tom "guilty," though he is, in fact, innocent, and he is killed while "attempting to run from the police" during the appeal process. Tom Robinson's family is devastated by the murder, and Atticus is angered by the miscarriage of justice born of racial prejudice. In our discussion after this extraordinary film, one of my classmates said his father had taught him that "all you need to know about the relationship between people of different races is this: 'Birds of a feather flock together.' This is simply the law of nature. This is why the Archdiocese of Chicago has Polish parishes, Irish parishes, German parishes, Italian parishes, and Black parishes. People of similar backgrounds want to live, work, and worship with their own kind! It has always been this way and it always will be. It's that simple: birds of a feather flock together." He said nothing about the death of Tom Robinson, as if his life did not matter. I have never forgotten that conversation.

I did not write about the Black Lives Matter movement in my Pastoral Letter, "The Racial Divide in the United States: A Reflection for the World Day of Peace 2015." At that time, the movement had not yet attained the high visibility and considerable influence that it has today. Readers of this reflection would benefit from having an awareness of the main themes addressed in my 2015 Pastoral. That letter is an invitation to readers, inviting them:

- To imagine how African Americans experience the Catholic Church, which almost always uses European-based religious art depicting God, Jesus, Mary, the saints, and angels as white and almost never depicting them as African, Asian, or Hispanic;
- To allow the new awareness of the racial divide to move Catholics to think about the way the followers of Jesus Christ should speak and act in the face of the racial divide;
- To come face-to-face with accounts of the events surrounding the deaths of numerous African American men in altercations with white law enforcement agents and the international protests that followed;
- To review the Catholic Church's teachings (*Brothers and Sisters to Us*, *What We Have Seen and Heard*) concerning the racial divide in America;

- To discontinue the church's common practice of referring to People of Color with such biased terms as "minorities," "minority" Americans, and "minority" Catholics, since all are Americans and all are Catholics;
- To refer to people as who they are rather than who they are not (e.g., African Americans, not "a minority group," or Baptists, not "non-Catholics");
- To commit themselves to praying, listening, learning, thinking, and acting in ways that will help to bridge the racial divide.

During this past year, the racial conflicts addressed in "The Racial Divide" seem to have been exacerbated. It was my hope that my previous pastoral letter would be a contribution to the urgently needed conversation within the Catholic Church in the United States about the ongoing challenges Black and white Americans continue to face. These challenges have become even more acute with the high visibility of additional violent, often fatal, altercations between white law enforcement agents and African American men, and with the alarming number of young People of Color who die at the hands of other African Americans. As a result, in different settings around the country, I have been frequently asked, "What do you think of the Black Lives Matter movement?" "What is the position of the Catholic Church concerning the Black Lives Matter movement?" "Why are Catholic leaders silent about such an important, albeit controversial, social development?"

Some voices, Black and white, have condemned this movement as a violent ideology urging attacks on police officers, encouraging the disruption of the daily lives of innocent citizens by blocking traffic on major thoroughfares, closing down places of business, interrupting gatherings of political candidates, and, perhaps unwittingly, participating in Black genocide by its strong support for the "right" of women to terminate their pregnancies. Other voices have compared the movement to the historic civil rights movement of the 1960s—even though the current movement's loud, brash, "in your face" tactics may lack the discipline and clearer focus of that earlier movement. The movement has staged more than a thousand protests (like "die-ins" in shopping malls), which are intended to make everyone aware of the movement's grievances.

Despite the profound differences and seeming incompatibility between the teachings of the church and the Black Lives Matter movement, there may be ways in which the church and the movement might benefit from a conversation. Because each group speaks from a unique perspective and with a unique tone of voice, a genuine conversation may be difficult. Still, Catholics might, at the least, become better informed about a rapidly growing movement that *Time* magazine placed fourth on its list of eight candidates for Person of the Year in December 2015. We do well to recall the words of Blessed Paul VI's first Encyclical, *Ecclesiam Suam*, "Dialogue in such conditions is very difficult . . . we have no preconceived intention of excluding the persons who profess these systems (those that are contrary to Catholic doctrine). For the lover of truth, dialogue is always possible" (#102).

Any effort to invite a conversation about the Black Lives Matter movement and the Catholic Church in the United States must begin by acknowledging that such an effort raises many questions that cannot be answered in a brief reflection. My modest goal is to share with you some themes that might foster a conversation which might otherwise not take place. What follows does not presume to provide a complete overview of all of the relevant questions posed by bringing these topics together. Instead, this reflection should be seen as a companion piece to my pastoral letter, "The Racial Divide in the United States."

All Lives Matter

All human beings, as conscious subjects, feel strongly that their individual lives matter. Our lives matter to us as individuals, to our families, friends, neighbors, co-workers, and others. Ideally, all of our lives should matter to every other human being. But every morning's newspaper cries out that in today's world not everyone embraces this truth. Certainly, from the theological perspectives of the authentic teachings of Judaism, Christianity, and Islam, your life and my life should matter to everyone on this planet. In the Gospels, Jesus of Nazareth, drawing from Deuteronomy and Leviticus, teaches us to love God with our whole being and love our neighbor as we love ourselves (Matt. 22:37–39, Deut. 6:5, Lev. 19:18). When he is asked who is our neighbor, Jesus tells all of us the story of the man who is beaten, robbed, and ignored by the members of his community who should have helped him. Yet a man, who was considered an enemy, had pity on him, bound his wounds, took him to an inn saying, "Take care of him. I will pay whatever it costs." Jesus asks us, "Who was the true neighbor to the man violently attacked?" We know what our response should be, "The one who showed compassion." Jesus then tells us, "Go and do likewise!" (cf. Luke 10:36, 37).

The teaching of Scripture and Jesus Himself make it clear that for a Christian, for a Catholic, and for the Catholic Church, all lives should matter. Many Americans believe this should be the end of the question. Obviously, if all lives matter, then Black lives matter! Yet this seemingly obvious truth has not been a sufficient answer to those whose voices are raised in protest in the Black Lives Matter movement. Why is that? Several supporters of the movement have cited George Orwell's *Animal Farm* for the answer. They remind us that the mantra of the totalitarian world of the novel is "All animals are equal." But, eventually, the mantra is changed to "All animals are equal. BUT, some animals are more equal than others."

The Black Lives Matter Movement

The Black Lives Matter movement began as a hashtag which became a protest slogan and fueled an internet-driven international protest confronting what its originators and others believe to be indifference to the deaths of young, unarmed Black men at the hands of white law enforcement representatives. The phrase is more a call to action against racial profiling, police brutality, and racial injustice than a specific organization. The media and the public often associate a variety of unconnected groups with Black Lives Matter, when they are actually not structurally connected. According to the #BlackLivesMatter website, the first appearance of Black Lives Matter occurred when a Facebook post by Ms. Alicia Garza, Ms. Patrisse Cullors, and Ms. Opal Tometi used the expression after Mr. George Zimmerman was acquitted in the shooting death of Trayvon Martin, 17, an unarmed African American youth. These women and other activists created the Black Lives Matter hashtag and social media pages. Later, after Mr. Michael Brown Jr., 19, another unarmed African American youth, was fatally shot in Ferguson, Missouri, by Mr. Darren Wilson, a former police officer, and Mr. Eric Garner died in what has been called a police chokehold, the movement gained greater prominence. Demonstrators and marchers around the country and around the world shouted "Hands up! Don't shoot!" "I can't breathe!" and "Black Lives Matter!" to call attention to what is perceived by many people to be systemic bias and racial prejudice in the criminal justice system and particularly in the behavior of some representatives of law enforcement. The complaint is not that all young Black men are always innocent of wrongdoing. We all know this is not true. The complaint is that even someone who may have broken the law should not be "tried, convicted, and executed" on the streets.

A particularly egregious example of this occurred in Chicago. On October 20, 2014, Mr. Laquan McDonald, 17, who was armed with a knife, died after being shot sixteen times by Chicago Police Officer Jason Van Dyke. The shooting was videotaped on the police car dashboard camera. However, the video, which showed Mr. McDonald walking away from the officer, was not initially released to the public. The Black Lives Matter movement joined with those expressing anger over what many considered a politically motivated delay. On November 24, 2015, over thirteen months after the shooting, the video was finally released. As a result, the police officer was charged with first-degree murder. Days later, he was released on bail. There were massive protests and demonstrations in downtown Chicago demanding the resignation of Mayor Rahm Emanuel and the dismissal of Police Superintendent Garry McCarthy. Superintendent McCarthy did resign. However, the mayor remained in office pledging significant reforms in the Chicago Police Department, which has frequently been accused of racial bias.

The protest expression, "Black Lives Matter" became a dramatic way of calling attention to a reality largely ignored by the larger society. Namely, there are many circumstances in which society seems to operate as if it does not believe that the lives of young Men of Color really do matter as much as the lives of young white men. The intent of the frequent use of the phrase is to confront the consciences of those who might reply, "Of course, Black lives matter because every human life matters." Expressions such as this are perceived by participants in the movement as a way of ignoring the terrible reality that the actions of some police, the decisions of some criminal justice agencies, the activities in many prisons, and efforts to make it difficult for Black people to vote strongly suggest that Black lives really do not matter. More than one commentator has proposed that Black Lives Matter is a form of shorthand. The true intent of "Black Lives Matter" is a plea to all Americans to work to refashion our country so that the lives of People of Color actually do matter as much as the lives of white people. Help us all live in communities in which everyone experiences equal safety, education, and employment opportunities, and equal political power as well as equal treatment by the criminal justice system. The movement consciously embraces those who often seem to be at the margins of the Black community such as African Americans who are disabled, undocumented, homosexual, and transgender.

Since anyone can shout "Black Lives Matter," the phrase has sometimes been used in ways that cause many who might be sympathetic to the concerns of Black people to criticize the Black Lives Matter movement. Some individuals and groups chanting "Black Lives Matter" have used language that enflames violence against those charged with law enforcement. Whenever anyone associated with the Black Lives Matter movement encourages attacking police officers, they are rightly condemned because police officers' lives matter! When Governor Chris Christie of New Jersey was seeking the Republican presidential nomination, he said, "I don't believe that that movement should be justified when they're calling for the murder of police officers." Other political leaders have expressed similar concerns. Leaders within the movement, however, stress that they reject violence and say those who speak of harming police are speaking in their own names and not in the name of the movement. Their critics argue they are being disingenuous.

Significantly, Dr. Ben Carson, the distinguished pediatric neurosurgeon who was briefly—by a strange fate and stranger fortune—a leading Republican presidential candidate, has argued that many people involved with Black Lives Matter are misguided. The only African American seeking to succeed President Barack Obama argues that it is not unjust treatment by white police that fills America's urban communities with people who daily face growing hopelessness. Law enforcement and the judicial system are not the reasons why young African American men and women are unemployed, lacking the skills needed to compete in the modern job market. Dr. Carson believes that many African American families are suffering from self-inflicted wounds. As a pioneering specialist in the health care of infants, he has expressed particular concern about the number of Black lives that are extinguished by abortion.

Dr. Carson has singled out failed public schools as a source of African American suffering because they are not really teaching children how to learn. He argues that the actions of rogue police officers take Black lives one at a time. However, the public school system has destroyed Black lives not in the ones and twos, but in whole generations. According to Dr. Carson, the failures of public schools do not kill as quickly, but they kill as surely as bullets do.

Dr. Carson also faults the entertainment industry, which earns huge amounts of money by glamorizing negative images of African Americans, portraying men as thugs and women as immoral sexual objects. He urges Black Lives Matter supporters to use their influence so that Black teenagers will start talking to Hollywood with their wallets. They should let the motion picture industry know that demeaning women is not art and it should not be profitable. Glorifying violence and prison life is not art, and these kinds of films should not make money from African American communities. Dr. Carson believes the popular film, *Straight Outta Compton*, is a recent example of a film that does not provide African American people with characters worthy of respect and imitation.

Black Lives Matter supporters counter Dr. Carson with the argument that his ideas are determined by his age, social standing, conservative Republican ideology, and his strict adherence to his Seventh Day Adventist faith. One person on a radio talk show said, "He thinks like a white person!" While it is not clear what percentage of Black Lives Matter activists actually vote, it is clear that Republican politicians and Republican-leaning media are very critical of the movement and presume they will not lose votes because of this. Whereas politicians in the Democrat Party and Democrat-leaning media are more tolerant of the movement (despite podium-upstaging tactics), and, knowing that many African Americans vote as Democrats, they are concerned not to alienate potential supporters. Nevertheless, when the Democratic National Committee endorsed the Black Lives Matter movement representatives declined the endorsement.

The Catholic Church and Black Lives Matter

There are about 70,000,000 Catholics in the United States. At most, about 3,000,000 of these are African Americans. There are many dioceses where there are no Black Catholics at all, and many others where there are very few. This means that many white Catholics in certain states and in rural communities have virtually no contact with African American Catholics. Many of them only experience the Black Lives Matter movement indirectly by way of the media. It is probably not a major presence in their consciousness, nor is it a part of their daily concern. As one university student from a very small rural community said to me, "Growing up I never met any African American people. Everyone in my neighborhood, in my parish, and in my school was white. I do not remember anyone saying much of anything one way or another about Black people. It was as if they did not exist, except on TV. I never wondered why there were no Black people in our parish church. If I thought about it at all, I probably thought they must have their own churches and they are happy there. It never occurred to me that African Americans would have been unwelcome in my parish until I went to college, met many Black students, and began to read about racial prejudice in the Catholic Church. When I heard about Black Lives Matter, I wondered why it was necessary to single out the lives of one particular group. It took me awhile to appreciate the deeper meaning of this expression."

Because African Americans make up such a small portion of the Catholic Church, it may be quite difficult for the church to interact in a significant way with the Black Lives Matter movement. People have long memories of past rejection and discrimination. It is not likely that the number of Black Catholics will increase significantly in the near future. Even if the church were to mount an aggressive evangelization effort, it would probably make only small inroads in African American communities. Those with long histories of membership in the Baptist Church and the African Methodist Episcopal Church are not likely to leave these church families for Catholicism. The growing numbers of younger African Americans with no church affiliation are not likely to be attracted to the Catholic Church in significant numbers.

The barbaric slaughter of the innocent on June 17, 2015, in Mother Emanuel African Methodist Episcopal Church in Charleston by twenty-one-year-old Dylann Roof, a white supremacist pictured wrapped in the Confederate flag, horrified many Americans. However, many of those horrified are unaware that the reason why the AME Church exists is the simple fact that the children of people who had been enslaved were not allowed to become members of mainline Christian communities, including the Methodist, Episcopal, and Catholic Churches. This fact is a part of African American consciousness. A past marred by racial oppression and systematic discrimination cannot be undone by pastoral letters, no matter how heartfelt they may be. The evil of America's original sin of enslaving free human beings, like the evil that the Nazi Holocaust inflicted on the Jewish people, has left a permanent scar on the nation's psyche. As a result, "white" Christianity lacks credibility to many members of the traditional Black Church. And sadly, I know African American Catholics who, based on their personal experiences, do not believe that their Black lives matter in the Catholic Church as much as white lives matter.

If all African American Catholics (clergy and religious included) suddenly disappeared, most white Catholics might not even notice the disappearance because they were more or less unaware of African American Catholics. Most have no personal contact with African American Catholic laity. They never see African American sisters, brothers, deacons, or priests. They might not even know that there are a small number of African American bishops. If all of the white Catholic laity, sisters, brothers, deacons, priests, and bishops (including Hispanics) suddenly disappeared, the African American Catholic experience would, of course, be quite different. Black Catholics would notice it immediately. This is because the church in the United States would be transformed from a large, influential, national religious institution into a small, largely African American religious community comparable to the Jehovah's Witnesses who, according to the Pew Research Center, have about 2.5 million American members.

Historically, the Catholic Church has not been actively engaged in conversation with African American communities at the level of ideas, major movements, and the emergence of Black consciousness. While several popes and many Catholics condemned the anti-Christian practice of enslaving human beings to work the lucrative plantations of the South, the larger Catholic community maintained a distance from the abolitionist movement in which the church played no leadership role. In 1889, Daniel Rudd initiated a series of Black Catholic Congresses. The Fifth Congress in Baltimore in 1894 said, "We hope to hail the day when the American people, the hierarchy of the Catholic Church, and the laity shall rise up in might and stamp out the prejudice which is today destroying the life blood of the country." However, that did not happen. The church did not take a significant role in the Niagara Movement (1905–09) led by W. E. B. Du Bois, which forcefully worked for the welfare of People of Color, demanded equal rights, and laid the foundations that led to the National Association for the Advancement of Colored People. Nor did the church address Marcus Garvey's Back to Africa movement (1918–20), which urged all Americans of African background to establish new lives in Liberia.

The Harlem Renaissance (1919–40) produced many eloquent voices portraying the African American experience, including Alain Locke (author of the classic essay, "The New Negro"), Claude McKay (a Jamaican-born poet and essayist who became a Catholic in Chicago and was devoted to the Catholic Youth Organization), Zora Neale Hurston (a visionary writer and folklorist of international renown), Langston Hughes (the poet laureate of the Harlem Renaissance; "I, Too, Sing America!"), and Countee Cullen (the brilliant, haunting voice of the Harlem Renaissance, who gave us "Incident," the poem, which is as timely as this morning's headlines, that introduces this pastoral letter).

Later came Richard Wright (*Native Son*), Ralph Ellison (*Invisible Man*), and James Baldwin (*The Fire Next Time*). They were followed by the many challenging political, legal, moral, spiritual, and historical writings, including those of Associate Supreme Court Justice Thurgood Marshall (*Brown v. the Board of Education*), Malcolm X ("By Any Means Necessary"), Martin Luther King Jr. ("Letter from a Birmingham Jail"), and Alex Haley (the Pulitzer Prize–winning *Roots: The Saga of an American Family*). These are only a few of the major voices. Of course, in time, there were many more, including important women such as Lorraine Hansberry (*A Raisin in the Sun*), Maya Angelou (*I Know Why the Caged Bird Sings*), Toni Morrison (the Pulitzer Prize–winning *Beloved*), and Alice Walker (the Pulitzer Prize–winning *The Color Purple*). An examination of Catholic journals and periodicals does not suggest that the church was particularly attentive to, or in dialogue with, these essential Black voices, with the possible exception of Dr. King. Formal statements by the Catholic Church have not been significantly informed by the voices that have articulated the depth and meaning of the African American experience. This lack of a history of dialogue underscores the difficulties the church might encounter seeking a genuine conversation with the Black Lives Matter movement.

Until recently, my personal awareness of the Black Lives Matter movement has been derived from various forms of media. During this past year, however, I have made a conscious effort to establish contact with individuals who, while not in leadership positions, have varying degrees of association with the movement. By means of emails, phone conversations, and face-to-face meetings, I have gained (in an admittedly limited way) a partial knowledge of what some Black Lives Matter movement activists think about the Catholic Church, church teachings, and the degree to which Catholics have demonstrated by their deeds that Black lives matter to them.

There are no reliable statistics concerning how many African Americans are actively involved in Black Lives Matter. It is generally believed that the number is rather small and that the key voices of the movement are young people in their twenties and thirties, many of them women. There is also no reliable way of determining how many Black Catholics are supportive of the positions espoused by the movement. But I know for a fact that some young Black Catholics are sympathetic to some of the issues raised by movement members. My main impression from direct contact is that the movement does not give much thought to the Catholic Church. Movement supporters assume the church does not give much thought to them either. "We live in different worlds." While there is a degree of awareness of the church's various social, educational, and health care ministries that make a positive contribution to Black communities, the primary impression some movement supporters have of the church is that it is a large, white, conservative (mainly Republican) institution that stands aloof from confrontational movements such as Black Lives Matter.

(As a matter of fact, many Catholics are Democrats.) Movement members think the church is more a part of the problem than of the solution because it has a necessary allegiance to "white privilege." The movement sees an incompatibility between itself and the church's "out of touch with the times" moral teachings on marriage (rejecting "marriage equality," i.e., same-sex "marriage"), contraception and abortion ("women's reproductive justice," "women's right to choose" to end their pregnancies), and homosexual activity ("gay rights" and "Lesbian, Gay, Bisexual, and Transgender concerns").

Members of the Black Lives Matter movement see the church as a complex bureaucracy tied to the status quo and unwilling and unable to "speak truth to power." One activist said, "When the church does speak about social justice it is always in measured, balanced, reserved and qualified language." When I asked which church documents they had actually read, they said they had only read excerpts online. I explained that the church's social doctrine may be more forceful than they think. I also pointed out that Catholic beliefs about the nature of marriage, the meaning of human sexuality, and the dignity of human life from conception to natural death are not mere cultural norms or social issues. The church cannot and will not change these moral doctrines. These beliefs represent what the church firmly holds to be fundamental moral principles rooted in human nature, natural law, biblical revelation, and the teachings of Jesus Christ. However, does this necessarily mean that a representative of the church cannot have a meaningful conversation with representatives of the movement about these and other issues where there may be greater accord?

In my conversations, I learned that the traditionally Black Protestant churches do not play the same role in the Black Lives Matter movement that they played during the civil rights era. While there is an appreciation of the presence of ministers and priests on the streets during urban disturbances, this movement does not embrace traditional Christian theological ideas about praying to keep the peace and change hearts. One person wrote, "Turning the other cheek is not in our playbook." They are not interested in a "passive respectability" type of Christianity. They embrace a radical theology of inclusion inspired by a revolutionary Jesus. They prefer a Jesus who spent more time confronting the power structure of Judaism and the Roman Empire than a Jesus who was turning the other cheek.

Even though one of the young men with whom I spoke was raised in a Catholic family (he is now agnostic), neither he nor any of the others had ever met or even seen an African American priest, deacon, or sister. Before their contact with me, none of them had any awareness that there was even one African American Catholic bishop. To my surprise, one participant in the conversation who has serious musical interests said she really liked Gregorian chant and church organ music though she likes rap, hip-hop, and jazz more. I was not surprised that all of them had a favorable impression of our Holy Father, Pope Francis. They, like many Catholics, had not actually read any of the pontiff's writings. Their high regard is influenced by their erroneous impressions, shaped by secular media, that the pope is seriously considering changing fundamental moral and doctrinal teachings of the church. I assured them that, while the Holy Father has brought a renewed pastoral spirit of compassion and mercy to his pontificate, there was nothing to substantiate media speculations about a coming theological revolution.

The Teachings of the Church

Throughout his pontificate, St. John Paul II seemed to bestride the world like a moral giant proclaiming the Gospel that all lives mattered, including Black lives. During his 1987 pastoral visit to the United States, I was present when the Holy Father thanked nearly 2,000 representatives of the African American Catholic community for the ways that they enrich the church. He spoke forcefully against racial prejudice in American society and encouraged Black Catholics to contribute their cultural gifts to the wider church. He lamented that "even in this wealthy nation, committed by the Founding Fathers to the dignity and equality of all persons, the Black community suffers a disproportionate share of economic deprivation."

Later, in his 1995 encyclical, *Evangelium Vitae*, the Holy Father outlined the philosophical and theological framework for the church's belief in the incomparable worth of every human life, including every Black life:

> Man is called to a fullness of life which far exceeds the dimensions of his earthly existence, because it consists in sharing the very life of God. The loftiness of this super-natural vocation reveals the greatness and the inestimable value of human life even in its temporal phase. Life in time, in fact, is the fundamental condition, the initial stage and an integral part of the entire unified process of human existence. It is a process which, unexpectedly and unde-servedly, is enlightened by the promise of and renewed by the gift of divine life, which will reach its full realization in eternity (cf. 1 Jn 3:1–2). At the same time, it is precisely this supernatural calling which highlights the relative character of each individual's earthly life. After all, life on earth is not an "ultimate" but a "penultimate" reality; even so, it remains a sacred reality entrusted to us, to be preserved with a sense of responsibility and brought to perfection in love and in the gift of ourselves to God and to our broth-ers and sisters.
>
> The Church knows that this Gospel of life, which she has received from her Lord, has a profound and persuasive echo in the heart of every person—believer and non-believer alike—because it marvelously fulfills all the heart's expectations while infinitely surpassing them. Even in the midst of difficulties and uncertainties, every person sincerely open to truth and goodness can, by the light of reason and the hidden action of grace, come to recognize in the natural law written in the heart (cf. Rom 2:14–15) the sacred value of human life from its very beginning until its end, and can affirm the right of every human being to have this primary

good respected to the highest degree. Upon the recognition of this right, every human community and the political community itself are founded.

In a special way, believers in Christ must defend and promote this right, aware as they are of the wonderful truth recalled by the Second Vatican Council: "By his incarnation the Son of God has united himself in some fashion with every human being." This saving event reveals to humanity not only the boundless love of God who "so loved the world that He gave His only Son" (Jn 3:16), but also the incomparable value of every human person. (*Evangelium Vitae* #2)

I was present in the gallery on September 24, 2015, when His Holiness, Pope Francis became the first pontiff in history to address both chambers of the Congress of the United States with remarks that, to the surprise of his listeners, focused on four influential Americans: President Abraham Lincoln, Dorothy Day, Trappist mystic Thomas Merton, and Dr. Martin Luther King Jr. Each of them affirmed, in different ways, that Black lives mattered. While President Lincoln's pragmatic, political motives for opposing human bondage have been idealized and romanticized, his efforts to bring an end to slavery and his Emancipation Proclamation demonstrated an atypical regard for Black lives even though he did not equate them with white lives. The Catholic Worker founder, Dorothy Day, was consistently outspoken in her opposition to racist attitudes in America. Her Catholic Worker movement was prophetic in its concern for the poor, many of whom were People of Color. In *Conjectures of a Guilty Bystander* and "Letters to a White Liberal," Cistercian Father Thomas Merton wrote searing condemnations of racial prejudice and provided the spiritual and theological foundation for his unambiguous affirmation that Black lives matter, if not in those words. Dr. King sacrificed his life for the cause of racial justice and the still deferred dream that African Americans would be judged by the content of their character and not by the color of their skin.

By calling to mind the legacies of these four remarkable

Americans, not usually referred to in papal addresses, the Bishop of Rome clearly wanted to associate himself with their beliefs that Black lives do indeed matter. To underscore the point, he said:

> Politics is, instead, an expression of our compelling need to live as one, in order to build as one the greatest common good: that of a community which sacrifices particular interests in order to share, in justice and peace, its goods, its interests, its social life. I do not underestimate the difficulty that this involves, but I encourage you in this effort. Here, too, I think of the march which Martin Luther King led from Selma to Montgomery fifty years ago as part of the campaign to fulfill his "dream" of full civil and political rights for African Americans. That dream continues to inspire us all. I am happy that America continues to be, for many, a land of "dreams," dreams which lead to action, to participation, to commitment; dreams which awaken what is deepest and truest in the life of a people.

By word and deed (especially during his November 25–30, 2015, pastoral visit to Kenya, Uganda, and the Central African Republic), Pope Francis has demonstrated that the lives of the people of African descent matter very much to the church.

On June 10, 2015, during the bishops' meeting in St. Louis, the president of the United States Conference of Catholic Bishops, Archbishop Joseph E. Kurtz, issued a letter saying:

> I cannot help but think of recent events that have taken place around our beloved country. We mourn those tragic events in which African Americans and others have lost their lives in altercations with law enforcement officials. These deaths have led to peaceful demonstrations, as well as violent conflicts in the streets of our cities. . . . Sadly, there is all too often an alienation of communities from those sworn to protect them.
>
> Our efforts must address root causes of these conflicts. A violent, sorrowful history of racial injustice, accompanied by

a lack of educational, employment and housing opportunities, has destroyed communities and broken down families,
especially those who live in distressed urban communities. . . .
The Church has been present in these communities, active
in education, health care and charities.

Archbishop Kurtz recalled the 1979 US Bishops' pastoral letter,
Brothers and Sisters to Us, which named racial prejudice as a grave
sin that denies the truth and meaning of the Incarnation of the
Word of God in Jesus Christ.

Unfortunately, the words of that letter still ring true: "Racism
is an evil which endures in our society and in our Church." The
bishops called for decisive action to eradicate racism from society,
and considerable progress has been made since 1979. However,
more must be done. Let us again call upon our Catholic people to
pray frequently in their homes and in their churches for the cause
of peace and racial reconciliation.

Speaking about the landmark Civil Rights Act of 1964, Archbishop Kurtz said it was "a monumental step forward" for human
dignity. He stressed that continued work is necessary to fight the
"destructive influence of racism." He said that the Gospel requires
"ongoing personal and social transformation." This ongoing
personal and social transformation is critical within the church
when it comes to living the truth that Black lives matter, precisely
because all lives matter.

Abortion and Black Lives

Because the Catholic Church believes that all lives matter, from
conception to natural death, the Catholic community has been
deeply involved in efforts to argue forcefully in the public square
in defense of developing human life in the womb and in increasing its opposition to the death penalty. The Black Lives Matter
movement would generally agree with the church's concerns
about the death penalty, which is imposed disproportionately on
offenders who are poor People of Color and lack adequate legal

representation. The movement would appreciate Pope Francis's Year of Mercy plea to world leaders to abolish the death penalty altogether. However, the movement is outspoken in its defense of what it calls "reproductive justice" and "reproductive rights" and in its embrace of the 1973 *Roe v. Wade* decision of the Supreme Court. Like many Americans, including, sadly, some who consider themselves Catholics, the Black Lives Matter movement rejects the arguments of those who speak in defense of human life in the mother's womb.

Like many defenders of abortion "rights" in the larger secular society, many in the movement express a strong acceptance of the position that the fetal organism does not have the legal status of a human person at any stage of gestation. As a result, that life can be ended at any time. The position that fetal life is not human—or, at the very least, becoming human—is asserted without serious biological, philosophical, or theological argument. The spiritual dimension of a human being (the existence of a spiritual soul?) is ignored or rejected. The fetus is referred to as "just tissue," especially in the first trimester of pregnancy. However, the court permits terminating pregnancy even in the third trimester. Yet, when a mother suffers a miscarriage, she does not say, "I am so sad because I lost my fetus." She says, "I lost my baby!" This dichotomy suggests that the nature and being of the developing life has no objective reality. Its "whatness," its "beingness" is determined by and dependent on the intentionality of the mother. It should be noted that currently thirty-eight states have fetal homicide laws.

Black Lives Matter advocates, along with most others who favor abortion, place their focus not on the ethical question of what is being done to the life in the womb but on the legal question of a mother's "rights" to control her own body and determine when, or if, she will have children. Movement spokespersons are generally opposed to any federal or state law that would place limits on a mother's "right" to have an abortion. Their critics say that little consideration is given to the idea that the time to exercise this "right" is before becoming pregnant. They reject any assertion that Black women are killing their own children. This position has led some African Americans to protest against "black genocide" and declare that the most dangerous place for an African American is in the womb. According to the Centers for Disease Control, in 2010, the most recent year for which statistics are available, 765,651 abortions were performed in the United States. Black women continue to have the highest abortion rate of any racial or ethnic group. In that same year 138,539 African American women ended their pregnancies by abortion. For every 1,000 live births, there were 483 abortions. Although African Americans represent only 13 percent of the population of this country, between 2007 and 2010, almost 36 percent of the abortion deaths in the nation were Black infants.

Black Lives Matter argues that the goal of recounting these disturbing statistics is to shame Black women for exercising their "fundamental right" to make their own reproductive choices. They believe that defending the "right" of women who wish to end their pregnancy is greater than the "supposed right to life" of the fetus. The "right" of one Black woman to end her pregnancy, they argue, places no burden on another Black woman who believes, for whatever reason, that abortion is wrong, immoral, or sinful. Legal abortion does not prevent a woman who opposes abortion from carrying her child to term.

They believe some pro-life politicians make every effort to deprive poor, young, African American women of their "right to choose" while opposing urgently needed social programs such as health care, sex education, food benefits, public assistance, and equal pay for women. They protest that it is programs such as these that are needed if Black women are going to be able to choose to become mothers and have the ability to raise healthy children.

The movement argues that traditional Christianity is selectively "pro-life." Where are the tens of thousands of white Christians marching in "pro-life" rallies when Black children are gunned down in the street by white police? Don't those lives matter as much as the lives of those yet to be born? African American women and men, who disagree with Black Lives Matter concerning abortion, firmly stand their ground. "If you genuinely believe that Black lives matter, you should be working to see that every Black infant is accorded the very first civil right, the right to life."

Crime and Black Lives

When pressed, representatives of the Black Lives Matter movement are willing to concede that ALL lives matter. They say they know that the lives of Syrians who die trying to escape a civil war, the lives of those murdered by radicalized Islamic terrorists in Paris and San Bernardino, and the lives of white police officers slain in confrontations with young African American men ALL matter. Their goal is to confront white people who say all lives matter but do not live this truth with the words of *Animal Farm*, "All animals are equal. BUT, some animals are more equal than others."

Many Catholic priests, deacons, religious, and members of the Christian faithful who serve in urban communities around the country raise the same burning question that is raised by many others. Why does a movement that is rightly calling attention to violent, deadly conflicts between white police officers and young African American men seem to almost ignore the obvious reality that most young Black men who die violent deaths do so, not at the hands of racist white police, but at the hands of other young Black men?

Ninety-three percent of Black murder victims are murdered by other Black people. Eighty-four percent of white murder victims are killed by other white people. Black and white commentators often raise the question of self-inflicted violent crime in Black communities. They are distressed when Black Lives Matter responds that it is painfully aware of the many violent crimes in Black neighborhoods. The movement knows that many people think their outrage should be focused on the many acts of violence within the community rather than the relatively few acts of violence inflicted from outside the community. They counter that even though the number of white police who inflict violence on Black youth is small by comparison, their voices must be raised in protest over the violent actions of white police. These officers, who are committed to serving and protecting all citizens, are not only violating this commitment, but also are frequently doing so without punishment.

The number of white police officers who intentionally shoot and kill Black men is small when compared to the estimated 7,000 Black people who are murdered each year by people from their own communities. In an opinion column in the February 12, 2016, edition of the *Wall Street Journal*, Heather Mac Donald argues that Black Lives Matter is a myth and its claims are fiction. To make this point, she cites statistics of the high rate of violent crime in some Black communities, the fact that police officers are disproportionately endangered by Black assailants, and that Hispanic and Black officers are much more likely to shoot African Americans than white officers because of the mistaken belief that the African American is armed.

Black Lives Matter supporters argue that the high homicide rates in impoverished Black neighborhoods are fed, in part, by the structural racism that has been in place for generations since the Great Migration, maintaining segregated neighborhoods, inadequate housing, dreadful public schools, and bleak employment opportunities. Young people with nothing to do and no hope are easily ensnarled in the world of gangs and selling drugs, which leads to internecine murders. The movement believes that these factors do not excuse violent crime in Black communities. However, they do help to explain a tragic pattern seen in many cities from Baltimore to Chicago to Los Angeles. This is seen as a systemic pattern over which the poor have very little control. If those who have political power really cared about Black lives, they would address these issues and, by doing so, help reduce urban violence.

Nevertheless, some African American community leaders believe the movement would gain more credibility if some of its members made it a high priority to contribute directly to grassroots efforts to at least diminish the scourge of Black youths killing one another. It has been encouraging to see young men in some African American communities wearing T-shirts with the message, "Let's stop killing each other!" Those who minister in Catholic parishes in African American communities might be able to support more effectively the Black Lives Matter movement in its efforts to draw attention to white officers who display a reckless disregard for the lives of African American lives if the movement were able to devote some of its considerable energy to decreasing what is sometimes called "Black-on-Black crime."

Readily available deadly weapons are a major contributor to the frequent murders in some Black communities. One way in which the Catholic Church may increase its credibility in the eyes of those who believe the church really does not think the lives of Black people matter is through the church's support for reasonable gun control legislation. Many Catholics share the view of many other Americans that any effort to regulate the buying, selling, and transporting of guns in our society is an attack on their Second Amendment right to bear arms. However, a growing number have seen the need for change. A Religion News Service and the Public Religion Research Institute poll in 2013 found that 62 percent of American Catholics support some measures to strengthen gun control. Many bishops have expressed their support for various gun control measures such as background checks and a ban on assault weapons. Pope Francis, in his address to Congress, said:

> Why are deadly weapons being sold to those who plan to inflict untold suffering on individuals and society? Sadly, the answer, as we all know, is simply for money: money that is drenched in blood, often innocent blood. . . . In the face of this shameful and culpable silence, it is our duty to confront the problem and to stop the arms trade.

The gun lobby argues that people and not guns kill people. While this is true, the evidence from other countries clearly confirms that when gun purchasers have been properly screened by background checks, when proper attention is given to the care of those with mental health needs, when violent offenders are monitored, and when people have fewer guns, the number of murders declines.

Concluding Dialogue

In the section of this letter titled "The Catholic Church and Black Lives Matter," I said that until recently, I had no personal contact with individuals directly associated with the Black Lives Matter movement. I saw it as a grassroots movement that I viewed with genuine interest and concern. I wondered then, as I do now, if its long-term impact on the lives of People of Color and on the fabric of the nation would be positive or negative. It was at that time that I became acquainted with a young attorney who is a Catholic and who had a close relative who was deeply involved with Black Lives Matter. He was the primary person who facilitated my contact and conversations with a small group of women and men who are involved with the movement but who are not, in any sense, representatives of or leaders of the movement. It is important to keep in mind that what I have written is a personal reflection and not an exhaustive, fully researched critique. It is simply an effort by one human being, who is a Catholic bishop and a Person of Color, to call this movement to the attention of members of the church who might easily overlook it. I have called this reflection "The Racial Divide Revisited" because it continues the conversation I initiated with my 2015 Pastoral Letter, "The Racial Divide," by engaging the Black Lives Matter movement in a very initial way.

I am grateful to my acquaintance for making my conversations with movement members possible, and I respect his desire not to be identified. However, after I shared with him the contents of this pastoral letter, he asked me a number of pointed questions. My responses to some of his questions will serve as the concluding dialogue of this reflection.

Is it really your expectation that members of the Black Lives Matter movement and members of the church are going to sit down and discuss your pastoral letter?

While that would be a remarkable development, it is not my realistic expectation. My hope is that Catholics who read this pastoral letter will find it a useful resource for having a conversation among themselves and with people of different racial backgrounds and points of view about a timely subject to which they may not have previously given much attention.

What is your response to those who may say you have provided them with a helpful overview of a complex issue, but you have not provided them with a plan or program to help them effectively address the issues you have raised?

This is true because I do not have such a plan or program. I would hope individuals would devise plans appropriate for their situation. I hope they will do what I asked at the conclusion of the prior pastoral letter. They should commit themselves to praying, listening, learning, thinking, and acting in ways that will help them bridge the racial divide. They may already know someone who, unbeknown to them, is associated with the movement.

Is the Catholic Church abandoning schools in African American neighborhoods because these schools have failed to produce converts to the church?

I do not agree with the premise of your question. The church is not abandoning these schools. The entire Catholic school system in this country has undergone radical changes in the last fifty years. Maintaining schools has become much more expensive. Catholic families have fewer children. More Catholics send their children to free public schools with state-of-the-art facilities. And, most significantly, we have seen the virtual disappearance of the religious sisters who established and staffed these schools. Economic and staffing limitations have led to consolidating and closing large numbers of schools in many communities.

In the past, many people thought the church's commitment to maintaining schools in poorer, urban communities would serve as a means of evangelization. However, that has not proven to be the case. African American parents have been appreciative of the church for providing an alternative to the often inferior urban public schools, but this has not led them to turn away in significant numbers from traditional Black churches for Catholicism. The church's ministry of education has provided generations of young

African Americans with superior educational experiences, making it possible for them to attain greater opportunities. A number of dioceses have made a deliberate choice to maintain urban schools at considerable expense while realizing these schools will not produce many converts to the faith. Contributing to the enrichment of the lives of African Americans, who are not Catholics, has become part of the church's ministry of education. This has been done because Black lives matter to the church. (The same could be said of the church's health care ministry, the vast network of social services, the Campaign for Human Development, Catholic Charities, and the St. Vincent de Paul Society. These services to anyone in need, at least implicitly, affirm that Black lives matter.)

Do you personally believe that the church as an institution (at the level of the Vatican, the Bishops' Conference, and parish leadership) really does believe that Black lives matter?

In the end, the church "as an institution" or the government "as an institution" is only as committed to living Christ's law of loving our neighbors as we love ourselves as the individuals who make up the institution. In this pastoral I have stressed that the Gospel requires "ongoing personal and social transformation." This transformation takes place in the hearts of individuals, and those individuals can change institutions. Even though they would be unlikely to use the expression Black Lives Matter because of unfamiliarity with it or because of certain ideas associated with it, I do believe that many people at every level of the church have a desire to purify the church of bias, prejudice, and discrimination. Nevertheless, we have a very long way to go. Otherwise, the Holy Father would not have called us to a Holy Year of mercy, forgiveness, and reconciliation. Nor would he have asked us to envision the church as a hospital on the field of battle tending the spiritual wounds of the injured (including those injured by prejudice in the church), not unlike the Good Samaritan.

Do you think that racial prejudice is the primary reason there are so few African American Catholics?

While historically speaking, it is certainly an important reason, I am not able to say it is the primary reason. Historic events and cultural, educational, emotional, and spiritual factors are also important reasons. Obvious examples of this are worship, liturgy, and theological discourse. Catholic worship is shaped profoundly by European culture, which may make it less inviting for people whose cultural experience is Afrocentric. Catholic theology is also formulated with categories of thought derived from ancient Greece and medieval Europe. This may be one reason why the Scripture-centered vocabulary of Black Protestant churches is so attractive.

You have argued in the past that the expressions "minorities" and "minority groups" commonly used by Black and white people and the Catholic Church are not neutral expressions. You have suggested that they are used in a biased and selective way, which make it more difficult to bridge the racial divide. Have you had much success in influencing the church, for example, to refer to people and groups as who they are rather than who they are not? Not the "majority"?

No, I have not. But I did not expect sudden changes in long-standing behavior. After all, the media and the government constantly use these terms. Indeed, People of Color often speak of themselves as "a minority group." Nevertheless, my point remains true. Every American citizen is an American, not a minority American. Every member of the church is a Catholic, not a minority Catholic. "Minority" effectively means "not white." It is as demeaning as "non-Catholic." The change in vocabulary that I am urging can only come about after a considerable amount of profound "consciousness raising."

You have also indicated that one way for the church to show that Black lives matter might be to depart from the long-standing practice of depicting God, Jesus, the angels, and the saints as Europeans and make greater use of African, Asian, and Hispanic religious art. Have you sensed much interest in acting on this idea?

No. However, I never expected any immediate interest. Again, changes like this take time, perhaps over generations. All I have been doing is planting seeds for consideration. I think the proposal is valid and truly "catholic." John Nerva's "Communion of Saints" tapestries in Our Lady of the Angels Cathedral in Los Angeles constitute one of the few prominent examples of racially inclusive quality Catholic religious art in the country. If efforts are not made to follow this example (including images of God and angels), the church will be the poorer for it.

Are you optimistic about the future of Black lives in America?

Yes, I am. As a human being, as a Christian, and as a priest, I am naturally optimistic. Christ is our hope! There are many indicators to suggest grounds for optimism. You have only to look at where Black lives were in 1916, 1950, 2000, and today to see the reasons for optimism. At the same time, I am a realist. I do not have a naïve vision of a future marked only by racial harmony and accord. The points of conflict and the great disparity in education, employment, income, housing, health care, and social mobility are such that we will continue to see steps forward followed by steps backward for years and years to come. This is so not only because of the many, including some Catholics, who are not committed to ongoing personal and communal spiritual and moral transformation (due to indifference?), not only because of the few who oppose ending the racial divide deep within their souls, but also because of the undertow of history.

When President Obama was elected, several articles appeared hailing the dawn of the "postracial era" in the United States. I said to anyone who would listen that this was not the case. I also pointed out that while Mr. Obama has embraced the African American experience, it is strange that the fact that he is actually biracial is almost always ignored by the media.

A 2015 *New York Times*/CBS News poll makes it clear that seven years after the president's election we are still not in a "postracial era." The survey indicated that nearly six in ten Americans, including significant majorities of Black and white people, think race relations are generally not good. Nearly four in ten think the situation is getting worse. By comparison, two-thirds of Americans surveyed shortly after President Obama took office said they believed that race relations were generally good and getting better.

During Mr. Obama's 2008 campaign, nearly 60 percent of Black Americans said race relations were generally bad. Shortly after his election, that number was cut in half. It has now soared to 68 percent, the highest level of discontent among African Americans during the president's years in office. It is close to the numbers recorded in the aftermath of the civil disturbances that followed the 1992 acquittal of Los Angeles police officers charged in the beating of Mr. Rodney King. Almost half of those questioned said Mr. Obama's presidency had had no effect on creating greater racial harmony. About a third said his presidency had driven people of different races further apart. Only 15 percent said race relations had improved. There is much to ponder here and no one can adequately explain why this is so.

Nevertheless, I remain optimistic because of the encouraging signs I see around the country. And, of course, as Christians, who affirm the redemptive truth of the Incarnation of the Word of God in Jesus Christ, the transformative power of the amazing grace poured out by the Holy Spirit, and the powerful nourishment that we receive when we are fed by the Bread of Life in the Eucharist, we must never grow weary of grace-filled efforts. The church has a grave responsibility to contribute to the ongoing conversion and spiritual transformation of us all. Working tirelessly day by day, we are co-workers with Christ.

I hope all who read this pastoral letter share my optimism. But our optimism must always be tempered by these words of Dr. Martin Luther King Jr., in his "Letter from a Birmingham Jail":

> I have just received a letter from a white brother in Texas. He writes: "All Christians know that the colored people will receive equal rights eventually, but it is possible that you are in too great a religious hurry. It has taken Christianity almost two thousand years to accomplish what it has. The teachings of Christ take time to come to earth." Such an attitude stems from a tragic misconception of time, from the strangely ir-

rational notion that there is something in the very flow of time that will inevitably cure all ills. Actually, time itself is neutral; it can be used either destructively or constructively. More and more I feel that the people of ill will have used time much more effectively than have the people of good will. We will have to repent in this generation not merely for the hateful words and actions of the bad people but for the appalling silence of the good people.

Therefore, let us prepare to go up to Jerusalem with the Lord to celebrate the Paschal Mystery. We must pray that the Holy Spirit, who will come upon us at Pentecost, will give us the strength that we need not to maintain an "appalling silence." Instead, we must follow the imperatives that I shared in my earlier pastoral letter. We must PRAY, LISTEN, LEARN, THINK, and ACT in such a way that all people everywhere will know that we truly believe that Black lives matter precisely because all lives matter!

3

Old Wounds Revisited

The Catholic University of America

S<small>EPTEMBER</small> 21, 2017

The first time I mentioned in a public lecture the fact that Roger Taney, the Chief Justice of the Supreme Court who penned the odious 1857 Dred Scott *decision, was a Catholic, several people in the audience expressed dismay and shock. "He couldn't have been a Catholic!" But the truth is that he was. Unfortunately, many Catholics of that period supported the immoral practice of enslaving free human beings. It was a flaw at the foundation. That flaw has had a lasting impact up to the present day.*

It is unlikely that the Chief Justice or his fellow Catholics, who owned enslaved free human beings, could have imagined that 163 years later, in 2020, African American people would be suffering from Covid-19, the disease caused by the coronavirus, in alarmingly higher numbers than other Americans. And this disproportion is due, in part, to health conditions that have their source in slavery.

The oppression of slavery and fragmentation of families, segregated housing and schools, poverty, low-paying jobs, lack of educational opportunities, inadequate health care, diets lacking in good nutrition, and generations of stress—all have created circumstances that make African Americans more likely to be infected by the coronavirus and die from Covid-19 than white Americans. By some accounts, although African Americans are 13 percent of the population, they are 42 percent of the deaths. In states like Mississippi and Louisiana, over 65 percent of those who die from Covid-19 are African Americans.

A direct legacy of the flaw at the foundation is the fact that large numbers of African Americans necessarily work as janitors, bus drivers, hotel maids, nurses, and first responders. They are considered part of the critical workforce who must continue to work. One of the best ways to prevent the spread of the very contagious virus is for people to shelter in place and stay at home. But many People of Color simply cannot stay at home the way white people who work on computers in their offices can. African Americans who are poor live in crowded conditions and necessarily take public transportation to work in higher numbers than white people. This means greater contact with infected individuals.

This same legacy has contributed to higher instances of heart disease, high blood pressure, diabetes, and obesity in African American communities than in white communities. These health conditions create a higher risk of life-threatening illness in those infected by the virus.

When I delivered this address in 2017, no one was thinking that in three years we would be engulfed by the coronavirus pandemic. In the face of the current crisis, I now see a direct connection between the flaw at the foundation examined here and the disturbingly high instances of Covid-19 in African American communities.

The Horizon of Possibilities

We are living in a unique moment in our history, a moment when, sadly, the racial divide[1] in our country is becoming more acute. If we are to move ahead in a positive way from this moment, we must learn from the past by studying the choices, decisions, beliefs, and experiences that have brought us to this moment. Hopefully, this will allow us to nurture better choices, decisions,

---

[1]The Racial Divide: While I am fully aware that the reality referred to by the words "racism" and "racists" are very real in our country and in our church, I have long preferred to speak of "the racial divide" in my published writings and in my public addresses. The expression seems less confrontational and less judgmental. The words "racism" and "racists" at times make some listeners or readers feel excluded from the conversation before it really begins.

beliefs, and experiences to shape our future. My remarks this afternoon will have a moving viewpoint in five parts:

The Horizon of Possibilities;

A Flaw at the Foundation: *Dred Scott* and Robert Taney;

The Horizon of Possibilities: Once Ignored Monuments Stir Fierce Debate;

"Our" History and Culture;

The Horizon of Possibilities within Christian Communities: What Can the Church Do?

In his book *Sapiens: A Brief History of Humankind,* Yuval Noah Harari notes that a wide spectrum of beliefs, practices, and experiences is available to communities and individuals at different moments in history. However, most individuals and communities only embrace a small portion of the choices that are actually within their horizon of possibilities, paying little attention to the wide spectrum of possibilities hidden from view due to cultural and other limitations.[2]

Listen! Learn! Think! Pray! Act! Faithfully attending to these imperatives will help all of us become aware of the widest range of options within our horizon of possibilities. Jesus of Nazareth has given us the most fundamental option that all people should exercise from their horizon of possibilities. Drawing on Deuteronomy 19:7–18 and Leviticus 6:4–5, Jesus teaches us the Law of Love (Matthew 22:35–40). We must love God with our whole heart and our whole being. And we must love our neighbor as we love ourselves. It is a threefold law. Love God! Love ourselves! Love our neighbor! And in the story of the man who shows compassion to the stranger, beaten, robbed, and ignored by his countrymen (Luke 10:25–35), Jesus teaches us that our neighbor is any fellow human being of any background anywhere. Communities, whether religious or secular, that overlook, ignore,

---

[2]See Yuval Noah Harari, *Sapiens: A Brief History of Humankind* (New York: HarperCollins, 2015), 45.

or reject this Law of Love from their horizon of possibilities make decisions, erect laws, and create social structures that have a dangerous flaw at the foundation.

Most Catholics readily affirm the truth of this Law of Love. Most also acknowledge that Jesus' words become more and more difficult to obey as we face complex social, moral, political, and personal situations about which Catholics themselves may disagree. The events of 2020 concerning freedom of speech, public Confederate monuments, white supremacists, neo-Nazis, and the Ku Klux Klan are particularly challenging and complex for Christians seeking to obey the Law of Love. Daily headlines, the evening news, and all forms of social media have placed the racial divide in the United States right in front of us in ways we would not have expected as we approach the fiftieth anniversary of the cruel murder of Dr. Martin Luther King Jr., on April 4, 2018. Was his precious blood spilled in vain? Do Black lives really matter? President Donald Trump, by his inconsistent comments, has become a lightning rod in the midst of this turmoil, resulting in intense media coverage of old wounds reopened. We cannot know what is in his heart, and it is not for us to presume to sit in judgment of the choices he makes within his horizon of possibilities. Our reflection on his words respects both the office and the person of the president.

We have no window into the interior world of another person. It is almost impossible to know with certainty what individuals, with whom we have had no personal conversation, think and feel at the deepest levels about the racial divide in this country. From Charleston to Charlottesville, we have been observers of a public quarrel and dispute without having the opportunity for a serious and honest conversation with any of the participants. Almost all of our impressions are formed by information gleaned from public media, which are necessarily selective in their presentations. In some instances, however, individuals have expressed their beliefs with such intense emotion, force, and frequency that it is difficult not to conclude that they are revealing their true selves. Paradoxically, some reject Christ's Law of Love from their horizon of possibilities, while proclaiming themselves Christians in the public square.

As Catholics, our goal is to always nurture choices, decisions, beliefs, and experiences that are faithful to Christ's Law of Love. Our chances of succeeding in this unique moment of history will be better if we follow these critical imperatives: Listen! Learn! Think! Pray! Act!

A Flaw at the Foundation: *Dred Scott* and Robert Taney

The racial divide we are experiencing so acutely has a long history. If we are to understand the present, we must examine the past. Could there be a flaw at the foundation? Could the extreme racial divide that we are witnessing today be a residue of a foundational flaw born of moral blindness due to wrong choices people have made from their horizon of possibilities? Robert B. Taney, a Catholic, who rose to prominence under President Andrew Jackson, was eventually appointed Chief Justice of the Supreme Court. Apparently, early in his life, Taney had some qualms about the enslavement of free human beings, thus "freeing" his own enslaved free human beings as a young man. A native of Maryland, he shunned the Confederacy and supported the Union all of his life. Yet one hundred and sixty years ago, on March 6, 1857, he wrote the majority opinion in the 7–2 *Dred Scott v. John F. A. Sandford* decision in what is generally considered to be the most odious and shameful ruling in the Supreme Court's history. He declared that people of African ancestry living in America had absolutely no legal standing before the court and could not sue for their freedom because they were nothing more than the property of their "owners." It is stunning to think that a Catholic, who surely was taught the Law of Love, could pen these words:

> The question is simply this: Can a negro [*sic*], whose ancestors were imported into this country, and sold as slaves, become a member of the political community formed and brought into existence by the Constitution of the United States, and as such become entitled to all the rights, and privileges, and

immunities, guarantied [*sic*] by that instrument to the citizen? One of which rights is the privilege of suing in a court of the United States in the cases specified in the Constitution.

It will be observed, that the plea applies to that class of persons only whose ancestors were negroes [*sic*] of the African race, and imported into this country, and sold and held as slaves. The only matter in issue before the court, therefore, is, whether the descendants of such slaves, when they shall be emancipated, or who are born of parents who had become free before their birth, are citizens of a State, in the sense in which the word citizen is used in the Constitution of the United States. . . .

They had for more than a century before been regarded as beings of an inferior order, and altogether unfit to associate with the white race, either in social or political relations; and so far inferior, that they had no rights which the white man was bound to respect; and that the negro [*sic*] might justly and lawfully be reduced to slavery for his benefit. He was bought and sold, and treated as an ordinary article of merchandise and traffic, whenever a profit could be made by it. This opinion was at that time fixed and universal in the civilized portion of the white race. It was regarded as an axiom in morals as well as in politics, which no one thought of disputing, or supposed to be open to dispute; and men in every grade and position in society daily and habitually acted upon it in their private pursuits, as well as in matters of public concern, without doubting for a moment the correctness of this opinion.

Yet the men who framed this declaration were great men—high in literary acquirements—high in their sense of honor, and incapable of asserting principles inconsistent with those on which they were acting. They perfectly understood the meaning of the language they used, and how it would be understood by others; and they knew that it would not in any part of the civilized world be supposed to embrace the negro [*sic*] race, which, by common consent, had been excluded from civilized Governments and the family of nations, and doomed to slavery. They spoke and acted according to the then established doctrines and principles, and in the ordinary language of the day, no one misunderstood them. The unhappy black race were separated from the white by indelible marks, and laws long before established, and were never thought of or spoken of except as property. (See 60 US (19 How.) 393 (1857))

Many Southerners thought that Chief Justice Taney's opinion definitively resolved the issues concerning the status of enslaved free human beings before the law. Instead, it was met with widespread outrage and fueled the fires that led to the Civil War. Eventually, the Emancipation Proclamation (1863), the Civil Rights Act (1866), and the Thirteenth, Fourteenth, and Fifteenth Amendments to the United States Constitution (1868) nullified Taney's infamous ruling, giving human beings of African ancestry full citizenship (on paper only!), thus making them, for the first time, African Americans!

Nevertheless, this ruling by the first Catholic Chief Justice, which seems glaringly false today, created a flaw at the foundation of the country's relationship to People of Color. It is not possible for us to know how the clear teaching of Jesus Christ, to love our neighbors as we love ourselves, escaped Justice Taney and the six justices who concurred with him, unless we consider the possibility that they simply could not conceive of Dred Scott as their neighbor because of his African heritage. He was not really a person, only property.

Unfortunately, there were, within the horizon of possibilities of the Catholic Church, firmly held opinions that made Taney's decision possible. There was a "flaw at the foundation," which was, sadly, supported by teachings at the highest levels of the Catholic Church. We learn from history, and credible historical documents suggest that one of the first extensive shipments of human beings from West Africa in the transatlantic slave trade was probably initiated at the request of Bartolomé de Las Casas, a Catholic priest from Spain, who wrongly thought that African people were more suited for slavery than Indigenous people. Later, as a bishop, he showed repentance for this grave sin. ("I soon repented and judged myself guilty of ignorance. I came to realize that Black slavery was as unjust as Indian slavery.") In 1548, Pope Paul III declared that both clergy and laity had the right to own enslaved free human beings. The Catholic colonies of Spain and Portugal were the major agents of slave trade in the Americas.

More than that, the Catholic Church placed books critical of enslaving free human beings on the Index of Forbidden Books between 1573 and 1826. The church excommunicated Capuchin missionaries because they urged that enslaved free African people in the Americas should be given their freedom. Blessed Pius IX, during whose pontificate (1846–78) the *Dred Scott* decision was handed down, wrote, "Slavery itself . . . is not at all contrary to the natural and divine law, and there can be several just titles of slavery, and these are referred to by approved theologians and commentators of the sacred canons. . . . It is not contrary to the natural and divine law for a slave to be sold, bought, exchanged or given." (See 1866 Instruction of the Holy Office in Response to questions from the Vicar Apostolic of the Galla tribe in Ethiopia, www.kingscollege.net)

Prominent American bishops (including John Hughes, New York, 1842–64; Francis Kenrick, Baltimore, 1851–63; St. John Neumann, Philadelphia, 1852–60; and Anthony O'Regan, Chicago, 1854–58) did not condemn the Supreme Court's decision.

Indeed, historian John Strausbaugh, writing about Archbishop Hughes, observed that the archbishop's position was that as long as slavery was legal in the South, owning slaves was not a sin. He did not admire President Lincoln and found no place in his heart for people of African ancestry. Strausbaugh notes that as the conflict between the abolitionists and the Irish workers intensified, anti-abolitionist forces in New York would "scare workers with terrible predictions that if the millions of enslaved Blacks in the South were freed, they'd flood into northern cities and take away all the work."

With the flood of Famine Irish into the Lower East Side in the 1840s and 1850s, the immigrants' struggle to set themselves apart from blacks and be accepted by whites turned mean and hard. The Irish now developed a fierce strain of anti-black and anti-abolitionist sentiment. Clinging desperately to their low-level jobs, Irish workers hated the abolitionist movement they feared would unleash millions of freed black workers to flood the city and replace them.[3]

Hughes said that if the president's goal in the Civil War was to end slavery, then Irishmen "will turn away in disgust from the discharge of what would otherwise be a patriotic duty."

Listen! Learn! Think! Pray! Act!

The Horizon of Possibilities: Once Ignored Monuments Stir Fierce Debate

Hundreds of monuments honoring men from the Civil War era have been on public display for decades. The almost visceral debate about them that has recently been raging in certain parts of the country has emerged because of a different response to the horizon of possibilities. Beliefs, attitudes, feelings, and judgments about the character of the individuals immortalized in bronze were different for different individuals and communities during their lifetime, during the Lost Cause era, and during the 1950s. Clearly, today's debate is born from the fact that different individuals and communities attribute different meanings to the monuments because the images provoke different psychological selections from their horizon of possibilities.

A bronze sculpture of Justice Taney stood in the North Garden in Mount Vernon Place in Baltimore since 1872, until the City Council voted to remove it quickly and quietly, and did so on August 18, 2017. How could a monument "honoring" the man

---

[3]See John Strausbaugh, *City of Sedition: The History of New York City during the Civil War* (New York: Twelve Books, 2016), 195.

who vigorously defended the lie of white supremacy while leading the nation's highest court have remained on public display for so long without an outcry? A primary reason may not be political or cultural. It may be simply a matter of inattentiveness. People of all backgrounds (including Catholic clergy, religious sisters and brothers, and laity) may have passed by the statue of Robert Taney, and the now controversial monuments to General Robert E. Lee and other Confederate leaders, with a degree of indifference and inattentiveness. Questioning the appropriateness of the statue was within their horizon of possibilities, but they did not advert to that possibility.

Many, if not most, Americans strolling through parks and public squares pay little or no attention to the weather-worn statues and monuments of men sitting in formal chairs or on horseback. They are simply decorations, part of the ambience of the park, like the beautiful flowers and ponds full of gliding ducks and graceful swans. Some might take a photograph; a few might read the name of the "famous" person. Very few give much thought to exactly who the person was or what he did to merit such a place of honor. Those who do know whom the monument immortalizes almost certainly do not consult reliable historical accounts of the person's life and give serious thought to whether this person represented the noblest ideals of the country or adhered to positions that must be rejected and condemned, such as racial division, oppression, and superiority.

In the case of Confederate monuments, there have always been some individuals and groups who knew well who the dignified figure on horseback was. He reminded them of their pride in their identity, their heritage, their history, and their culture. There are others who have been equally aware of whom the monuments celebrate. They know when the monuments were erected and why. For them, these statues are a reminder of the commitment of some to the Lost Cause, a defense of the Civil War as an honorable struggle for the Southern way of life, and a denial of the central role human slavery played in the war. The Lost Cause was the old order of the Confederacy, of which racial superiority, sustained by Jim Crow laws, and an apartheid-like form of absolute racial segregation, were an integral part.

Of the approximately seven hundred Confederate monuments (and numerous displays of the Confederate flag) in the United States, mainly in the South, a good number were erected when the post–Civil War Reconstruction era was overtaken by a return to political power of white southerners in the years between 1890 and 1920, a time when the disenfranchisement and lynching of People of Color were commonplace. A romanticized antebellum revisionist view of history prevailed that could not imagine that the enslavement of free human beings was the primary cause of the Civil War. Nor would they acknowledge the truth that human bondage was the financial engine that sustained the genteel world of the old South, which is well documented in Edward E. Baptist's *The Half Has Never Been Told: Slavery and the Making of American Capitalism*. This worldview is meticulously re-created in Margaret Mitchell's 1936 novel, *Gone with the Wind*, in which the Irish Catholic O'Hara family has no qualms about owning enslaved free human beings as workhorses on their plantation, Tara. Solomon Northup's 1853 memoir, *Twelve Years a Slave*, provides a far more accurate account of the horrors of human bondage on a southern plantation.

A great number of Confederate monuments, however, were built later, beginning in 1950 and into the 1960s as an expression of opposition to decisions by the federal government and the rulings of the Supreme Court under Chief Justice Earl Warren, including striking down as unconstitutional racial segregation in public schools (*Brown v. Board of Education*) and laws forbidding interracial marriage (*Loving v. Virginia*).

During a speaking engagement in the Diocese of Charleston, South Carolina, I went on pilgrimage to the Mother Emanuel African Methodist Episcopal Church. I stood in silent prayer in the sanctuary, which endured the slaughter of the innocent on June 15, 2015, when Dylann Roof extinguished the lives of nine African American Christians. He later said he was a white supremacist whose goal was to start a race war. The pictures of him proudly waving a Confederate flag enkindled anew the long-standing debate about the meaning of this flag, to some a banner of honor, pride, history, and heritage; to others a reminder of the horror of enslaving free human beings from West Africa to labor in the plantations of the South and to later suffer under systematic racial oppression. This led to efforts by some elected officials to vote to remove the flag from public buildings, over the objections of others. The Charleston City Council voted to remove the flag from the capitol grounds. When the current president was running for office, he approved the relocation of the flags to a museum. Since then, other communities have voted to remove Confederate flags and monuments from high-visibility locations because they are widely seen as exacerbating the racial divide. The Dylann Roof assassinations triggered a dramatic shift in the horizon of possibilities for many Americans.

On February 6, 2017, the Charlottesville, Virginia, City Council voted to move a prominent statue of Confederate General Robert E. Lee from the city's central square because it was considered, by some, inappropriate to honor someone who supported the enslavement of free human beings and who led an army to war with his own country, the United States.

On Friday, August 11, 2017, marchers who opposed the removal of the monument paraded through the University of Virginia carrying torches and proclaiming "white lives matter," "Jews will not replace us," and the German nationalist Nazi slogan, "blood and soil." On Saturday, August 12, 2017, there was a "Unite the Right" rally in Charlottesville to protest the removal of the Lee statue. A large number of people turned out to oppose this rally, which was widely seen as a white supremacist gathering. The event became violent when white supremacists clashed with counter-demonstrators (including Black Lives Matter and antifascist groups). A speeding car drove into the crowd of people who opposed the white supremacist groups, killing Heather D. Heyer, 32, and injuring at least nineteen others. The police apprehended the driver, James Alex Fields Jr., of Ohio, described as a Nazi sympathizer, and charged him with second-degree murder.

Meanwhile, two state troopers were killed when their helicopter, which was monitoring the rally, crashed. Since the City Council voted to remove the Robert E. Lee statue, Charlottesville has attracted members of the Ku Klux Klan, neo-Nazis, and other white supremacist groups. After this violent conflict, there was widespread condemnation by civic, political, and religious leaders of the extremist groups that were unambiguous about their racial bias and hatred.

The initial response of the US president on Saturday, August 12, 2017, to these events was characterized as forceful but vague. "We condemn in the strongest possible terms this egregious display of hatred, bigotry and violence on many sides." Many criticized him for not specifically condemning white supremacy in any form, especially neo-Nazis. They were deeply troubled by his reference to violence "on many sides," which seemed to imply that everyone involved in the conflict was equally at fault. David Duke, the former Ku Klux Klan Grand Wizard, expressed gratitude to the president for the honesty and courage "of this initial statement and for telling the truth about Charlottesville and condemning the leftist terrorists involved with Black Lives Matter and Antifa."

On the following Monday, August 14, 2017, facing intense criticism, the White House issued a new statement in the president's name: "Racism is evil. And those who cause violence in its name are criminals and thugs, including KKK, neo-Nazis, white supremacists, and other hate groups, and are repugnant to everything we hold dear as Americans. Those who spread violence in the name of bigotry strike at the very core of America."

But on Tuesday, August 15, 2017, during a press conference about another matter, the president criticized the media for mischaracterizing white supremacist protesters in Charlottesville, stating that some of those marching alongside of them were "very fine people." This response surprised many and was quickly criticized by leaders of foreign governments, Republicans, Democrats, Christian and Jewish organizations, and the Joint Chiefs of Staff for seeming to suggest there is a "moral equivalence" between neo-Nazis, white supremacists, and the demonstrators (a mixture of various groups including some of whom advocate violence) protesting against them. Business leaders in the president's Economic Strategic and Policy Forum and the members of the president's Committee on the Arts and the Humanities all resigned in protest. Nevertheless, as recently as Thursday, September 14, 2017, the president renewed his assertion of blame on both sides.

After a meeting with Senator Tim Scott of South Carolina, the only African American Republican in the Senate, who had challenged the president on his claim that "both sides" were responsible for the Charlottesville violence, the president said, "Especially in light of the advent of Antifa, if you look at what's going on there . . . you have some pretty bad dudes on the other side also," in an apparent reference to the antifascist activists who confronted the neo-Nazis and white supremacists. "Now because of what's happened since then, with Antifa, you look at really what's happened since Charlottesville, a lot of people are saying . . . 'Gee, Trump might have a point.' I said, 'You've got some very bad people on the other side,' which is true." Senator Scott said he met with the president to express his strong opposition to his assertion that "both sides" were to blame for the conflict. He had no expectation of changing the president's mind, and he had not done so. Listen! Learn! Think! Pray! Act!

"Our" History and Culture

Turning his attention to the controversy that prompted his comments about "both sides," the president lamented the changing of "our" culture, history, and heritage that is implied by removing historic monuments honoring Confederate generals like Robert E. Lee. He asked whose statues would be next to go. In impromptu remarks on August 15, he said, "George Washington was a slave owner. So will George Washington lose his status? Are we gonna take down statues to George Washington? How about Thomas Jefferson? What do you think of Thomas Jefferson? Do you like him, because he was a major slave owner? Are we gonna take down his statue? So it's fine. You're changing history, you're changing culture. . . . You really have to ask yourself where does it stop?" During a rally in Phoenix on August 22, 2017, he stated that the media are "trying to take away our history and our heritage." The president's comments did not distinguish between individuals who, like Jefferson, ignored the moral evil of enslaving free human beings while devoting themselves to the ideal of one United States and other individuals, like Lee, who led an army against the United States attempting to undermine the possibility of "a more perfect union."

It would be helpful to have a better understanding of what the president means by "our" heritage. One would think that if the president, who represents the nation, says "our" he means "us," all Americans. However, his words can be interpreted as an expression of identity politics, referring not to all, but to specific exclusive religious, racial, or social groups. When African Americans exclaim, "Black lives matter," it is often labeled identity politics. Identity politics is not new to the American landscape. It is a reflection of a kind of tribal kinship that some people feel for people who are similar to them. Intentionally or not, identity politics is manifested in the speech of many opposing groups at this critical juncture of our history. When the current president proposed and then defended the known-to-be indefensible argument that our first biracial president, Barack Obama was not born in this country, his critics called this an example of identity politics, portraying the former president as foreign, exotic, other, "not one of us."

When the president uses "our" in the context of Charlottesville, he is accused of racial identity politics because of a history that may not be clear to many. Because of that history, "our" could be interpreted to mean American citizens whose ancestors came from Europe and who are presented as the most important actors in the early history of the nation. Is "our" history, heritage, and culture, the history, heritage, and culture of all Americans or is it essentially Eurocentric? Is our American "nationality" derived from citizenship and commonly held core or foundational values no matter from what part of the world our ancestors came? Significantly, in 1790, when the country was determining how those who immigrated to this land could become citizens, the first naturalization law stated that only "white" Europeans could be naturalized, excluding all others.

As for the citizenship of non-Europeans born in this country, that was determined by each state. Thus, some people of African ancestry were granted citizenship. As we have seen, Justice Taney's *Dred Scott* Supreme Court decision determined the law at the national level, declaring that no one of African ancestry was or ever could be a citizen. In 1861, at the time of the Civil War, this was settled law. The Confederacy was committed to maintaining this law excluding People of Color from citizenship. When the Thirteenth, Fourteenth, and Fifteenth Amendments affirmed an egalitarian vision of America, acknowledging it to be a multiracial democracy, the Ku Klux Klan stood in violent opposition. When the president, defending Confederate monuments, speaks of "our history and culture," his listeners who affirm white supremacy and white privilege may hear it as a defense of this historic racial divide. The common practice of speaking of some Americans (e.g., African Americans, Hispanic Americans, Asian Americans) as "minorities" or "minority groups" and not others (e.g., German Americans, Jewish Americans, Irish Americans) unintentionally reinforces both this divide and identity politics. If you understand the meaning of *"E pluribus unum"* ("out of many, one"), there cannot be "minority" Americans, only American citizens of many backgrounds who are all equal to each other. Different Americans, depending on the questions they ask and the responses they affirm from their horizon of possibilities, may reach very different conclusions about what they mean by "we," us," and "our."

One of the best correctives to the perhaps unintentionally one-sided references to "our" history, heritage, and culture was provided on Friday, May 19, 2017, when Mitch Landrieu, the mayor of New Orleans and a Catholic, was moved perhaps by the Holy Spirit to give a prophetic, landmark address explaining to the city and to the world his reasons for removing the last four of the city's several Confederate monuments. In a clear plea for supporters of Confederate monuments to focus on new and different experiences, questions, beliefs, and attitudes within their horizon of possibilities, he said:

> But there are also other truths about our city that we must confront. New Orleans was America's largest slave market: a port where hundreds of thousands of souls were bought, sold and shipped up the Mississippi River to lives of forced labor, of misery, of rape, of torture. America was the place where nearly 4,000 of our fellow citizens were lynched, 540 alone in Louisiana; where the courts enshrined "separate but equal"; where Freedom riders coming to New Orleans were beaten to a bloody pulp. So, when people say to me that the monuments in question are history, well what I just described is real history as well, and it is the searing truth.
>
> And it immediately begs the questions, why there are no slave ship monuments, no prominent markers on public land to remember the lynchings or the slave blocks; nothing to remember this long chapter of our lives; the pain, the sacrifice, the shame . . . all of it happening on the soil of New Orleans. So for those self-appointed defenders of history and the monuments, they are eerily silent on what amounts to this historical malfeasance, a lie by omission. There is a difference between remembrance of history and reverence of it.
>
> Consider these four monuments from the perspective of an African American mother or father trying to explain to their fifth grade daughter who Robert E. Lee is and why he stands atop of our beautiful city. Can you do it? Can you look into that young girl's eyes and convince her that Robert E. Lee is there to encourage her? Do you think she will feel inspired and hopeful by that story? Do these monuments help her see a future with limitless potential? Have you ever thought that if her potential is limited, yours and mine are too? We all know the answer to these very simple questions. When you look into this child's eyes is the moment when the searing truth comes into focus for us. This is the moment

when we know what is right and what we must do. We can't walk away from this truth.

Listen! Learn! Think! Pray! Act!

The Horizon of Possibilities within Christian Communities: What Can the Church Do?

The resurgence of neo-Nazis, white supremacists, and the Ku Klux Klan has reopened old wounds and made Christian communities more deeply aware that some Americans make choices from their horizons of possibilities that are diametrically opposed to the choices made by others. Many Catholics may have thought that Jesus' Law of Love, calling every human being to love God with our whole being and to love all people as we love ourselves, had been more genuinely embraced by all communities as the most important choice made from their horizon of possibilities. They may be shocked to learn that some Catholics associate themselves with ideologies of hate even though they are contrary to the Gospel. This summer, Father William Aitcheson of Arlington wrote movingly of his conversion story in "Moving from Hate to Love with God's Grace." He wrote that as a young Catholic he was a member of the Ku Klux Klan, and his actions (including cross burnings and a letter threatening the life of Coretta Scott King) were despicable. Expressing repentance for these and other misdeeds, he described the radical transformation in his life brought about by God's forgiveness and the mercy of Jesus Christ.[4] This story of conversion is the story of a person who, from the horizon of possibilities before him, rejected his earlier choice to hate and embraced Christ's Law of Love, the unconditional requirement for anyone who calls himself a Christian.

The Bishops of the United States will soon issue a new pastoral letter as the first major follow-up to the 1979 pastoral, *Brothers and*

---

[4]See *The Arlington Herald,* August 21, 2017.

Sisters to Us: US Bishops' Pastoral Letter on Racism in Our Day, which condemned racial prejudice as a sin and a heresy that endures in our country and in our church. Among the goals of the bishops are to help Catholics focus on peace and justice in our communities and to promote active listening to the concerns of people in neighborhoods where there are tensions between people of different races and between local citizen and law enforcement. The church wishes to contribute to building stronger relationships among people of different races in our communities in order to anticipate, prevent, and even resolve recurring conflicts. The bishops approach these efforts chastened by the awareness of the Catholic Church in the long, sad history of the United States supporting the racial divide, seemingly embracing Justice Taney's vision. Catholics, including John Carroll, the first bishop of Baltimore, Georgetown University, and many other individuals and institutions "owned" enslaved free human beings. The church did not oppose segregated neighborhoods, segregated churches, segregated schools, or segregated and unfair employment. The church refused to accept People of Color in convents, seminaries, and the ranks of the clergy. Evangelization in African American communities has not gained momentum, in part, because people have long memories. As I have said many times, the Catholic Church has made extraordinary efforts to correct its past grave misdeeds. The church has made many significant contributions that have supported African American people by means of civil rights, education, employment, housing, health care, and social advocacy. Nevertheless, it is with regret that I must say that I do not believe there are any grounds for hoping that the number of African American Catholics will increase significantly in the coming generations. Indeed, the number may actually decline.

Sadly, in 1979, many Catholics had never heard of *Brothers and Sisters to Us*, and many of the goals proposed in that pastoral letter were never seriously pursued or achieved. The bishops could publish the 1979 letter tomorrow, and large numbers of Catholics would think it was brand new. It was never read, discussed, prayed about, or acted on in their dioceses or their parishes. There are no easy answers to the question, "Why is this so?" But a partial answer may be the fact that individuals and communities did not personally appropriate the full implications of Christ's Law of Love from the horizon of possibilities proclaimed to them in the Gospel. We Catholics, like other Christians, sometimes have only a superficial cultural commitment to our faith. We do not experience our faith in Jesus Christ and his command to love at the deepest levels of our being. Only this deep existential commitment to follow Jesus as the Way, the Truth, and the Life will impel us to truly live the Catholic faith we profess in all of the complex and difficult situations of our lives, including those that will require us to oppose anyone and anything that serves to maintain the racial divide.

This requires that we open our hearts to the purifying power of the Holy Spirit and the healing grace of Christ. This is the path that leads to true conversion. This means practicing the Law of Love with ourselves, our family members, our neighbors, our fellow parishioners, our co-workers, the faculty members and students here at Catholic University. This lifelong process will be more effective in all aspects of our lives if we are faithful to the imperatives: Listen! Learn! Think! Pray! Act!

What can the church do? Every individual, organization, institution, and structure in the church can do something to counter the intensification of the racial divide. There is no excuse for doing nothing. However, discerning what we can and should do may not be easy. But if we are following the path of true Christian, ecclesial, intellectual, and moral conversion, we should be able to scrutinize with care the horizons of possibilities before us and prayerfully make the best choices in matters great and small. Everyone can do something.

Let me conclude with ten suggestions for your consideration.

1.   Do not be a part of the conspiracy of silence. If family members, friends, fellow students, co-workers, or representatives of the Catholic Church do or say things that reinforce the racial divide, find a respectful but effective way to communicate that you think what they are doing is wrong. It is reopening old wounds. And

you do not want to be a part of it. Your silence may be construed as approval.

2.   Renew and strengthen the focus of your spiritual formation for the courage needed to bridge the racial divide. Read the Gospels regularly and be attentive to the specific and very clear directives from Jesus of Nazareth (e.g., "Do unto others as you would have others do unto you!" [Luke 6:31, and other ancient texts]). This means not presuming to know what is in the heart of others. It also means not being quick to brand historical figures (e.g., past popes, justices, bishops, elected civic leaders, people of different racial and ethnic backgrounds) as "racists" or as guilty of "racism." It is usually very difficult to understand fully the horizon of possibilities that influenced the words and deeds of people of a radically different moment in history.

3.   In the debate about Confederate monuments, keep in mind that we are ALL redeemed sinners. Remember that far more important than tearing down the likenesses of imperfect people from the past is the need to tear down the remnants of their attitudes that continue to abide in our minds and hearts today. Tearing down systemic bias and racial, ethnic, and religious prejudices that endure in so many aspects of American and Catholic life may ultimately be more important than tearing down monuments.

In communities where there are controversial Confederate monuments, Catholic clergy and laity should not remain silent. They should be active participants in the conversation about the future of these monuments, bringing their informed Catholic faith to bear in the public square.

Some argue that the illegal destruction of monuments is wrong, no matter how offensive they may be. They say elected representatives of local communities should make this decision in dialogue with all. Should they be removed altogether? Placed in a museum? Still others propose erecting appropriate additional statues or monuments of the African American experience on the same site to provide a more balanced and truthful view of Civil War history and human bondage. Some voices insist: "The people of both races should just 'grow up' and get over offensive monuments.

Leave them where they are! History is history. We cannot rewrite it. Simply acknowledge the painful, disputed history and resolve not to repeat it. You can never tear them all down, and the majority of people pay no attention to them anyway. Focus your time and resources on improving education, increasing employment, developing housing and health care in Communities of Color!" Others insist: "Destroy them all as a disgraceful reminder of the tragedy of the racial divide in our nation's history."

4. Catholic educational leaders should take this issue seriously by examining history books used in Catholic schools. Are they truthful, fair, and balanced? Are they silent on the moral blindness of George Washington, Thomas Jefferson, Andrew Jackson, Justice Taney, General Lee, and others on the evil of enslaving free human beings for the sake of enriching their so-called owners? Do they minimize or omit altogether the heroic achievement of outstanding People of Color like Nat Turner, Harriet Tubman (whose likeness may never grace the $20 bill), Frederick Douglass, Richard Allen, Absalom Jones, Jarena Lee, Julia A. J. Foote, and Maria W. Stewart?

Is church history presented in these texts from a completely Eurocentric perspective, giving little or no attention to the flourishing churches in sub-Saharan Africa and to African American Catholic history?

If this is the case, they should change to more accurate textbooks, or supplement parish school textbooks with more complete and more accurate history to purify false, incomplete, and misleading accounts. This is essential for the proper formation of the religious consciousness of young people. The horizon of possibilities in their lives of faith will be largely determined by their education in Catholic schools and parish religious education programs. The shape of the church and the world to come is in their hands.

5. Catholic universities and colleges have many opportunities to expand the horizon of possibilities for their students, including making sure they are taught the authentic and full meaning of Christ's Law of Love and its practical implications in address-

ing the racial divide. Every effort should be made to uproot any practices or structures that reinforce racial prejudice and ethnic or religious bias. Attracting and retaining African American students and faculty members continues to be a challenge in most Catholic institutions of higher learning. An atmosphere of true hospitality and welcome that does not tolerate any expressions of white supremacist attitudes must be consciously maintained. Those Catholic universities that have known connections to human slavery and institutionalized racial prejudice would do well to address the flaw at the foundation in the manner of Georgetown University under the leadership of its president, Dr. John DeGioia. The university's Working Group on Slavery and Memory and Reconciliation faced with honesty a painful history with a heartfelt apology, contacting and assisting the descendants of free human beings once owned and sold by the university, renaming halls that once honored Jesuits who were involved in the sale of human beings and honoring the first man whose name appeared on the sale document, and a free Woman of Color who established a school for African American girls at the university in 1820.

6.   Seminaries must be vigilant and make sure that men who harbor racial prejudice are not advanced for ordination and that faculty members understand clearly that no actions or attitudes of racial bias will be tolerated. Working with dioceses and vocation directors, seminaries must continue to seek out, encourage, and welcome seminarians of different racial backgrounds. Encourage presentations on and discussions of these issues. Seminary leadership understands well that if they appear indifferent to the current displays of racial hatred, the candidates for the priesthood will consider that indifference an appropriate horizon of possibilities for their lives and ministry. The August 16, 2017, letter of the Very Reverend Thomas Knoebel, president-rector of Sacred Heart Seminary and School of Theology in Hales Corners, Wisconsin, provided an excellent example of leadership after the disheartening events in Charlottesville. He wrote:

> The most recent events of this past weekend in Charlottesville, Virginia, as well as the growing number of incidents

of racial, ethnic, and religious hatred and violence in recent years, remind us that we have a long way to go before the vision of God the Father and his Son Jesus is fully realized in our midst. As one of the most ethnically and racially diverse seminaries in the United States, Sacred Heart has a privileged opportunity, as well as the ethical and moral responsibility, to live out the universality of our common Christian faith here in our own community.

In addition to any personal conversion of mind and heart to which each of us may need to commit ourselves, may I ask that we each consider some practical suggestions to strengthen the inclusive community that Sacred Heart is, and always strives to become.

a.) Pray daily for all those who suffer from racial, ethnic or religious prejudices or violence in our community, country and world.

b.) Continue to foster, in every way possible, the positive inter-religious, inter-racial and inter-ethnic spirit that characterizes Sacred Heart.

c.) Take advantage of the marvelous opportunity Sacred Heart affords to build a friendship across racial and ethnic boundaries, not only for your sake, but for theirs.

d.) Share your own experiences of racism, religious intolerance or ethnic prejudice, whether on your part or of others, with persons of a different race or ethnicity. Listen to their own experiences.

e.) Faculty can make sure that they include academic and formational authors, speakers or sources that are racially and ethnically diverse, and make sure that these moral issues are addressed when appropriate in their courses.

7. Learn about Father Augustus Tolton (April 1, 1854– July 9, 1897) of Chicago, and pray and work for the cause of his canonization. He would be the first American saint of African ancestry, and the story of his heroic virtue in the face of racial oppression would expand the horizon of possibilities for Americans of all backgrounds striving to live by the Law of Love.

8.   Visit and make use of the extraordinary resources of the new Museum of African American History and Culture in Washington, DC.

9.   Parishes building new churches and dioceses erecting new cathedrals would do well to ponder the question: Why are all of the images of God the Father, Jesus Christ, Mary, Joseph, the Apostles, the saints, and even the angels (who have no bodies, race, or gender!) presented almost exclusively with European features? Everyone knows that God the Father is not, in fact, an elderly European man with a flowing white beard. Why is he exclusively pictured that way? The horizons of possibilities of potential African American Catholics are certainly limited by Catholic Church art that suggests quite definitively that no one in the Kingdom of Heaven looks like them? This could easily be changed. But it seems unlikely that it will be. The church would do well to make regular use of ethnic and racially diverse images in sacred art. There is no more effective way of saying, "All are welcome!"

10.   The Catholic Church and Catholic institutions should lead the way in discontinuing the practice of referring to any American citizens as "minorities" or "members of minority groups." This arbitrary designation of Americans of some backgrounds but not all is, perhaps unwittingly, a vocabulary of control, power, and privilege. It identifies American citizens by who they are not instead of by who they are.[5]

I invite everyone here in the community of the Catholic University of America, the church's university, to think about and discuss what I have said and share my thoughts with others. Go deep into your interior world and enter into silent dialogue with the Holy Spirit and pray for the expansion and enrichment of your personal horizons of possibilities so that as members of the Body of Christ, the church, you can help to heal old wounds reopened and bridge the racial divide.

---

[5]See Matthew Frye Jacobson, *Whiteness of a Different Color: European Immigrants and the Alchemy of Race* (Cambridge, MA: Harvard University Press, 1998), and Noel Ignatiev, *How the Irish Became White* (New York: Routledge, 1995).

Paul Laurence Dunbar (1872–1906) knew well the old wounds of which I have spoken from painful personal experience, and wrote eloquently of them in his poem "Sympathy."

I know why the caged bird sings, ah me,
When his wing is bruised and his bosom sore,—
When he beats his bars and he would be free;
It is not a carol of joy or glee,
But a prayer that he sends from his heart's deep core,
But a plea, that upward to Heaven he flings—
I know why the caged bird sings!

Listen! Learn! Think! Pray! Act!

4

We, Too, Sing America

The Catholic Church and the Museum
of African American History and Culture

JANUARY 15, 2017

When I traveled to Baltimore in November 2016 for the fall meeting of the United States Conference of Catholic Bishops, I was, as always, looking forward to the discussions of the topics on our agenda and the opportunity to visit with other bishops to learn about the different ways they were facing the challenges in their dioceses. However, most of all, I was anticipating my first visit to the newly opened African American History and Culture Museum. I had set aside two days for the visit because I had read about how much there was to see and how long it would take to absorb its rich contents.

The museum was designed by Sir David Frank Adjaye, a British citizen, the son of a Ghanaian diplomat, who was born in Dar es Salaam, Tanzania. I was not aware of any internationally known architects of African descent before I learned about the works of Mr. Adjaye. This is quite significant to me because, growing up in Chicago surrounded by the amazing buildings of Louis Sullivan, Ludwig Mies van der Rohe, Frank Lloyd Wright, and Helmut Jahn, I had often thought that I would like to be an architect. I remember talking with my spiritual director in the seminary about what I might do, if I did not become a priest. I said I might become a doctor or an architect. He told me it would be very difficult, if not impossible, for a person of my race to pursue either of those careers.

During the breaks between our meetings, the conversations sometimes turned to the recent election of Donald Trump as president. Not surprisingly, the bishops, like other Americans, had different perceptions of the new president. In one conversation there was discussion about single-issue voters. Several participants had the impression that some Catholics did not admire some of Mr. Trump's attitudes but at the same time they had voted for him because of the single issue of abortion. Even though he had not always opposed abortion, his current position against abortion was far more acceptable to them than the position of Mrs. Clinton, who vigorously supports a woman's right to have an abortion. There was no consensus in this small group about the pros and cons of single-issue voting.

After my heart-moving time in Sir David's Yoruba-crowned masterpiece, I visited with African American friends whom I knew from years working in Washington. They, too, discussed the presidential election. Some voted for Mrs. Clinton and some voted for Mr. Trump. While none of them supported Mrs. Clinton's views on abortion, they said they voted for her because on issues of social justice for People of Color, for the poor and disenfranchised, the former secretary of state displayed more genuine empathy and concern.

Now as I revisit this essay for publication, we are approaching another presidential election. Former Vice President Joseph Biden is running against President Trump. The electorate is again polarized. I hear voices saying, "How can a Catholic, in good conscience, vote for Mr. Biden, a Catholic who not only supports abortion rights but also has no moral objections to same-sex marriage?" "How can a Catholic, in good conscience, vote for Mr. Trump, who seems to encourage racial bias and division in the country and who governs more like a king than a democratically elected president?"

The Bishops' Meeting, the Election, and the Museum

The new Smithsonian Museum of African American History and Culture has stirred a great deal of interest. Dr. Martin Luther King Jr., whose eighty-eighth birthday we celebrate today, who had a dream of racial conflict resolved in harmony, would surely see this museum as a significant contribution to the fulfillment of that dream. As an African American and as a Catholic bishop, I have looked forward to visiting the museum and examining its treatment of the church. After the presidential election, I traveled to Baltimore for the fall meeting of the United States Conference of Catholic Bishops. Afterwards, I traveled to Washington, DC, where I once served as personal theologian to James Cardinal Hickey, to visit the museum. Once in the museum, I realized it would take many visits to comprehend its overwhelming sweep and wonder. I also quickly realized that there was very little in the museum about the Catholic Church or about African American Catholics. The church is in the museum more by its absence than its presence. The museum aims to be a museum for all people, a timely reminder that the African American story is at the heart of the American story. Since the museum displays only 3,500 of the 40,000 objects in its collection, I hope there will be more about the Catholic Church and African American Catholics in future exhibits.

This journey came in the wake of the most controversial, the most negative, the most emotional, the most painful, and the most polarizing presidential campaign in my adult lifetime. It was a campaign during which the racial divide in the United States was never far from the attention of the ever-vigilant media. Would this election affirm or repudiate the historic presidency of Barack H. Obama? Would the Democratic candidate be able to motivate the unprecedented numbers of African American and young voters to return to the polls? Could the Republican candidate attract significant African American voters with his question, "What the hell do you have to lose?" Or could he be victorious without their votes? A number of commentators suggested that there was a degree of racial tension in the air fueled by some campaign rhetoric and a long, sad season of altercations between law enforcement officers and People of Color resulting in the deaths of youthful African Americans and the fatal assaults of white policemen. It was in this context that the bishops chose to celebrate the opening Mass of our General Assembly at St. Peter Claver Parish, a modest church in Baltimore's African American community. A striking Afrocentric crucifix, with a corpus carved by Juvenal Kaliki of Tanzania, was used during the Mass. It was also on display throughout the meeting of the bishops' conference.

Because of its small size, many may not have noticed it. Following the long-standing custom, at the Mass many of the bishops stood during the singing of "Lift Every Voice and Sing" (the African American National Anthem).

We sang, in part:

> Lift every voice and sing,
> Till earth and heaven ring . . .
> Stony the road we trod,
> Bitter the chast'ning rod,
> Felt in the days when hope unborn had died;
> Yet with a steady beat,
> Have not our weary feet
> Come to the place for which our fathers sighed?
> God of our weary years,
> God of our silent tears,
> Thou who hast brought us thus far on the way;
> Thou who hast by Thy might,
> Led us into the light,
> Keep us forever in the path, we pray.
>   —James Weldon Johnson (1871–1938)

The election results surprised and even shocked pollsters, late-night talk show hosts, *Saturday Night Live*, and many voters who anticipated a different outcome. The results may not, however, have surprised the winner's enthusiastic supporters, who had stood in line for long hours in order to overflow his rallies and announce their unconditional commitment to him and his election. Though I and, I assume, other bishops participated in a number of informal conversations during the bishops' meeting, there were no public discussions of positive or negative views about the one who won or the one who lost. Several postelection surveys indicated that 55 percent of Catholics voted as Republicans and 45 percent voted as Democrats. (At this point, however, we should probably be slow to put much trust in polls.) It would be presumptuous to suggest that the votes of the bishops would be in similar percentages. It would be equally presumptuous to think that all of the bishops voted for the same candidate. Apparently, 43 percent of eligible Americans, including Catholics, did not bother to vote!

The guests at a dinner I attended with friends from my years in Washington were Democrats, Republicans, and Independents, with very different backgrounds, who were eager to discuss the election. Following my general practice, I never said for whom I voted (major party candidate, independent, or write-in). More than once I heard exchanges such as, "How could you, as a Catholic, have voted in good conscience for him? He is going to be the worst president ever." "How could you, as a Catholic, have voted in good conscience for her? She would have been the worst president ever." "What do the election results say about the changing character of our country?"

Happily, the conversation turned to my planned visit to the museum the next day. One of the guests had been present for the gala dedication and grand opening on September 24, 2016. She said that it was quite moving to see President Obama and First Lady Michelle Obama and former President Bush and former First Lady Laura Bush presiding at the dedication amid warm and friendly exchanges. When another guest commented that it was truly great that Barack Obama, the first biracial president, was dedicating the museum, someone pointed out that the true engine behind the project was President Bush, who signed the bipartisan legislation in 2003 at the urging of Congressman John R. Lewis (Democrat, GA), over the strong opposition of North Carolina Senator Jesse Helms (Republican). In fact, the impetus for this museum started one hundred years earlier when African American veterans of the Civil War urged the erection of a memorial to Black veterans in 1915. Though Leonidas C. Dyer, a Republican representative from Missouri and an ardent foe of the widespread practice of lynching African American men, introduced legislation for a monument in honor of Negroes[1] in 1916, it gained no support. Efforts

---

[1]Negro (derived from the Latin *niger* meaning dark or black) is a word first used by the Portuguese who were very active in the "selling" (see note 2) of free human beings from West Africa. Spanish and Portuguese speakers began using this word

by writer James Baldwin and baseball player Jackie Robinson in the 1960s to press for a museum did not prevail. Finally, in 1986, Congressman Mickey Leland, a Democrat from Texas, sponsored and successfully passed legislation for a museum. But he perished in a terrible plane crash in 1989, and Congressman John Lewis aggressively took up the baton.

This should not come as a surprise considering the long-standing thesis that People of Color had no history and no culture. The towering figure, Thomas Jefferson (1743–1826), is depicted in the museum standing in front of the Declaration of Independence, of which he was the principal author, and bricks representing the hundreds of enslaved free human beings he "owned."[2] He wrote, "Never yet could I find that a black had uttered a thought above the level of plain narration; never seen even an elementary trait of painting or sculpture. . . . Misery is often the parent of the most affecting touches in poetry.—Among the blacks is misery enough, God knows, but no poetry. I advance it, therefore, as a suspicion only, that blacks . . . are inferior to the whites in the environment both in mind and body."[3]

The German idealist philosopher Georg W. F. Hegel (1770–

(never used by Africans in the past or the present) in the mid-sixteenth century. Its usage continued as a standard designation from the seventeenth to the nineteenth centuries. It was commonly used by prominent African American leaders, including W. E. B. Du Bois (who fought tirelessly and unsuccessfully with newspapers for an uppercase N in the same manner that many writers today have fought for an uppercase B in Black), Booker T. Washington, Dr. Martin Luther King Jr., and African Americans in general into the 1960s. In the 1970s, it fell out of usage in part because of the general rejection of the pejorative rendering of the word. That pejorative is a word now shunned by polite society, banned from the pages of respected newspapers and journals, and unspoken by TV newscasters. Nevertheless, it is alive and well, a word used frequently in particular neighborhoods, communities, and households. It falls freely from the lips of certain "entertainers." It is, by turns, considered a term of endearment, a crude slang expression, and the most heartbreaking of insults. It is a paradox that, in Barry Jenkins's acclaimed film *Moonlight*, which many enthusiastic critics thought should win the Academy Award, the poor, disadvantaged, bewildered young African American characters all constantly call each other and themselves by this very name.

[2]Thomas Jefferson, *Notes on the State of Virginia*, Query XIV, The Avalon Project, Yale Law School, https://avalon.law.yale.edu.

[3]Thomas Jefferson, *Notes on the State of Virginia*, Query XIV, The Avalon Project, Yale Law School, https://avalon.law.yale.edu.

1831) was a contemporary of Jefferson, whose rigorous writings have influenced generations of American Christian theologians. In *The History of Philosophy*, Hegel states that Egypt is not really a part of Africa and that people from sub-Saharan Africa have no history, no culture, no collective memory, and, for all practical purposes, lack what is needed to be properly called human. He dismisses all of African history and culture, saying, "At this point, we leave Africa not to mention it again. For it is no historical part of the world; it has no movement or development to exhibit."[4] We can thank the astounding achievement of the museum's founding director, the historian Lonnie G. Bunch III, for proving just how wrong Jefferson and Hegel were. As Bunch said, the primary goal of the museum is "to help all Americans remember and, by remembering, to stimulate a dialogue about race and help foster a spirit of reconciliation and healing."[5]

One of the dinner guests, who had visited the museum earlier, asked me if I was going to the museum by myself. When I replied, "Yes," he said, "That's good." When I asked why, he said, "Well, for me, the experience was emotionally very stressful. Like the United States Holocaust Memorial Museum, the National September 11 Memorial and Museum, and the National Civil Rights Museum built around the Lorraine Motel in Memphis where Dr. Martin Luther King Jr. was violently murdered, this museum confronts visitors with disheartening realities. Some people leave the lower-level History Galleries in tears, or in shocked silence!"

The Museum: A Visual Wonder

As I approached the museum, designed by Tanzanian native and British architect David Adjaye, I was struck immediately by its unique design and location. It is a visual wonder. The architect

---

[4]Cf. Olufemi Taiwo, "Exorcising Hegel's Ghost: Africa's Challenge to Philosophy," *African Studies Quarterly* 1, no. 4 (1998): 3–16.

[5]Mabel O. Wilson, *Begin with the Past* (Washington, DC: Smithsonian Institution, 2016), 17.

clearly did not want to repeat the white marble design typical of structures on The Mall. It is next to the Egyptian-African-style obelisk monument to our first president, George Washington, who "owned" enslaved free human beings at his estate in Mt. Vernon, Virginia. The memorial to our third president, Thomas Jefferson, who "owned" enslaved free human beings at his estate, Monticello, is nearby. A Greek temple on the horizon is the monument to our sixteenth president, Abraham Lincoln, who issued the historic Emancipation Proclamation, while arguing that perhaps the best thing for the "freed" former enslaved human beings whom he considered "inferior" would be their return to Africa. (It was from the steps of this monument that Dr. King proclaimed, "I have a dream!") Also within sight are the Capitol and the White House, which were both built, in part, by enslaved people. These buildings, as well as the largely African American city of Washington, can be seen from within the museum through strategically placed windows that look out onto the National Mall and beyond. These vistas fulfill the museum's commitment to use African American history and culture as a lens into what it means to be an American.

Drawing closer to the imposing structure, I was initially unaware that the most critical portion of the museum is in several lower levels that are not in view, almost like a sunken ship. The upper level consists of three upside-down pyramid-like layers that complement the nearby obelisk. The outer walls are ornamented with a bronze-colored aluminum grillwork. This three-leveled structured Corona echoes elements found in African art and architecture at once suggesting hands lifted up in prayer, a Yoruba crown, and figurative verandas found in Nigerian Yoruba royal courts. The outer panels of the grillwork suggest the West African grillwork crafted by African people in Louisiana and South Carolina. The skin of the museum shimmers in shades of sepia, copper, deep red, and gold, depending on the sunlight, offering a silent tribute to the creative craft and building skills of African Americans long "hidden in plain sight," since enslaved free human beings were never given credit for their craftsmanship.

When I headed down into the three lower levels of the History

Galleries, I realized that 60 percent of the museum is underground in the largest exhibition in any Smithsonian Museum. Though the gallery space is vast, it has low ceilings, dark walls, and many passageways. Mr. Adjaye, the architect, said he wanted visitors to feel like they were entering a crypt. It also made me think of the lower level of the European vessels used to transport enslaved free human beings across the Atlantic Ocean in the Middle Passage. Almost everything on these levels is displayed in small areas that require the visitor to move around walls and passageways that are deliberately dark and cramped, just as the enslaved free human beings chained side by side and on top of one another in unspeakable squalor were cramped into darkness. Graphic commentaries paint a picture of the sickness and death on the transport vessels. Mothers giving birth while still in chains. The sick, the dying, and the dead were thrown overboard into shark-infested waters. An estimated 2 million people lost their lives during the Middle Passage of this African Holocaust.

The History Galleries

The three underground History Galleries are the heart of the museum, providing a heart-wrenching record. They cover three periods: "Slavery and Freedom," "Defending Freedom, Defining Freedom: Era of Segregation 1876–1968," and "A Change in America: 1968 and Beyond." In these galleries, it becomes apparent that money and the complete disregard for the value and dignity of a human person were at the center of an enterprise that uprooted more than 12,500,000 West Africans from their homeland, family, culture, language, and religion and brought them, in chains, to the Americas. Once here, men, women, and children worked unceasingly under the hot sun and the lash on sugarcane, cotton, and tobacco plantations; and all manner of other difficult labor were rewarded with degradation, humiliation, and backs torn open and bleeding from the taskmaster's whip, while plantation owners grew wealthy. In *The Half Has Never Been Told: Slavery and the Making of American Capitalism*, Edward E. Baptist examines

America's original sin as a huge financial enterprise bringing great wealth to those who "owned" the people who served as the machines of capitalism.

Examining the first federal census of 1790, I noticed that it does not mention African people at all. It records only "free white males of sixteen years and upwards, including heads of families," "free white males under sixteen years," "free white females," and "all other free persons." "Slaves" are mentioned at the end without any mention of age, gender, or place of origin. They were simply property. I can understand very well why the enslaved African people in the diaspora compared their unhappy fate to the Children of Israel in bondage under the Pharaoh of Egypt, and sang, "Go down Moses, Way down to Egypt land, Tell all pharaohs to let my people go!"

The Role of the Church

In the History Galleries, it is not possible to miss the important role played by religion during the history of African people in America. They brought African traditional religions with them. By some estimates, 30 percent of enslaved people from Africa were of the Islamic faith. It is a surprising turn of history and grace that the enslaved free human beings took comfort in variations of Christianity even though their oppressors could not see the contradiction between their Christian piety and their absolute cruelty to their human "possessions." Individuals who felt "like a motherless child a long way from home" found, in Christianity, a way to make a way out of no way. Excluded from mainline Protestant churches and Catholic churches, they established their own Baptist communities, and Richard Allen founded the African Methodist Episcopal Church, which remains the heartbeat of many African American communities to this day. The resilience and the forgiving hearts at Charleston's Mother Emanuel AME Church after the June 17, 2015, slaughter of the innocent by the self-proclaimed white nationalist and confessed murderer Dylann Roof bears witness to this heartbeat.

As I examined the exhibits about the strong power and support of the "Black Church," for People of Color after emancipation, the references were always to Black Protestant churches not Black Catholic churches. The Black Baptist Church raised up many prophetic voices and dynamic leaders, like Dr. King. The museum does not select any African American Catholics for comparable recognition. White Catholics could not easily be prominent leaders of the abolitionist movement since Catholic families, religious orders, and bishops (including John Carroll, the first bishop of Baltimore) owned slaves of their own. Beginning with the civil rights movement of the 1960s, I found the occasional white Catholic priest, nun, or layperson appear in photographs and videos of civil rights demonstrations. In several places, mention is made specifically of the Sisters of the Holy Family, founded twenty years before the Civil War, as a community specifically for African American women (rejected by white religious orders) by Henriette DeLille, a free Woman of Color in New Orleans. But I did not see any pictures of Mother Henriette DeLille, Father Augustus Tolton, Pierre Toussaint, Mother Mary Lange, Julia Greeley, or Sister Thea Bowman in the History Galleries. All are African Americans proposed for canonization.

I did find a small shrine containing an altar and votive candle stand from St. Augustine Parish in New Orleans, where Catholic Free People of Color opposed all Jim Crow racial segregation laws. In 1895, when the archbishop of New Orleans, Francis Janssens, established a separate parish for Black Catholics in the Faubourg Tremé neighborhood, St. Augustine's Creole parishioners asserted their right to worship in an integrated community. Black Catholics competed with white Catholics to buy pews. Black Catholics succeeded in getting half of the center pews for their families and all of the seats along the side aisles for enslaved people. This produced, for a time, one of the most integrated Catholic congregations in the nation.

Then, as now, African American Catholics were all but invisible in the larger, influential Black Church. At the same time, African Americans were and remain all but invisible in the larger, influential

Catholic Church. The September 2016 CARA study on cultural diversity in the Catholic Church in the United States notes that, of the nearly 70 million Catholics in America, only about 2.9 million are African Americans.

"It Would Be Alright If He Changed My Name"

Moving through the History Galleries, it is difficult not to notice the evolving names. In different moments in history, we see African, Negro, Colored People, Blacks, Black People, People of Color, Afro-American, Africans in the Diaspora, and African American, or a plea for just plain American. Many years ago, a bishop asked me, "Have all 'Blacks' now agreed that they wish to be called 'African Americans?'" He was surprised when I said, "No, they have not, and they probably never will." The changing names is a part of the outward expression of the unique inner struggles of the people of African ancestry to find a way to speak about their experience in this country, from the Middle Passage, to enslavement, to the era of Jim Crow, to bondage in urban blight in northern cities, to the fragile gains of the civil rights era, to participation in middle-class, educated, professional life, to the racial divide of the present day. In different periods of this history, one can see a people going through a process of self-affirmation. Uprooted from their homelands, they have moved from a negative self-identity, in which they almost rejected their own identity as incompatible with the Western European American hybrid culture that surrounded them, to a total rejection of that culture and its worldview. They have gone from a complete immersion in what is sometimes called "the Black Experience," to the personal appropriation and transcendence of that experience, leading to the emergence of Black consciousness and a growing use of the name African American.

When the aggressive Black Power movement of the 1960s first began to use "black" ("I'm black and I'm proud!") in place of Dr. King's eloquent use of "the Negro" or "Colored People," everyone did not embrace that change. Many individuals and geographical communities continued their customary use of the

Portuguese derivative "Negro" (insisting against great opposition on an uppercase "N"), or "Colored People" because they were uncomfortable with (even embarrassed by) the word "black." As the word "black" gained greater acceptance in the 1970s, the people to whom it referred often preferred to write it with an uppercase "B," to give the name more dignity. They were frustrated seeing statements about "Jews, Hispanics, Asians, and blacks." Writers argued, in vain, with editors of journals and newspapers insisting on an uppercase "B." They also tended to disdain the term "blacks," preferring Black People or Black Americans. A key reason for the emergence of "African American" is the fact that it provides a sense of origins (Americans of African origins) similar to "Irish Americans" (Americans of Irish origins), while conceding that Africa is a continent and not a country like Ireland. Of course, with the name African American, favored by many professionals, came an uppercase name. A number of "white" or "European American" commentators find this entire evolution of names incomprehensible. "You wanted freedom, you wanted rights? Well, now you have them. Why not just call yourselves Americans, like everyone else?" The response is often, "Maybe we will, just as soon as we are treated like everyone else!" I find myself thinking of Nina Simone singing, "I told Jesus it would be alright if He changed my name!"

Face-to-Face with Dear Emmett Till

For me, personally, the most devastating experience in the History Galleries was surely coming face-to-face with the original coffin of dear Emmett Till, which I had not seen in sixty years. In August 1955, when he was fourteen years old, Emmett's family in Chicago, where I grew up, sent him to Money, Mississippi, to visit relatives. While there, he was suspected of flirting with a twenty-one-year-old white woman. The woman's husband abducted the young man, beat him beyond recognition, shot him, and dumped his body in the Tallahatchie River, where it was found several days later. When his hideously disfigured body was returned to

Chicago to his grief-stricken mother, Mamie, she insisted that the casket should be open for a public viewing "so the world can see what they did to my child." My uncle, who was born in the South, took me and my brother, Lawrence, to the visitation. We stood in line for hours outside of A. A. Rayner Funeral Home. My uncle repeatedly told us, "I don't want you to ever forget this night!"

When we finally reached the bier, I peered into the glass coffin and beheld the terrifying remains of a vicious murder. He did not look like a human being! Emmett's mother was sitting in a chair sobbing uncontrollably, crying "My baby, my baby, why, why did I send him down south?" I looked into her red-rimmed eyes not knowing what to say. As we rode home, my uncle told Lawrence and me, "When you grow up, whatever you do, don't go south, don't live or work in the South. The same thing could happen to you. They would just as soon kill you as look at you. Heed my words!" I have never forgotten those words. I have never forgotten the totally unrecognizable, bloated, mutilated face behind the glass in the coffin. I have never forgotten the raw anguish on Mamie Till-Mobley's face. It all came back to me when, as a bishop and a former priest of the Archdiocese of Chicago, the Apostolic Nuncio, Archbishop Gabriel Montalvo, said to me in 2000, "Your Excellency, the Holy Father, Pope John Paul II has appointed you to serve as the second Bishop of Lake Charles, Louisiana." For a moment, I was stunned, "Don't go south! Don't go south!" Nevertheless, I did go south where, fortunately, much has changed. I embraced the People of God with an open mind and an open heart. Happily, while there were a few very painful experiences, the vast majority of the people of Southwest Louisiana warmly welcomed me. My five years serving there were happy ones. I came to know members of the Christian faithful who have remained dear to me to this day.

Those responsible for the lynching of Emmett Till were tried and acquitted. Later, protected by double jeopardy laws, they admitted their guilt in a 1956 article in *Look* magazine and remained free. Of course, dear Emmett was only one of an estimated 3,446 African Americans lynched between 1882 and 1968!

As I walked through the History Galleries for a second time, I noticed a number of exhibits that required greater study, including an important section on Frederick Douglass, who escaped from bondage in Maryland and became a social reformer, abolitionist, orator, writer, and statesman. There was a display of a beautiful silk lace and linen shawl given to Harriet Tubman by Queen Victoria. Harriet escaped from enslavement in the early 1800s. She returned to the South so many times, leading other African Americans to freedom, that she became known as a "conductor" on a metaphorical Underground Railroad. I also saw how easy it is to walk by exhibits without reading the lengthy explanations or watching the informative videos. As I passed a full-size railroad car, I heard a number of people observe, "Oh, that must be Harriet Tubman's Underground Railroad." In fact, it is a real train car displaying the segregated, crowded, unsanitary sleeping conditions endured by African Americans traveling by night, while paying the same fare as white passengers in comfortable deluxe cars.

When I left the History Galleries, I realized that many more hours had passed than I realized. Walking out, I thought of Pulitzer Prize winner Suzan-Lori Parks's remarkable theater piece, *The Death of the Last Black Man in the Whole Entire World AKA The Negro Book of the Dead* (a 1990 work recently revived at New York's Pershing Square Signature Theater). The work is as relevant as this morning's newspaper. In the play, various African American characters carry a large green watermelon across the stage from scene to scene. This delicious fruit, used in the past and even in the present as a belittling racial stereotype, becomes a potent symbol of the burden of racial oppression. One character tries to move, but he cannot because the heavy watermelon on his lap makes him a captive. He says, "This [burden] does not belong to me. Somebody planted this on me. On me, in my hands." When he finally stands up, he is still not free.

The lower and upper portions of the museum form a coherent whole. Nevertheless, it is possible to think of it as two museums in one. It takes a great deal of time to examine everything closely, read the commentaries, and watch the videos in the lower History

Galleries. But those who fail to take the time will be intellectually, emotionally, and spiritually impoverished.

The Upper Galleries

As you make your way up to the upper floors that fill the Corona, there is a noticeable change in the feel of the museum. It is lighter in color, more spacious, more upbeat, and even more entertaining. While these Culture and Community Galleries are filled with astonishing exhibits, many of which document the struggle, pain, and suffering that African Americans endured in every area of life, they are not dominated by the dark shadow of apartheid-like systematic and systemic racism that pervades the History Galleries. These galleries display the triumph of the human spirit over the gravest adversities. The vast upper floor galleries are devoted to the truly astounding contributions People of Color have made in the areas of music, art, sports, and the military. Depending on the visitor's age, there will be surprises around every corner. No major achievement in television, Broadway theater, recordings, or championship sports goes uncelebrated.

In the Community Gallery and the Cultural Gallery on levels 3 and 4, the role of religious institutions, entrepreneurship, art, recreation, the pioneering achievements in television, music (including jazz, be-bop, hip-hop, rap, opera, and other classical music), motion pictures, and daily life for African American people are all examined in depth. In the art section of the museum there is a painting, *Stations of the Cross*, by Allan Rohan Crite, the dean of African American artists, renowned for his Afrocentric religious art. His mantra was, "I tell the story of man through the Black figure." But, when he painted *Stations*, this devout Episcopalian chose to paint Jesus and Mary with European features. The history of educational institutions, the Black press, business, unions, and organizations like the National Association for Colored Women and the National Association for the Advancement of Colored People are creatively displayed. The struggle of African Americans in the military (including the heroic achievements of the Tuskegee

Airmen, the first African American military aviators in the Armed Forces) is critically examined. Great achievements in sports from Jackie Robinson desegregating Major League Baseball in 1947 to Althea Gibson winning at Wimbledon in 1957, to the triumphant story of Muhammad Ali, to the contemporary tennis triumphs of the Williams sisters are all there. Also present is Louis Armstrong's golden trumpet, Chuck Berry's red Cadillac Eldorado. and the set of the famed Oprah Winfrey TV program. (The museum's theater bears her name in appreciation for her gift of $21 million of the museum's $540 million cost.)

These upper galleries contain far more than this. I do hope that younger visitors will not be so enthralled by these amazing, encouraging, and delightful displays that they will avoid or rush through the true core of the museum on the lower levels in order to revel in the exciting panoramic vision of the great accomplishments of a gifted, free, and hope-filled people.

My thoughts turned back to the presidential election and the meeting of the American bishops a few days earlier. Once the forty-fifth president of the United States is inaugurated, many people will be watching to see what he means by making America "great" again. Some commentators think several of his public statements and a number of his proposed cabinet members evoke an era when America was primarily "great" for those who lived on one side of the racial divide. Other commentators suggest that the new president's postelection words and deeds indicate that "great" may mean building on the greatness of our commitment to a more prosperous economy, increased employment, greater attention to the needs of the poor, and bridging of the racial divide. The leadership of the new president and the responses of the American people may result in positive or negative future exhibits in the museum.

The Church and the Museum

During our Baltimore meeting, the bishops of the United States discussed their intention to explore ways of addressing the racial divide, which was a concern of many during the presidential campaign and remains a concern of some after the election. There are plans for developing a new pastoral letter as the first major follow-up to the 1979 pastoral, *Brothers and Sisters to Us: US Bishops' Pastoral Letter on Racism in Our Day*, which condemned racial prejudice as a sin and a heresy that endures in our country and in our church. In addition, a group of bishops has been asked to help Catholics focus on peace and justice in our communities. The goal is to promote active listening to the concerns of people in neighborhoods where there are tensions between people of different races and between local citizens and law enforcement. The church wishes to contribute to building stronger relationships among people of different races in our communities in order to anticipate, prevent, and even resolve recurring conflicts. The bishops approach these efforts chastened by the awareness that many Catholics never heard of *Brothers and Sisters to Us* in 1979 and that many of the goals proposed in that pastoral letter have not been seriously pursued or achieved.

Knowledge can play a central part in bridge building and fostering peace and justice in our communities. The extraordinary Museum of African American History and Culture is a wellspring of knowledge that could be a valuable resource for bishops and the Catholic Church seeking to bridge the racial divide and find new paths to peace and justice in our communities. In the years ahead, many Catholics will have the opportunity to visit the museum. However, millions more will not be able to. Many can benefit from the museum by visiting online, through videos, books, and articles.

Here are some practical suggestions:

1. Many bishops frequently travel to Washington, DC, for meetings at the bishops' headquarters. If they were to make a visit to the museum a priority, they would be moved by what they would learn. They would see a clear connection between the history presented and the Gospel challenge to Christians to work for reconciliation and harmony among all people.

2. Many priests, deacons, sisters, and the Christian faithful also often have reasons to be in Washington, DC, a vacation destination

for many Americans. Representatives of diocesan leadership could plan a summer visit to Washington, placing a museum visit at the center of their itinerary. Because of the scope of the exhibits, visitors of all racial and ethnic backgrounds will leave with a deeper appreciation of our common humanity, a more accurate understanding of past events, and a renewed motivation to obey the mandate of Jesus Christ, "Love your neighbor as yourself."

3.   Catholic colleges, high schools, and elementary schools, and diocesan offices of education could benefit immensely from the museum's educational resources, which include print materials, videos, and online connections. The unique resources of this museum can be brought into classrooms, adult education programs, parish bulletins, and other educational ministries.

4.   Catholics who make use of the museum's resources should complement the museum exhibits by documenting the many important, more recent efforts made by the Catholic Church to correct past acts of institutional bias and prejudice. This will be an incentive to contribute to the church's contemporary efforts to convey to all people the inclusive and welcoming message of the Good News.

5.   Bishops, priests, sisters, deacons, seminarians, teachers, parents, and students should learn the stories of great African Americans not mentioned in the museum, including Mother Henriette DeLille, Father Augustus Tolton, Pierre Toussaint, Mother Mary Lange, Julia Greeley, and Sister Thea Bowman. (All are candidates for canonization.) Communities that have artifacts relating to these heroes of faith might consider offering them to the museum for consideration. The faithful should be urged to pray for their canonization.

6.   While this museum is exceptional, there are museums and historic sites concerning African Americans in different parts of the country. A visit to any one of them would be equally valuable as a starting point for dialogue. (See, e.g., the National Civil Rights Museum in Memphis and the Museum of African American History in Boston.)

7.   Creative ways of sharing the museum's vision can be used with members of law enforcement, civic leaders, and neighborhood communities of diverse racial backgrounds. (For example, show the PBS video *Still I Rise*, which examines African Americans since the death of Dr. King, in the parish center and facilitate honest discussion. The book, by the same title, is also available.)

8.   Catholic educational resources used in schools (especially elementary schools), parishes, and diocesan educational programs should be reviewed for historical accuracy. Are the textbooks used in schools silent about the fact that presidents, bishops, and religious orders "owned" enslaved human beings? Are texts and programs silent about the accomplishments of African Americans? The denial of history makes the establishment of peace and justice in our communities more difficult.

9.   Attention should be given to ethnic and racial diversity in the religious art in our schools and churches. Are all sacred images Eurocentric? It is difficult for the Catholic Church to preach the dignity of all people before God while, indirectly through iconography, suggesting that the Kingdom of Heaven has no place for People of Color. The display of Juvenal Kaliki's Tanzania crucifix during the bishops' meeting was noteworthy.

10. The museum depicts a history during which African American people were generally treated as outsiders, as "minorities." But by telling the full story, it affirms that People of Color, as American citizens, should not be treated as a "minority group" unless German Americans, Polish Americans, and Irish Americans are treated as "minority groups." A true understanding of the story told in this museum should help the Catholic Church make a conscious effort to correct the long-standing practice by the church of selectively referring to some Americans (namely Hispanic People and Black People) as members of "minority groups." No ethnic group constitutes the "majority" of the population. Every American is equally an American. Arbitrarily calling some Americans "minorities" is demeaning and inaccurate.

Conclusion: Eat in the Kitchen

The museum's excellent restaurant, the Sweet Home Café, continues the history exposition with executive chef Jerome Grant's *tour de force* menu devoted to authentic African American cuisine. The wonderfully diverse menu is a delicious extension of the important artifacts and documents seen in the exhibit galleries. Many museum visitors who saw things they had never seen before also tasted foods they had never eaten before. I enjoyed a plate of Georgia shrimp and Anson Mills stone-ground grits, smoked tomato butter, caramelized leeks, crispy tasso, and homemade cornbread. The walls of the café display large black-and-white photographs of brave young African Americans "sitting-in" on stools in restaurants in the Deep South, stoically awaiting taunts and severe beatings at the hands of those who refused to serve People of Color. These nonviolent demonstrations, which I remember very well, sparked a true revolution in the manner of the nonviolent revolution led by Mahatma Gandhi in South Africa and India.

Looking around the restaurant, I noticed that almost all of the tables were racially "segregated." Black people were sitting together and white people were sitting together. I noticed the same thing in the groups walking through the museum. I told myself that this was, hopefully, no more than a random happenstance and that I should not make too much of it.

As I made my way out of the Museum of African American History and Culture, I turned over in my heart the words of the brilliant Harlem Renaissance poet Langston Hughes that adorn the wall of the museum. These words are from a favorite poem of Dr. King's who, in a more perfect world, would be enjoying his birthday dinner today with his children and his children's children.

> I, too, sing America.
> I am the darker brother.
> They send me to eat in the kitchen

When company comes,
But I laugh,
And eat well,
And grow strong.
Tomorrow,
I'll be at the table
When company comes.
Nobody'll dare
Say to me,
"Eat in the kitchen,"
Then.
Besides,
They'll see how beautiful I am
And be ashamed—
I, too, am America.

5

Reverend Dr. Martin Luther King Jr.

What If He Were Still Alive Today?

FEBRUARY 23, 2020

When Muhammad Anwar el-Sadat, the president of Egypt, was assassinated in Cairo, Egypt, on October 6, 1981, there was a worldwide expression of admiration for the winner of the 1978 Nobel Prize for Peace, who had initiated serious peace negotiations with the Israeli prime minister Menachem Begin. Under their leadership, Egypt and Israel made peace with each other in 1979. American commentators compared him to the Reverend Dr. Martin Luther King Jr. I remember a political cartoon with the caption, "We intend to walk in the footsteps of Dr. King and President Sadat." The drawing showed huge footsteps striding across the landscape and within one footstep were tiny images of various political and religious leaders with magnifying glasses looking for their footsteps.

I do not think it was the intent of the cartoon to suggest that either of these men were perfect human beings or that either of them actually achieved their high and distant goals of peace and racial justice. A glance at the headlines concerning the relationship between Israel and Egypt, Israel and the Palestinians, and the racial divide in the United States makes that clear.

I think the point of the cartoon was that Reverend King and President Sadat were, like Mahatma Gandhi and Nelson Mandela, the kind of bold, confrontational, risk-taking, visionary, prophetic leaders who are so rare that it is unlikely that you will see another like them. As one television commentator said of Reverend King after his death, "He was the kind of leader who may emerge once in a century, when the man and the moment meet in such a way that he becomes the catalyst for unexpected change and deeper insight into a complex situation. He is like Moses, the deliverer, of whom the Bible says there arose since in Israel no other prophet like unto him."

When I originally wrote this essay in 2018 marking the fiftieth anniversary of the cruel murder of Reverend King, I wrote about the ongoing racial divide in this country in a manner that attempted to comment on the contemporary racial crisis from dear Martin's perspective. Implied in this literary device was the presumption that we should have little reason to hope for or expect another to arise like this Baptist preacher to shine the bright light of the Gospel on the difficult path before us with the same brilliance.

Instead, it was and remains my hope that other individuals, groups, and religious communities who share Dr. King's dream would shine their own intense light, however modest, on the nonviolent path that leads to the overthrowing of all forms of racial prejudice, discrimination, and social injustice in our country and in our church. However, I must acknowledge, with regret, that my modest efforts through my writings and lectures over many years have had little or no significant impact.

The Reverend Dr. King at 91

Today, in the United States, it is not so rare for a man to live to be 91. On January 15, 2020, the Reverend Dr. Martin Luther King Jr. should have celebrated his 91st birthday! But the fierce events of fifty-two years ago, on April 4, 1968, make that impossible.

When I think of the violence, the hatred, and the evil that engulfed the balcony of the Lorraine Motel on that terrible day in Memphis, Tennessee, I do not think of the word "assassination." That word is too clean, too detached, and too antiseptic to convey my vivid memories as a youthful seminarian. The image of Dr. King's body sprawled on the balcony with a towel over the gaping hole in the side of his face and so much blood flowing from his wound made it obvious to me that he was dead. It was murder, murder most foul.

Regretfully, I never had the privilege of hearing Rev. King speak in person. However, in 1966, he came to my hometown of Chicago, two years before he was murdered. He came for the Chicago Freedom Movement, a Southern Christian Leadership Conference effort to bring the forces of the civil rights movement to bear on the long-standing reality of the city's education, housing, and employment policies notorious for their systemic racial segregation and discrimination. During his visit, I read every article and watched ever television program I could. I was galvanized by his presence and his words.

I was watching on August 5 when he led a march through an all-white neighborhood in an environment of intense racial hostility. He and the nonviolent protesters were cursed and spat upon as the crowd hurled bottles and bricks at them. When Dr. King was hit in the head with a rock, he said: "I have seen many demonstrations in the South but I have never seen anything so hostile and so hateful as I've seen here today." In 1983, Dr. King's assessment of the situation in Chicago was documented in Arnold R. Hirsch's *Making the Second Ghetto: Race and Housing in Chicago, 1940–1960*. Less than two years later, after King's visit to Chicago, this Nobel Peace Prize laureate, this advocate for nonviolence and civil disobedience for the cause of justice, this troubadour for the end of racial discrimination was dead.

He was only thirty-nine years old.

I know that last month, for many Americans, and, yes, for many Catholics, his death meant little more than a "day off" in January. For many others, his death marked a critical turning point in American history. For my family and for me personally, April 4, 1968, was a day of emotional turmoil and immense sadness which remains vivid in my memory to this day.

But, what if . . . what if Rev. Dr. King were still alive today? What if that gunshot wound had not been fatal and he had survived and lived through all of the events of the 1970s, '80s, '90s, to the dawn of the new millennium, and on to this present day? What if this towering Baptist minister, at 91, were in our midst, as one like Moses, "whose eyes were not dimmed, nor his natural forces abated" (cf. Deuteronomy 34:7)?[1]

---

[1] This lecture is obviously an exercise in imaginative thinking. Writing in this format allows the author to imagine possible points of view and thoughts. It does

He would have enjoyed thirty-eight more years with his wife, Coretta Scott King, until her death in 2006. He would have been proud of his nine-year-old granddaughter, Yolanda Renee King's impressive presentation in Washington, DC, on March 24, 2018, at the March for Our Lives against gun violence initiated by students galvanized by the senseless gun murders at Marjory Stoneman Douglas High School. When Yolanda said, "I have a dream too; no more gun violence," he might have sighed with relief since he once felt that his own life would be cut short by gun violence. He might have uttered a silent prayer of gratitude thinking back on that day in April 1968.

The ninety-one-year-old Preacher of the Gospel, looking back fifty-two years at our country, would see both progress and regression. He would take note of the eight-year presidency of Barack Obama, the country's first biracial president. He might have been quite surprised and encouraged by the fact that a youthful African American senator from Illinois was elected and reelected. He would surely appreciate the president's efforts to reform health care laws for the benefit of the poor and uninsured.

But it is unlikely that he would be surprised that the Affordable Care Act was flawed and controversial. He would not be shocked to see that the president's successor has attempted to dismantle the Affordable Care Act. Nor would he be surprised that the Catholic Church objected vigorously to the act's policy on abortion. Knowing the complexity of the racial divide, he would be quick to point out that those who thought President Obama's time in office was the beginning of a postracial America were quite naïve. After reading Ta-Nehisi Coates's *We Were Eight Years in Power*, he would have examined some of the author's more confrontational statements with a critical eye.

Considering the brevity of his time in national leadership (1956–1968), Reverend King gradually developed an ambitious agenda. By means of his speeches, writings, and nonviolent

---

not intend to suggest, in any way, that these are actual thoughts or words of Dr. King. Hence, the frequent use of phrases such as, "He might have said" or "He might have thought." Ultimately, the words and thoughts must necessarily be my own, since his mighty voice has been silenced!

demonstrations, he sought to bring about federal legislation to address social, racial, and economic injustice. Only then could there be meaningful hope for reconciliation between the races and economic and social classes. (Eventually, he added his opposition to the war in Vietnam to this agenda.) If he were alive today, he would be particularly disappointed at the persistence of economic disparity and injustice, the protracted war in Afghanistan, and the January 3 American assassination of Iran's notorious Maj. Gen. Qassim Suleimani, exacerbating tensions with Iran.

A New Era of Suffering

He would surely study the recently published Equality of Opportunity Project's extensive report examining racial differences in economic opportunities in a pool of twenty million children. The study examined them and their parents over several generations. The results clearly demonstrated that racial identity and racial prejudice continue to have a major influence on who does and does not make economic progress in this country.

Sadly, African American young boys almost always grow up to earn less than their white counterparts as adults. This is true even if they grow up in wealthy communities raised by wealthy parents. The Equality of Opportunity Project study concluded that African American boys have consistently had much lower rates of upward mobility than their European American counterparts. This has been a dominant factor shaping generations of racial income disparity. If he read Michael K. Honey's *To the Promised Land: Martin Luther King and the Fight for Economic Justice* along with this study and were to examine contemporary data on widespread discrimination against African Americans in housing, employment, and education, he might conclude that for every two steps forward there have been three steps backward. Indeed, if he read the 1968 report by the National Advisory Commission on Civil Disorders (the Kerner Report) and examined today's data, he would see a return to segregated schools, an increase in poverty rates, and the astonishing incarceration rates among African Americans due, in part, to sentencing policies that racially discriminate, with harsher sentences on crack users than for powder cocaine users.

The proposal of Housing and Urban Development Secretary Dr. Ben Carson that the phrase "free from discrimination" be removed from the department's mission statement would be unconscionable to Rev. King. He would see plainly that this proposal would undermine the historic 1968 Fair Housing Act. He would find appalling Dr. Carson's announcement that HUD would suspend until this year rules from President Obama's administration compelling communities to analyze patterns of segregated housing and provide plans for correcting this situation, if they wish to receive billions of dollars in federal aid. He would be grateful that HUD has been frequently challenged by the courts for permitting cities to confine African American families to little more than "federally financed ghettos "that provide very limited opportunities for finding good employment for parents and decent schools for children. These legal challenges have been essential to ensure the implementation of the spirit and the letter of the Fair Housing Act.

The drum major for justice and peace, who walked in the footsteps of Mahatma Gandhi working for nonviolent conflict resolution, would surely grieve over the deaths of so many young African American men in violent conflicts with white representatives of law enforcement. He would have seen the funeral two years ago on Holy Thursday in Sacramento, California, for Stephon Clark, 22, an unarmed African American man shot at twenty times by police on March 18, 2018. Mr. Clark was suspected of vandalism and thought to have a gun which turned out to be his mobile phone. Allegedly, he was not given sufficient time to raise his hands, and medical help for him was not called immediately. Video and autopsy reports indicate that at least six fatal shots struck him in the back. Many community members asked for a federal investigation. However, a spokesperson for the White House said the shooting death was "a local matter."

Making use of technology that he would not have lived to see had he succumbed on that Memphis balcony, he would go online to find that, in recent years, the list of African Americans who have died in altercations with law enforcement has grown too long to count. These include Terence Crutcher, Tulsa, Oklahoma; Philando Castile, Falcon Heights, Minnesota; Samuel DuBose, Cincinnati, Ohio; Sandra Bland, Prairie View, Texas; Freddie Gray, Baltimore, Maryland; Walter L. Scott, North Charleston, South Carolina; Akai Gurley, Brooklyn, New York; Laquan McDonald, Chicago; Keith Lamont Scott, Charlotte, North Carolina; Paul O'Neal, Chicago; Alton B. Sterling, Baton Rouge, Louisiana; Christian Taylor, Arlington, Texas; Tamir Rice, Cleveland, Ohio; Michael Brown Jr., Ferguson, Missouri; Eric Garner, Staten Island, New York. And so many more. A litany now too long to proclaim!

A thoughtful man of prayer, not inclined to make hasty judgments, Dr. King would readily acknowledge that each of these cases is different with different circumstances and different individuals. He would acknowledge that police are sometimes in very difficult situations in which they must make split-second decisions. They must act in an instance when they think their lives or the lives of others are in danger. He would acknowledge that some young African American men break the law and others are dangerous criminals. Nevertheless, he would be deeply distressed by this litany. He would not be unaware of the fact that when Dylann Roof, a self-proclaimed white supremacist, slaughtered nine innocent African Americans in Mother Emanuel African Methodist Episcopal Church in Charleston, South Carolina, on June 17, 2015, he was arrested by the police without a shot being fired.

He would be concerned about the widening gulf of suspicion between many People of Color and white law enforcement. He would be distressed by the fact that many in these communities believe strongly that at least some of these deaths could have been prevented by better police training, the use of Tasers, and shooting to disarm and not to kill. He would argue that suspected wrongdoers should not be tried, convicted, and executed on the streets.

He would understand the grief, even the rage in some

communities, but he would certainly not condone the violent and destructive acts of civil disobedience that have sometimes followed these sad deaths. He might be somewhat encouraged by the efforts of police departments in some major cities to increase the number of African American police and to work with African American communities to establish better channels of communication and understanding. He would definitely question the statement that "Most police fatal shootings of African Americans by police are legally justified."

Christianity and the Racial Divide

If he Googled "Christianity in America," he would first be struck by the recent Pew Research Center data indicating that the number of Americans who say they have no religious affiliation is increasing rapidly. Still, he would see significant growth and strength in some Christian communities and in some parts of the country. He would see megachurches attracting thousands of worshipers on Sundays and providing a wide variety of family services that he would not have considered when he pastored Ebenezer Baptist Church in Atlanta. He would see an ecumenical movement in which Christian communities seem to have moved away from the hopes for actual structural Christian unity evoked by the Second Vatican Council just five years before he escaped death in Memphis to an emphasis on practical, grassroots ecumenism focusing on shared concerns to meet human needs, especially the needs of the poor and marginalized.

At the same time, he would see a real polarization among Christians who identify as active in the church. This polarization is often over moral issues such as abortion, homosexuality, the nature of marriage, gender identity, and euthanasia; and policy issues such as the role of the United States as a world leader, immigration reform, care for the environment, international conflicts, and gun control.

Dr. King would not be blind to the fact that this polarization is contributing to the tensions surrounding the presidential impeachment trial and the coming 2020 presidential election and the raucous debates anticipating the election. As a political pragmatist, he would certainly acknowledge the serious objections that he might have with President Donald Trump's policies. He might well be on the forefront of those searching for a viable alternative candidate.

Studying current statistics, it would be obvious to Dr. King that there has been a general decline in the number of Protestants and Catholics who are actively involved in their churches. Perhaps he would be most concerned by the numbers that show a rapid secularization of American culture, which has tended to cause a large percentage of younger Americans to no longer participate in the Catholic or Protestant faiths in which their parents raised them. Young African Americans who support the Black Lives Matter movement would be quick to tell him that this movement is neither rooted in the Black Baptist Church nor guided by its ministers the way the civil rights movement was.

Looking specifically at the Catholic Church in the United States, Reverend King would surely applaud the church's long-standing commitment to Catholic schools, hospitals, and wide-ranging forms of social outreach to those most in need. He could not help but notice the various ways in which the Catholic Church has admitted and tried to overcome a past history during which the church, like other Christian denominations, accepted and tacitly approved the Jim Crow laws of old and the subsequent racial segregation and discrimination in many aspects of Catholic life. He would be happy with the publication of the bishops' 1979 pastoral letter, *Brothers and Sisters to Us*, which forcefully condemned racial prejudice as a sin and a heresy that has endured in our country and in the church. He would applaud *Open Wide Our Hearts: The Enduring Call to Love*, the bishops' 2018 pastoral letter against racism, though he might have argued in favor of calling it a pastoral letter encouraging racial reconciliation.

But, no doubt, he would caution that Catholics, like Protestants, must make sure that their challenging, gospel-inspired statements are studied by the faithful and actually implemented at every level of the community. *He might say the churches do not so much need to say more; they need to do more.*

If Reverend King were still an active force in the struggle for racial justice in this country, the burden of the years would not prevent him from taking a keen interest in the debate over Confederate monuments. He might have had a particular interest in the bronze sculpture of Chief Justice Robert Taney that stood in the North Garden in Mount Vernon Place in Baltimore since 1872. Justice Taney, a Catholic, sadly wrote the 1857 Supreme Court ruling that declared that the enslaved free human beings of African descent and their offspring had no standing before the courts since they were regarded simply as property. On August 18, 2017, the City Council voted to remove it quickly and quietly. Reverend King would have led the outcry. How could a monument "honoring" the man who vigorously defended the lie of white supremacy while leading the nation's highest court have remained on public display for so long without vigorous objection?

He would acknowledge that people of all backgrounds (including Catholic clergy, religious sisters and brothers, and laity) may have passed by the statue of Robert Taney, and the now controversial monuments to General Robert E. Lee and other Confederate leaders, with a degree of indifference and inattentiveness. Questioning the appropriateness of the statue was within their horizon of possibilities, but they did not advert to that possibility.

The debate about these statues has taken on new force in recent years, following the murder of members of the Mother Emanuel African Methodist Episcopal Church in Charleston, South Carolina, by Dylann Roof, a self-proclaimed white supremacists whose goal was to start a race war. Pictures of Roof posing with the Confederate flag enkindled anew the debate about the meaning of this flag, and renewed efforts to remove it from public buildings.

In August 2017, a decision by the Charlottesville, Virginia, City Council to remove a statue of Robert E. Lee inspired a "Unite the Right" protest rally by white supremacists, including neo-Nazis and members of the Klan. On August 12, in the midst of a clash between these white supremacists and counter-demonstrators (including members of Black Lives Matters and antifascists), a Nazi sympathizer drove a speeding car into the midst of the counter-demonstrators, killing Heather Heyer and wounding nineteen others.

It was in the aftermath of this incident that the president condemned violence "on many sides" and later explained that there were also "very fine people" marching among the white supremacists in defense of the statue of Lee. These statements drew widespread outrage. It is not hard to imagine that King would have raised his voice high in the face of all this.[2]

Conclusion: Everybody Can Be Great, Because Everybody Can Serve

If Reverend Dr. Martin Luther King Jr. had lived, I believe that our country would have benefited during these past five decades from his incomparable prophetic voice and his singular wisdom, which would have matured over the years. If he were alive and well today, I would try to seek him out, meet him, and thank him for his heroic witness and the powerful force he has been in challenging the conscience of a country that has a flaw at the foundation—the enslavement of free human beings. Not only would I thank him and embrace him, I would plead for the favor to sit down to a meal with him and talk heart to heart with him about many issues concerning the racial divide in the United States and in the Catholic Church that trouble my spirit. Most of all, I would simply listen to one who knows.

Of course, none of this is possible.

Reverend Dr. Martin Luther King Jr. is not alive and well enjoying his ninety-first year of life, as so many other Americans are.

He is long dead. He was cruelly and brutally murdered fifty-two years ago on April 4, 1968. He was only thirty-nine years old.

---

[2]These incidents are described in greater detail in Chapter 3.

I am aware that some Catholic people may feel that this "What If?" reflection is "too political." It is not appropriate for a Catholic priest and a Catholic bishop to be addressing these topics. This should be for the social activists and political commentators. I am aware that some Americans think of Dr. King and the movement he inspired as the work of Communist agitators. He himself was vilified as a "Communist sympathizer," an "Uncle Tom," a "house Negro," too tame or too radical. Reverend King was not popular during the last years of his life. A 1966 Gallup Poll found that the majority of Americans disapproved of him, especially because of his opposition to the war in Vietnam. Some say, the less said about him after fifty-two years the better. Others say he was a prophet speaking out against a moral blindness in the soul of America.

I believe the great Swiss Protestant theologian Karl Barth, who also died fifty-two years ago this year, was correct when he said a Christian must live with the Bible in his right hand and the morning newspaper in his left hand. I believe the great Trappist monk and mystic, Father Thomas Merton, OCSO, who also died fifty-two years ago this year, was correct when he frequently argued that Catholics and all Christians, precisely because we are followers of Jesus Christ, have a moral obligation to examine our consciences and uproot any vestiges of racial prejudice so they can be actively involved in the struggle to end racial prejudice and discrimination in our country.

Recent popes, including St. Paul VI, St. John Paul II, Pope Emeritus Benedict XVI, and Pope Francis, have all, by words and deeds, expressed their conviction that Catholics must live their faith in Jesus Christ not only in the churches but also on the streets. It is not enough for Catholics to pray for justice and an end to racial conflict and prejudice; we must work courageously to achieve that goal. Pope Francis has given a particular emphasis to this Catholic social gospel by urging the church to serve as a "field hospital" for humanity, reaching out and embracing the oppressed, the marginalized, and the excluded. If we do that, we contribute to the bridging of the racial divide.

The night before he was murdered, Reverend King uttered

these simple words. "We aren't engaged in any negative protests and in any negative arguments with anybody. *We are saying that we are determined to be men.* We are determined to be people." The Easter mystery of the Resurrection which we will celebrate on Easter Sunday, and every Sunday, is an affirmation of Dr. King's simple statement. Jesus of Nazareth lived, taught, suffered, died, was raised up, ascended to the Father, and poured out the Holy Spirit on us at Pentecost because of his love for us as human beings. It will take the power of that same Holy Spirit to achieve a human society based on justice, equal opportunity, and unselfish love for all people, a society Pastor King was fond of calling "the Beloved Community."

As he often said: "Everybody can be great, because everybody can serve. You don't have to have a college degree to serve. You don't have to make your subject and your verb agree to serve. You don't have to know about Plato and Aristotle to serve. You don't have to know Einstein's theory of relativity to serve. You don't have to know the second theory of thermodynamics in physics to serve. You only need a heart full of grace, a soul generated by love. *And you can be that servant!*"

6

There Are No "Minority" Americans

MAY 17, 2013

For many years, long before writing or speaking about the topic, I have written to editors of newspapers and journals asking why they insist on the selective use of the words "minorities" and "minority groups" when referring to certain groups of American citizens and not to others. I have argued, then and now, that if all citizens are Americans, how can certain groups be designated as minorities? The responses that I have often received said that there is nothing demeaning about the use of these terms. And, the fact that they tend to be used only in reference to certain groups (African Americans and Hispanic Americans, for example, and not, for example, to Jewish Americans or Irish Americans) is simply because of a historical evolution in usage. But this is certainly not the case.

The health crisis caused by the pandemic spread of the novel coronavirus has brought this further to light. Unfortunately, for a variety of reasons, the Indigenous peoples of this country, or the Native Americans (long misnamed as "Indians" by Western culture) have experienced very high instances of infection with the virus. The infection rates have been so high in some communities that efforts by community leaders to protect themselves from infections have led to conflicts with state and federal authorities. Media coverage of the difficulties that these citizens have experienced regularly speaks of them as members of "minority groups." They along with Hispanic Americans and African Americans are singled out as "ethnic minorities" who experience higher instances of serious Covid-19 disease. For a number of reasons, Polish Americans, German Americans, and Norwegian Americans do not experience these same higher instances of the illness. But if they did, there is no precedent for the media to list them as members of "minority" groups. They are simply Americans. But why is that?

Is it because they are assimilated into the culture of the country in such a way that their appearances, language, mores, and traditions allow them to blend in with other people of European background, which allows them to become just "Americans"?

We are all familiar with the expression the "majority rules." When disputed issues are addressed by the Supreme Court, when the House of Representatives or the Senate is considering a piece of legislation or an extraordinary act such as the impeachment of a president, a vote is taken and the majority rules. The minority must necessarily accept the position of the group with the most votes. This is generally considered to be fair play. Indeed, this is one of the reasons for recurring debates about the role of the Electoral College in presidential elections. The candidate who secures the majority of the votes from the voters themselves can still lose the presidency if the other candidate secures the majority of the votes in the Electoral College. While this may seem "unfair," it is not because it is what the Constitution dictates.

When we acknowledge the ordinary meaning of "majority rules," we can see that the term connotes power. When we persist in designating one group of Americans, arbitrarily as the "majority" group and others as "minority" groups, the very language implies that one group has more power than any of the other groups. I continue to find it difficult to believe that thoughtful Americans, especially Catholics, do not grasp that it is self-serving, manipulative, unjust and wrong to continue to refer to fellow Americans as "minorities."

On September 22, 1862, President Abraham Lincoln issued the Emancipation Proclamation, declaring,

That on the first day of January, in the year of our Lord one thousand eight hundred and sixty-three, all persons held as slaves within any State or designated part of a State, the people whereof shall then be in rebellion against the United States, shall be then, thenceforward, and forever free; and the Executive Government of the United States, including the military and naval authority thereof, will recognize and maintain the freedom of such persons, and will do no act or acts to repress such persons, or any of them, in any efforts they may make for their actual freedom.

During the subsequent one hundred and fifty years, People of Color have struggled in the midst of the worst forms of oppression and racism to realize the dream of being "thenceforward, and forever free." Sadly, the United States government and religious groups have done "acts to repress such persons" in efforts they have made "for their actual freedom." One of the almost unconscious ways in which this has happened has been in the way words have been used. From the time of the Jim Crow laws, to the civil rights movement, to the present day, insulting, demeaning, and dehumanizing words have been used to diminish the dignity of Americans of African descent as a group and as individuals. The most offensive of these expressions, which need not be mentioned here, has had the common consequence and goal of making people feel inferior, lacking in worth and value. One of the most subtle present-day examples of this is the expression "minority group," which causes some members of the community to think of themselves in terms of who they are not, rather than in terms of who they are.

Are there really "minority" Americans and "minority" Catholics? I have never used this term in reference to any group of American citizens or American Catholics. I believe it is erroneous and counterproductive. If we think carefully about what it means to be an American and to be a Catholic, we can see why these are questionable expressions.

Beginning in the 1960s, the media, the federal government, and Americans of certain racial and ethnic backgrounds (especially Hispanic, Asian, and People of Color) began to speak more and more of "minorities" and "minority groups" in solidarity with women and other groups who have experienced injustice based upon discrimination. These designations were used to help formulate the argument that in order to redress the grave injustices caused by systemic prejudices, special consideration should be given to members of these groups in matters related to education, employment, housing, financial assistance, professional advancement, and business contracts. Few fair-minded people will argue that long-standing practices of discrimination have made it impossible for certain groups of Americans to have equal access to the American dream.

Without prejudice to the validity of these important concerns, I believe that the common use of the word "minorities" as the collective designation of these groups of people perpetuates negative stereotypes and is contradicted by what it means to be an American citizen.

It does not take a particularly critical analysis to recognize the fact that words such as "minorities" and "minority groups" are used selectively and are not applied consistently in reference to all ethnic groups that make up a statistically small number of US citizens. At times, these expressions seem to be used as code words with subtle negative connotations. They also raise the question: Which American citizens are the "majority" group? There are no *"ethnic"* Americans in the same sense that one might speak of *"ethnic"* Japanese in Japan, for example. There is no single ethnic, racial, or cultural group that constitutes "true" Americans. Every citizen of the United States is fully and equally an American in the exact same sense of the word. Citizens who are descendants of passengers on the *Mayflower* are not, somehow, more truly American than descendants of "passengers" of slave ships, native people of the Seminole nation, or the most recent immigrants from Pakistan. If they are citizens, they are Americans, precisely because there are no *ethnic* Americans. A careful reflection on the meaning of the expression *"E Pluribus Unum"* excludes the possibility of designating "minorities" in this country, unless *all* citizens are so designated.

Obviously, this truth has not been fully accepted by all sectors of American society (including the Catholic Church) in the past or the present. European Americans, with roots in Ireland, Germany,

Italy, or Poland, for example, were once ostracized in this country as "immigrants," "foreigners," and "undesirable minorities." The same was true of Jewish people. But why are they generally not considered minorities today? The answer is not because any one of these groups now constitutes the statistical majority of the US population. As Matthew Frye Jacobson's *Whiteness of a Different Color: European Immigrants and the Alchemy of Race* notes, the process of gathering together those Americans whose ancestors were from various European countries with very little in common and making them the "majority" group and relegating everyone else as "minorities" is, historically, a rather recent and arbitrary development.

It is a development that, at certain junctures, excluded even European Americans of certain backgrounds as despicable *ethnic* minorities. In its present usage, the term "minority groups" often connotes the haves versus the have-nots, the powerful versus the powerless, the assimilated versus the nonassimilated, because they have not assimilated middle-class mores and the cultural heritage of Western Europe. As a result, even when the majority of the residents in a city are African American or Hispanic American, they are still "minorities."

It is obvious that the federal government, the media, the justice system, educational institutions, and the Catholic Church in the United States cannot be effective in their work without being aware of the complex ethnic, racial, and cultural diversity in the population of this country. However, an awareness of this diversity must never lead these institutions to the uncritical acceptance or even unwitting perpetuation of such terms as "minorities" and "minority groups," which are rarely neutral and which may contradict what it means to be an American by inviting stereotypes and reinforcing prejudices. As a Catholic bishop, I am very aware of the fact that many Protestant Christians today rightly prefer Catholic Christians to refer to them as what *they are*, "Christians of other traditions," rather than as what they *are not*, "non-Catholics." No one ever calls a Catholic a "non-Presbyterian."

In this new century, it might be most helpful if we could recall that *all* Americans are from different racial and ethnic backgrounds and that *no* group constitutes the *majority*. Indeed, many serious anthropological studies suggest that, despite their sociological prominence, ethnicity and race are very problematic categories. Frequent references to groups of Americans and groups of Catholics as "minorities" seem to designate them as who they supposedly are *not*. They are not a part of an arbitrary grouping of Americans of certain ethnic groups (those of European ancestry) who are designated as "the majority." Significantly, the majority of the world's population is not of European origin, and current demographic trends indicate that in the decades ahead Americans of European heritage may become a "minority" of the overall population.

The Catholic Church, faithful to scripture, teaches that in Christ there is neither Greek nor Jew, slave nor free, male nor female, neither north nor south, east nor west. All are redeemed sinners transformed by Christ as members of his mystical Body with equal dignity before God. It might be a good thing if the Catholic Church, other religious groups, and the media would lead the way in eliminating or at least challenging such expressions as "minorities" and "minority groups." This is more than a matter of "political correctness." Words, as conveyers of meaning, have great power for good or evil. It is not asking too much for a nation that proclaims itself to be "one from many" to affirm that in truth there are no majority/minority groups in this country because we really are *one*. We are simply Americans, proud of our amazingly diverse backgrounds, with every right to expect, even demand, to be treated with equal dignity in our churches, before the law and the Constitution, and in the public square.

7

Crossing the Cultural Divide

Evangelization in African American Communities

An Address
to the National Black Catholic Congress

NOVEMBER 18, 1998

Although this essay was written more than twenty years ago, a careful rereading reveals that its fundamental message remains the same. Namely, the Catholic Church has not been as effective as it would like to be in attracting, welcoming, and retaining People of Color as active members. A major reason for this is the fact that the religious meaning, value, and truths affirmed by the church are mediated and communicated to potential new members primarily through the philosophical categories, aesthetics, language, and thought patterns of Western European culture.

I remember discussing this reality with a dedicated priest of European American background many years ago. He said that he found my writings to be informative and thought-provoking. Then he said, "It was ever thus. And I don't see how anything can be done to change this." In his view the Catholic Church, as if by "divine providence," was blessed to move out of the Middle Eastern world of the Holy Land into Western Europe in the early centuries of its existence. This culture made it possible for the church to express anew its unchanging biblical faith with the help of Greek philosophy, to reorganize ecclesial life making use of key structures in the Roman Empire, and to give a new form to its house liturgies making use of aspects of Roman basilica architecture and ritual. Although the Second Vatican Council reaffirmed the importance of the different rites in the church and encouraged a certain amount of cultural adaptation of public worship for people from non-Western cultures, this, he argued, was done in a necessarily limited way.

One of my regrets about this piece, which was widely circulated and discussed, is the fact that the "Prologue" concerning the barbershop was printed separately in several publications. But the literary device of this opening was not written with the idea that this section would be read and discussed completely separated from the substance of the reflection that follows. This unexpected development led to misunderstandings and misinterpretations. I remember giving a talk on the need for greater sensitivity to racial diversity at a seminary. One of the seminarians informed me that he had read my article "The Barbershop." He said, after reading it, he and a classmate decided to visit "an inner-city barbershop" to experience the world of my article firsthand. He said that he was quite surprised by the experience. While some of the descriptions in my article were the same as what they saw and heard, much of it was not. They did not hear any in-depth discussions of complex racial issues. Nor did they hear any discussions of gangsta rap and the writings of James Baldwin, Malcolm X, and W. E. B. Du Bois. They were a little disappointed that it seemed like an ordinary barbershop, simply with African American clients. They were given very good free haircuts, which surprised them because their white barber said he would not know how to cut "Black hair."

Somehow, the seminarian did not realize that the entire narrative was not to be taken literally. It was an extended metaphor that allowed me to convey something of the ethos of certain dimensions of African American life. I was very disappointed when he said he never read the body of the essay. He never even heard of it. Though the Catholic community is fortunate to have the 2019 pastoral letter against racism, Open Wide Our Hearts: The Enduring Call to Love, *the issues addressed in the body of this chapter remain a challenge for the church's effective communication of the Catholic faith to African American people.*

Our Holy Father Pope John Paul II states in *Fidei Depositum*, his apostolic constitution which introduces the Catechism of the Catholic Church, that those who use it must "take into account various situations and cultures." If the catechism is to have any impact on our efforts to preach the Good News of Jesus Christ more effectively to African Americans, we must take the Holy Father's words very seriously. The pope's challenge is unambiguous. We cannot be effective evangelists if we are unwilling to learn firsthand about the fabric of the everyday lives of the people we hope to welcome in the name of the Lord.

I have written and spoken often on the subject of evangelization and African Americans, offering a variety of specific suggestions that might make our ministry of evangelization more effective. Rather than repeating those suggestions in this congress presentation prepared specifically for fellow bishops, I wish to invite you to reflect at a deeper level. Today I hope to contribute to a radically honest and genuinely realistic evaluation of what we must do at the dawn of the third millennium of Christianity if we are serious about reaching Black Americans. Knowing that this attempt to suggest implications of John Paul II's instruction to "take into account various situations and cultures" runs the risk of oversimplification, I will be satisfied if I can uncover the roots of fundamental concerns.

This will be done first by visiting a barbershop; second, by reflecting briefly on the meaning of evangelization; third, by examining the cultural divide that separates most potential Black converts from the fundamentally white world of the Catholic Church; and fourth, by offering specific recommendations for bishops to consider that might help create the rapport the church needs with Black people before we even begin to talk about effective evangelization.

The Barbershop

The neighborhood barbershop is often the center of life in poor Black communities. The beauty parlor is across the street. A laundromat, a currency exchange, a barbecue restaurant, a pool hall, and a liquor store are within a few blocks. The vacant lot where teenage boys play basketball begins in the alley behind the barbershop. There are several boarded-up apartment buildings in the neighborhood. One is a crack house. The storefront Baptist church and the funeral home are on the corner. The bus to the clinic and the unemployment office stops nearby. The all-Black Catholic school is outside the neighborhood. Though they are not Catholics, some parents drive their children there despite increasing tuition.

For most of my life as a priest and as a bishop, I have deliberately frequented these "neighborhood centers." Eventually just about everyone comes to the shop, especially on a Saturday. The atmosphere is congenial. Addressing one another as "Brother Austin" or "Brother Braxton," everyone speaks his mind. Copies of *Ebony, Jet, Black Enterprise, Sports Illustrated, Essence*, and the local Black newspaper are scattered about. Old, fading pictures of famous Black athletes, politicians, entertainers, and civil rights leaders are on the walls. There is also a dramatic painting of a militant, Black Jesus Christ, eyes ablaze with righteousness, fist clenched in the Black Power salute.

The enthusiastic conversation of the patrons and barbers moves randomly from topic to topic. Listen to what they say.

"Biting Evander's ear was wrong, and Mike Tyson should have known better. Evander Holyfield is a real class act. I'd like to see them fight again."

"How can we keep our children in school, so that they can get good jobs?"

"What can we do to get the landlords, the city, and the residents to combat the continuing deterioration of housing in our neighborhood?"

"White people will never understand the way most Black people feel about the Rodney King beating and the O. J. Simpson trial and that's that!"

"Let me tell you about the problems I am having at home with my wife and children."

"Do you know what the Man did at my job last night? It was an act of blatant racial prejudice. If I had the seed money or if I could get a loan, I would start my own small business."

"We have our share of violence and crime here. But it's nothing compared to the 'white-collar' crimes being committed by the invisible criminals who control the economic system that make it impossible for us to get ahead."

"Why did the police come down so hard yesterday on the Black brother who was a $1,000 crack dealer on the street and let the $500,000 supplier from outside the neighborhood sleep in a comfortable suburban bed last night?"

"What can I do to help my young, unmarried granddaughter, now that she is pregnant?"

"My neighbor's eighteen-year-old son was shot and killed last week for his Nike sneakers. Lord, what is this world coming to?"

Someone turns on the television. There are loud complaints about the many superficial comedies on the Fox TV station featuring all-Black casts.

"Sure, they will pay Black people to be on TV as long as we play prostitutes and murderers or make fools of ourselves. It's Amos 'n' Andy in living color."

"Show me one Black character on TV living a normal life, someone you can look up to as a role model for our children."

Surfing with the remote, one of the barbers stops at a Catholic program. "The Catholic channel on TV is something else. There is never a Black person on that show. No Black people in the audience. No Black people attending the church services either. And that tired music! They never talk about anything related to being poor or Black. And they wonder why we don't join their church?"

The barber cutting my hair informs the speakers that I am a Catholic priest. A relatively young man observes, "Well, well, well. I didn't know there were any Black priests. I didn't think the Catholic Church even allowed them." He asks why he hasn't seen one before.

"There are not that many of us," I explain. I told him that many priests and sisters, Black and white, do not wear distinctive garb today when they are not directly involved in their ministry.

"Then, how are we supposed to recognize them?" he asks.

Brother Austin, who owns the shop, turns on the Black call-in radio station where there is a heated debate about what color Jesus was. One participant argues loudly that Jesus and the apostles were definitely Black. Another says if he was Jewish he probably was not brown-haired and fair-skinned the way he is usually pictured. One of the men waiting for a haircut dismisses the radio debate saying, "No self-respecting Black man could fall on his knees before a white Jesus, when the white man was and is the oppressor."

At that point, a group of basketball players comes in to quench their thirst. They are wearing the jerseys of Michael Jordan, Shaquille O'Neal, Dennis Rodman, and other basketball "gods," who, they argue, inspire them more than any religion could. Their astronomical incomes and dazzling feats on the courts convince these teenagers that if they can play great ball, they do not need to go to college.

They turn the radio to a rap, hip-hop, and gangsta rap station. You may have managed to ignore this "in your face" confrontational and often vulgar music by such famous performers as the late, recently murdered, Tupac Shakur, the late, recently murdered, Notorious B.I.G., Snoop Doggy Dogg, Ice Cube, and Queen Latifah. However, this music idiom is the lifeblood of these young men, more meaningful to them than even the most energetic Black church music. They know the lyrics by heart and sing along, as they pound out the beat with their whole bodies.

As the ballplayers make their way back to the court, I ponder these rap lyrics and the culture of the streets which they powerfully convey. Sometimes violent, bluntly sexual, and almost always anti-white Establishment, they feed a smoldering rage and an impatient materialism that dictates how these young men walk, talk, dress, eat, and think: yes, even about God and the Christian faith. Because of circumstances too complex for easy analysis, many young Black males and more than a few females believe that everything of value for them can be found in the company of their "homeboys" on the street. Everything truly Black is there. The sometimes searingly brilliant poetry of rap lyrics provides the clearest expression of how they feel.

Two brothers take the chairs on either side of me in the

barbershop. They are in a serious conversation about Spike Lee's new documentary *Four Little Girls,* which is about the children who were murdered in the 1963 Birmingham, Alabama, church bombing and his provocative film *Get on the Bus,* which examined the Million Man March. The Catholic Church had no formal participation in this watershed event in the Black community, though Black Catholic laymen and priests were certainly there. The conversation turns to John Singleton's powerful movie *Rosewood,* a mythological retelling of the true story of an attempt to annihilate a prosperous Black town in Florida in 1923 by a white mob. One brother who looks directly at me says, "This movie gave me more hope than any church service." They ask me if I have heard of *Bring in 'da Noise, Bring in 'da Funk,* George C. Wolf and Saivon Glover's astounding Broadway phenomenon, in which tap dance is used to tell the story of a people from the slave ships to the present day. When I tell them I have seen it, they hang on my every word. As they are leaving, they give me a flyer about Wynton Marsalis's Pulitzer Prize–winning jazz oratorio *Blood on the Fields,* which explores the impact of slavery on Black people today.

A group of Black women come in from the beauty parlor, which has no TV, to watch the funeral of Dr. Betty Shabazz, widow of the murdered Malcolm X. They are caught up in a sisterhood of sorrow as they contemplate the tragedy of this singular light extinguished by the hand of her troubled grandson. Their hearts are broken as they watch Coretta Scott King, widow of the murdered Martin Luther King Jr., comforting Myrlie Evers-Williams, widow of the murdered Medgar Evers, and as poet Maya Angelou tearfully embraces each of Dr. Shabazz's six weeping daughters.

This untimely death caused a great mourning among Black women, including many Black Catholic women. But this death was not lamented in most Catholic churches because it was not a significant event for most Catholics. As they depart, one woman remarks to me: "Reverend, I go to Reverend Hampton's AME church myself, but I send my son to the Catholic school for the education and the discipline. But I would not want him to become a Catholic and become a priest. You can't get married and you can't have children. As badly as we need good Black husbands and fathers, I think that is such a waste and a shame."

Later, a senior from Howard University settles in for a haircut and turns on the public radio station to a roundtable discussion about Black intellectuals and their books. The session begins with praise for a new edition of the writings of James Baldwin. They assert that it's time for Black and white Americans to reread (or read for the first time) his classic essay *The Fire Next Time* and heed its warning, "God gave Noah the rainbow sign. No more warnings, the fire next time!"

The radio commentator turns to the growing African American intellectual presence at Harvard University. At the W. E. B. Du Bois Institute for Afro-American Research, Henry Louis Gates Jr., the cultural analyst, has assembled such scholars as William Julius Wilson, sociologist and public-policy expert, Cornel West, philosopher, and Evelyn Brooks Higginbotham, Black women's history expert. Everyone agrees that their new books are having a significant impact on Black thinkers.

Next, the radio panel gets into an angry exchange about Keith Richburg's *Out of America: A Black Man Confronts Africa.* This largely negative analysis of Black African politics and life brands Black Americans who have come to identify deeply with Africa as naïve romanticists. Such "Afrocentrism" is laughable in the author's view. Black Americans ought to be thankful that they are not in Africa with its crime, Black political corruption, and widespread disease. He urges Black American civil rights leaders to stop praising African politicians indiscriminately. He thinks some should be in prison for their treachery.

Martin Bernal's book *Black Athena: The Afroasiatic Roots of Classical Civilization* is briefly discussed. This ambitious scholarly work proposes a more radical Afrocentrism than the one rejected by Richburg. It has as its much-debated thesis the belief that the best of ancient Greek and Roman cultures, which are the foundation of Western European cultures, is profoundly influenced by even more ancient Egyptian cultures, which in turn have been shaped by sub-Saharan Black African cultures.

When the radio program ends, the Howard University student provokes a discussion about Black identity. One man observes that no sooner have white people adjusted to calling us *Afro-American* than they are expected to change to *African American*. What are they to make of current expressions such as *Americans of African descent* and *Africans in America?* He says some white people are bewildered. They have begun to think the question of naming has become a tiresome game of political correctness.

The university student interrupts him, asserting that the matter is not so simple; "It is tied to the story of how our people came to be in the United States against their will and how they have been treated here since the end of slavery." He recommends the W. E. B. Du Bois 1903 classic *The Souls of Black Folk,* which explores this dilemma of Black identity.

The student continues, "This long history is the reason why different groups and individuals use different designations based upon their experience. As a result, *colored people, Negroes, Blacks, Black people, AfroAmericans, African Americans, Africans in America, Americans of African descent, Africans in the diaspora, Americans, People of Color* and, yes, even *niggah* in the world of hip-hop and rap are all used, depending on the context of lived experience. One of the reasons for the emergence of *Americans of African descent* is the search for an inclusive expression that would be appreciative of the unique history of the various Caribbean peoples." A Catholic gentleman from Haiti spoke up. "Our people think of themselves simply as Haitians, not as African Americans."

One of the barbers asks, "Why can't we let go of all of this tortured history and simply call ourselves, Black and white, what we now all are—proud Americans?" Then he answers his own question. "Sadly, this is not true to what people experience each day. It is similar to asking why the Jewish people cannot put the Holocaust behind them simply a tragic episode of past history. They cannot do this because it was and is too traumatic. Slavery and its unending aftermath, like the Holocaust, is an unresolved and unreconciled memory of the past that informs how people wish to name themselves today."

As Brother Austin finishes my haircut, I think to myself that not one of the Black authors, artists, scholars, actors, politicians, or athletes discussed is a Catholic. I wonder if it is possible that being Catholic inhibits Black women and men from playing pivotal roles in the shaping of Black culture.

As I leave, the shop is filled with the rich aromas of soul food. A nearby restaurant chef has just brought dinner for the barbers so that they can take a much-needed break. As you leave the barbershop, you might ask yourselves as Catholic bishops how familiar or unfamiliar you are with the "various situations and cultures" that are revealed there.

What Do We Mean by Evangelization?

There are between 35 million and 40 million Americans of African ancestry. By our imperfect count, between 1.3 million and 2 million of these are members of the Catholic Church. Millions of Black Americans over thirty are members of Black Christian traditions, especially Baptists. At least half of the total population, or between 17 million and 20 million, are under thirty. Many of those under thirty are not members of any faith tradition. Young Black people who are attracted to religious faith, especially if they have been in prison, are far more likely to be drawn to some form of Islam, including Louis Farrakhan's Nation of Islam, than to the Roman Catholic Church. Yet, as in all communities, it is this younger, nonaffiliated group that we most urgently need to reach.

Some of the parents, grandparents, and aunts of the youthful devotees of popular Black culture may well be Catholics. Though they have found it difficult to pass their faith on to the younger generation, African Americans who are long-standing Catholics are often among the most devout and the most tenacious in holding on to their faith. Some have made their own a traditional Catholicism that makes them long for the day when the church was more uniform. They prefer the polyphony of Palestrina over the hand-clapping rhythm of gospel music. They might throw up their hands in disgust at the mere mention of the "Black Christ."

The majority embrace the reforms of the Second Vatican Council and believe that the church has only just begun to appreciate the powerful contributions that the cultures and experiences of Black people can make to Catholic worship and to all aspects of Catholic life. They are anxious to do more and be more in the church.

But how do we reach the millions of younger Black people for whom the Catholic faith seems irrelevant? I am not sure that any of us can answer that question. Before discussing some of the reasons why this question is so difficult to answer, we must ask ourselves what do we, as committed Christians and as bishops, really mean by evangelization? What do we expect to be different about the person who has been evangelized? Surely we expect more than mere church affiliation.

We all know people who register in a Catholic parish, identify themselves as Catholics, go to Mass a couple of Sundays a month, put their envelopes in the collection basket, have their children baptized, and live lives that seem much more focused on the "gods of secularity" than on the God of Jesus Christ. We would call them members of the church in a minimal sense. But would we call them evangelized?

I think we mean much more than that. Jesus Christ is at the center of the life of the person who has been effectively evangelized. The whole life and lifestyle of the evangelized person is gradually changed and transformed. This is because true and radical conversion is taking place. When the hearts and the minds of women and men are evangelized by the Good News, they become able to affirm the good and gracious nearness of the mystery of God in their lives, even in the face of pain, suffering, and confusion. This divine mystery, revealed in the depths of their being, in nature, salvation history, tradition, Scripture, and uniquely in Jesus Christ and his church, becomes intimately present in the lives of those who have put on Christ.

The Holy Spirit calls the truly evangelized to participate actively in the life, death, and resurrection of Jesus Christ through authentic personal prayer and the sacramental and liturgical life of the church. This paschal mystery converts their personal lives, calling them, as St. Paul writes to the Romans, to do the things they know they should do and not to do the things they know they should not do. Those for whom the Good News has fallen on rich soil live out their converted lives nurtured by genuine Christian example. As they grasp the radical catholicity of their faith, they seek to live lives of service to others, especially the poor. They strive to purify their hearts, uprooting biases and prejudices against any group or people, because these attitudes are incompatible with the love of God that fills their hearts. As they mature in faith, they develop an intellectual and emotional integration of what they believe and they become eager to share this faith with others. Rooted in Christ, they look beyond the certainty of death to the "life of the world to come."

If this is what we hope is unfolding in the life of a truly evangelized person, we must acknowledge the painful truth that many Catholic people, like many Christians of other traditions; are not truly evangelized. The Catholic faith, which has come to them as a part of their ethnic and cultural heritage, has never been personally appropriated and made their own. This reminds us that evangelization is an ongoing reality in our own lives as well. An important part of the "new evangelization," to which Pope John Paul calls the church as we approach the year 2000, must begin with ourselves and our people.

As leaders of the Catholic Church in this country, we are all aware of the fact that the annual increase in the number of Catholics is primarily due to the baptism of the children of Catholic couples and to the fact that Christians of other traditions who marry Catholics often decide to join the faith of their spouse. Only a small number of new Catholics are completely new, people who have heard about the faith from a friend or neighbor and want to learn about joining the church themselves.

Catholic bishops, priests, deacons, religious, and the Christian faithful have not, for the most part, been public evangelists. We do not see them visible on street corners, in shopping malls, at neighborhood social events, eagerly telling strangers about Jesus and his church. Nor do we tend to be door-to-door evangelists, knocking on doors for Jesus, putting flyers on car windshields, or placing signs on neighborhood bulletin boards with our tear-off phone numbers so that people can call us if they want to know about Jesus. Most of our people do not seem to be inclined to take out their Bible, council documents, Catechism of the Catholic Church, or rosary at lunchtime in the office, in the warehouse, or in the factory where they work in order to share their Catholic faith. Some Catholics might actually find this offensive.

Several points can be drawn from this. When we speak about evangelization and African Americans, our ultimate hope must certainly be for something more profound than a superficial denominational affiliation. We do not have large communities of Black Catholics with young couples having their children baptized as infants. Nor do we have large numbers of Black Catholics marrying Christians of other traditions who subsequently become Catholics. As a result, we do not experience a significant increase in the number of Black Catholics from the two paths by which our numbers increase in white Catholic communities.

Thus, when we say that the church or Black Catholics must evangelize in Black communities, are we asking that something be done that we are not doing in other communities? Are white Catholics evangelizing in white communities? Are we asking that Catholics open themselves to real changes in the way they see themselves, their relationship to their faith and to others? Are we asking Catholics to become involved with some form of public evangelization, be it on the street, door to door, or at work? Our people will not become more open to sharing their faith with people of different races until questions such as these are answered.

Worlds Apart: The Cultural Divide

Even if we could stir up an evangelizing spirit in our people, it might not result in a significant number of Black Americans embracing the Catholic faith in the decades to come. The reasons for this are manifold and as complex as those that have prevented the church from attracting significant numbers in countries such as Japan, China, and India for centuries. The greatest obstacle to the evangelization of Black Americans may be that the cultural, educational, economic, and political situations that define the relationship between the Catholic Church and most African Americans constitute a radical cultural divide.

The cultural divide is particularly acute between the Catholic Church as we know it and the culture and lived experiences of the vast majority of poor, younger, urban, and rural Black people who usually are not attracted to the Catholic faith. Jesus Christ clearly commanded his followers to teach all nations. Nevertheless, this universal faith as it is embodied by the Catholic Church in the United States has been profoundly shaped by "various situations and cultures" foreign to the contemporary Black experience.

These are essentially the cultures of ancient Greece and Rome that became the foundations of Western European cultures. The structure of Catholic theological reflection, the aesthetic principles by which religious art, music, literature, architecture, liturgical vestments, and the environment for worship are measured, the prism through which sacred Scripture is read, and the ascetical ideals that inform our understanding of spirituality, prayer, the interior life, the experience of God, our relationship with Christ, sin, and the work of God's saving grace in the sacraments have been primarily shaped by this Western European culture. This is inevitable because the church and the life of faith exist in time and space. The church transforms and is, in part, transformed by the "situations and cultures" in which it finds itself.

Anthropologists and philosophers of religion have traditionally argued that within the human spirit there are questions of meaning dealing with the purpose and destiny of the human person. For many people, the themes addressed by religion (God, eternity, moral judgments, afterlife, mystery, prayer, sacred time, sacred space, sacred narratives, sacred persons, and sacred ritual) have provided the context for seeking answers to these questions. Students of religion are always interested to know why certain religious traditions seem to illuminate these questions more adequately than others for individuals and people in different cultures, ethnic and racial groups, and historical contexts. We bishops also have reason to be interested in this question.

This relationship between the questions human beings ask and the answers provided by a particular faith tradition has sometimes been called the "existential fit." There have always been people who held that the questions themselves were absurd or at best could not be answered definitively who have then embraced atheism and agnosticism. Large numbers of young Black Americans say or imply that the questions are irrelevant to the struggles of their everyday existence. Or if they are relevant, the Catholic Church, looked upon with suspicion as a largely white, racist, middle-class reality, has not been able to raise the questions and illuminate the responses of its tradition in a way that touches the minds and passions of Black people. There is no "existential fit." This lack of "fit" does not mean that the truths of faith are not true. It may mean that the way the church articulates its faith and the degree of welcome that Catholics convey do not communicate the heart of the faith effectively to potential converts.

The basketball players in the "barbershop" are not likely to be engaged by another worldly apologetic that presents a Catholic Church unwilling or unable to do anything to help alter their present economic, political, and social plight. A church that offers little sustained help in the struggle and promises the joy of eternal life after they die is not an "existential fit" for the life experiences of these young people. Any preacher they follow will have to be at their side, engaged in the struggle, helping them find a God of the oppressed and an angel of freedom and justice, articulated in a theology that embraces, celebrates, and is informed by the Black experience. If God is to really be God for them, he must be God the liberator, who uproots injustice and oppression by his mighty power. A God of the status quo is dead for them.

There are many important related implications of this cultural divide. Three of them have a negative impact on evangelization. These are our segregated neighborhoods, our segregated Catholic schools, and, perhaps surprisingly, our segregated Catholic art.

Segregated Neighborhoods

Since most Catholics are white and since most Black people are not Catholics, the church's effectiveness in evangelizing Black people would almost certainly be greater if people of both races lived next door to one another as friends and neighbors. But this is rarely the case in the United States. Neighborhoods like the imaginary one in which the "barbershop" is located are all Black as a direct result of the cultural divide. These neighborhoods and the all-Black parishes in them were formed by the systematic segregation and re-segregation of our large urban communities.

As Black people moved from the South looking for employment in northern cities in the 1930s, '40s, and '50s, many factors fed a xenophobic dread of economic, cultural, religious, or racial diversity in city neighborhoods. Because the Catholic Church itself did not know the world of these Black, largely but not exclusively Protestant, migrants, it does not have a record of prophetic leadership during this time. John T. McGreevy's *Parish Boundaries: The Catholic Encounter with Race in the Twentieth-Century Urban North* documents the rapid movement of white Catholics to the suburbs to escape neighborhoods that were changing racially, economically, and culturally. Due in part to the cultural divide, white congregations and their pastors, often recent immigrants from Eastern or Western Europe themselves, did not find in their Christian faith an inspiration to welcome their new neighbors.

In spite of this, we must not diminish the enviable record of exceptional service of the white and Black bishops, priests, brothers, sisters, and Christian faithful past and present who have eagerly committed their entire lives to ministry in African American parishes. We think immediately of the Josephites, the Society of the Divine Word, the Oblate Sisters of Providence, the Sisters of the Blessed Sacrament, and the many diocesan priests and others who have been unselfish in their generosity. In and through God's grace they have accomplished and continue to accomplish great things in their local church communities.

Nevertheless, we are forced to acknowledge that there are a significant number of white priests today who make it clear that they do not wish to serve in Black parishes at any time during their ministry. This may not be due primarily to racial prejudice. It may be due in part to the real or perceived extreme differences between Black and white neighborhoods and their uneasiness about crossing the cultural divide. These priests may prefer suburban parishes where there are more people, more resources, better parish facilities, and more trained personnel because they are more like the communities in which they grew up and because they think it is easier to build post–Vatican II faith communities in such areas.

Some of our Black priests may feel the same way, wondering why they are expected to serve in what others consider undesirable parishes simply because the parishioners are "their people." Meanwhile, since the need for priests is great, bishops do not have the luxury of sending extra priests to be evangelists in Black parishes where there are only a few Catholics when they are so needed in the suburban parishes where there are so many Catholics. We are a long way from the day when white Catholics from the suburbs will cross the cultural divide and come eagerly to the city as evangelists and missionaries.

Segregated Catholic Schools

In the past, the all-Black Catholic schools that resulted from our segregated neighborhoods played a central role in the evangelization of African Americans. Black parents, seeking an alternative to the public schools and admiring the value formation for which the Catholic schools were renowned, sent their children to these schools. The pastors required the parents of the children who were not Catholic to study the Catholic faith. These adult "convert classes" resulted in the baptism of significant numbers of children and parents each year for almost a quarter of a century. But this trend was definitely reversed by the mid-1960s.

Today in our all-Black parish schools, where most of the students are not Catholics, there may be only one or two religious sisters, if any. There are almost no Black Catholic male teachers. Most of the lay teachers are white women who live in other neighborhoods. They may feel ill at ease about going beyond teaching general Christian values to actually enthusiastically urging the students to become Catholics. In some schools there seems to be an unwritten policy not to evangelize even if the children are unchurched. Many principals and pastors are uncomfortable with the old system of mandatory attendance at religion classes by parents. They also argue that it is unenforceable.

Even if pastors and catechists sense an openness to the Catholic faith on the part of a student, they may deem it unwise to prepare that child for baptism. Many Black children are brought to Catholic schools by working parents who live a considerable distance from the parish church. When there is not even one member of the family committed to the faith, it will be impossible for the sixth, seventh, or eighth grader to get to Sunday Mass and participate in the life of the church. With no support at all, it is unlikely that this fragile faith will survive, especially with the prospect of a public high school. In these circumstances, only the smallest number of Black students become Catholic each year.

Real as these difficulties may be, our Catholic schools must never be reduced to mere instruments of social progress. They have the great potential of becoming once again true and effective instruments of evangelization. If we abandon this confidence, we risk undermining the essential nature and purpose of the church's involvement in the ministry of education, which is to share the light and love of Jesus Christ with all.

Segregated Catholic Art

When I was the pastor of a parish in the Archdiocese of Chicago, I used to take the children from our all-African American school on a tour of our church three times a year. One of the first questions was always, "Father, why are all the angels and saints white? Aren't there any Black people in heaven?"

I thought of these children last month when I had quite a discussion about our beautiful new Mary, mother of Africa, chapel with a young Black man who had recently left the seminary. He asked, "Why should Black Catholics be so grateful for one chapel in our national basilica while the vast majority of the art in the basilica and in all of the Catholic churches present an image of the kingdom of heaven that is exclusively white?"

He continued, "Why can there not be Black angels, cherubs, and saints in all of our churches, Black and white? Imagine the impact on Black and white men and women if they saw images of God the Father, God the Son, and God the Holy Spirit represented in the deep mystery of what Paul VI called 'the gift of Blackness.' In Western iconography, darkness usually represents sin and evil. Demons, devils, and Satan are often presented in dark hues. Show me a church in which Satan is pictured as white! Would not our catholicity be well served by the common experience of seeing Jesus, Mary, Joseph, and the saints in different ethnic and racial appearances in all of our churches?"

The former seminarian asserted, "It cannot be argued that it is a matter of historical accuracy. Angels are pure spirits, without race, nationality, or gender. Western Christian art has never represented Jesus Christ, Mary, or the apostles as Jewish. God the Father is absolute spirit. He has no race or nationality. Scripture never describes him as an elderly, European-looking man. We know and understand the historical and cultural reasons for what was done in the past. But why should we perpetuate this all-white image of heaven in the present and the future? What would happen if the bishops recommended, even mandated, such diversity in all of our future churches, seminaries, chancery offices, and other institutions to convey a more authentically universal vision of the heavenly Jerusalem? Is this an insignificant issue?" asked the former seminarian.

"What if the situation were reversed? How would Catholics of European origin feel if, starting tomorrow, all of the images of the Trinity, Jesus, Mary, saints, angels, and all the inhabitants of heaven in their churches had Black, Hispanic, Asian, or Native

American features and none were white? Would they feel fully at home and welcome? Is this not what Black Catholics have lived with for generations? Is this not what they are going to live with for generations to come? Surely, the total absence of images of the holy and the sacred from a Black perspective in our churches has a negative impact on the church's efforts to evangelize Black Americans. The image of a magnificent Black angel in a cathedral might do more for the evangelization of Black people than handing out copies of a prayer book at the door. Who would want to join a faith in which all the spiritual personalities are visualized to look like the very people who enslaved and oppressed them?"

The thoughts of this young man are spoken in part from anger, hurt, and disillusionment. They may sound too strong and unrealistic to many of us. Nevertheless, we must hear these thoughts because they represent the deep-seated feelings of many Black people, young and old, whom we wish to reach. These same feelings are shared by growing numbers of Black Catholics. They are often expressed at gatherings such as this congress. We must also hear from them because they are a painful reminder of talented people like Brother Cyprian Rowe, who left the Catholic Church, in part, because of issues dealing with liturgy, art, and racial inclusiveness.

This examination of the cultural divide and some of its implications has been attempting to approach a very difficult question from a moving viewpoint. That question is not how do we make existing Black Catholic parishes more vital. Nor is it how can we make the liturgies, in which Black Catholics worship, more vital or more spiritually nourishing for those who are already coming to church. The question has been how can we reach the Black people, especially young men who pass by our churches week after week on their way to the barbershop without even noticing them.

Specific Recommendations

It may be useful to consider specific pastoral recommendations for the American bishops that may aid us in creating a greater atmosphere of openness to Black people on the part of the church and a greater openness to the church on the part of Black people. This openness and respect are part of the foundation that is necessary for crossing the cultural divide before the work of pre-evangelization can begin.

Perhaps no private institution has done more than the Catholic Church to secure a more just society. The church expends large sums of money each year in Black communities, subsidizing Catholic schools and in the work of Catholic Charities and a vast network of social service programs whose positive impact cannot be measured. Yet the church, as the church, is not a strong, visible presence to ordinary Black people in their neighborhoods.

There are things that we could do, perhaps as a conference, to make our presence better known and make our desire to cross the cultural divide more apparent.

1. We should give serious attention to our relationship with the Black media. Local dioceses and, where appropriate, the bishops' conference itself should consider preparing press releases tailored to *Ebony, Jet, Black Enterprise,* local Black newspapers, Black radio stations, the National Association for the Advancement of Colored People, and traditional Black churches. Imaginative advertisements on Black-oriented radio and TV stations would also make the church more present to people who literally do not know who we are.

Visible neighborhood signs directing people to the nearest parish and announcing "The Catholic Church Welcomes You!" establish immediate contact with the people on the street. A Catholic invitation to join the church on the sides of buses and in subway stations in Black neighborhoods would be seen by all.

2. The bishops of the United States should seriously consider leading the way in the elimination of the practice of calling people *minorities* and *minority groups*. Most People of Color find these words very offensive. African Americans almost never refer to themselves with these terms except when they are forced to do so by the legal language of set-aside and affirmative-action issues. Editorials in national newspapers, TV documentaries, and government studies

use these expressions frequently, oblivious or indifferent to their negative connotations.

These terms do not simply convey the neutral idea of numerically smaller groups in a given population. We have been conditioned to think of very specific groups in our culture when we hear these terms. Just as we no longer call Christians of other traditions *non-Catholics,* which describes them as what they are not, we should also avoid calling people *minority groups,* which describes them as what they are not, namely, not the majority.

The majority of the world's population is not European. Similarly, no particular European ethnic or national group constitutes the majority of the population in this country. In his call for candid discussions on the topic of race relations in the United States, President Clinton has pointed out that in the coming decades there will be no majority race, nationality, or ethnic group in America. We would do far better to refer to groups of people as who they are.

3. Think, for a moment, about the chancery offices, cathedrals, bishops' residences, seminaries, and parish plants in your diocese and ask yourselves how many Black people are employed as secretaries, custodians, cooks, and housekeepers. If our diocesan institutions and parishes hire only white-owned companies (with all white workers) for building, tuck-pointing, landscaping, and painting, if all the electricians, plumbers, carpenters, carpet layers, and window washers are white, it is noticed. No matter where our Catholic institutions are located, the presence or absence of Black workers is observed and thought about by Black and white people. The only way to ensure racial diversity in these workforces is to have someone who personally oversees and enforces the church's frequently stated commitment to this diversity. Think also of social gatherings at the bishop's residence. How often do white guests encounter Black guests there?

4. We should feature articles about African Americans frequently in our diocesan newspapers, whether or not we have a significant number of Black Catholics or even Black people in our dioceses. The articles would be primarily for the benefit of our Catholic people who are not African American. These articles

need not always be religious in nature. They could challenge stereotypes and help people learn about the Black experience. Many white suburban Catholic teenagers form most of their impressions of Black people from TV and movies, which usually reinforce prejudice and fear.

5. We must go beyond volunteerism. If the vision of this eighth National Black Catholic Congress is to be implemented, additional resources must be provided to support ongoing, organized efforts. If we are to make progress in getting to know the African American communities around us, we must be willing to invest greater resources and personnel over the long run. We cannot propose teams of full-time, well-trained door-to-door evangelists in Black neighborhoods without acknowledging that such persons must be adequately compensated. Very few of our Black parishes, if any, have the income to pay for this training and compensation. Funding will have to come from the larger church.

6. Our usually imposing parish building complexes may intimidate many people. Could we consider several strategic experiments with neighborhood storefront community-development and self-help centers? These could offer a wide range of recreational activities, social services, counseling, employment guidance, Bible classes, and simple, non-Eucharistic worship services tailored to meet the needs of young Black people right off the street. These experimental centers in three or four dioceses would need to be staffed by trained, paid, full-time deacons, sisters, or laypersons.

7. Our Campaign for Human Development does exceptional work in helping people to help themselves in many situations around the country. Many of us visit these sites and preside at the distribution of funds. Often the beneficiaries of CHD do not even know what the Catholic Church is, and they have no idea that it is the generosity of Catholic people that funds the CHD. There are obvious pre-evangelization possibilities in the midst of this good work, which often takes place in Black neighborhoods. CHD is not the activity of sincere social workers. It is the work of love of neighbor that flows directly from our commitment to Jesus Christ.

8. The year-long preparation for baptism mandated by the Rite of Christian Initiation for Adults is an exceptional resource for renewal in the church. Yet it may need to be adapted to be attractive to poorer, younger people. The RCIA is sometimes experienced as too long and involved. If this becomes discouraging, catechumens tend to drop out. Careful attention needs to be given to appropriate ways to adapt this very important process of entering into the life of the church without diminishing in any way the real and in-depth instruction and Christian formation that are essential for a life of faith.

9. Our episcopal conference has produced a number of detailed statements containing specific proposals, goals, agendas, and resolutions addressing the question of the church in Black communities and the concerns of this congress. If you reread them, you might be surprised and disappointed to note how many excellent ideas have been formulated that never have been systematically implemented.

These documents include: *Brothers and Sisters to Us*, our 1979 pastoral letter on the sin and heresy of racism that endures in our church and in American society; *Here I Am, Send Me*, our 1989 conference response to our mission of evangelizing African Americans; the National Black Catholic Pastoral Plan; *Go and Make Disciples*, our 1992 national plan and strategy for Catholic evangelization in the United States; and our 1997 statement, *A Pastoral Plan for Communication*, with an extensive section on evangelization. Although there is no need to say more, there is a great need to do more. Is this really a priority for the church in the United States?

10. My final recommendation may be the most important. We need to pray. I do not speak of occasional, vague, general prayers. I speak of prayers focused on conversion. First we should pray for ourselves and our people that God will bring about a true conversion of our hearts, our attitudes, and our way of doing things so as to remove any obstacles that we may unintentionally place in the way of evangelization. We should pray that the Holy Spirit helps us announce the Gospel in ways that speak to Black people, who really are brothers and sisters to us.

We should pray for vocations from African American families to the religious life, the diaconate, and the priesthood. We should pray as well for vocation directors and seminary and convent leadership that they will take special care to nurture potential vocations that come to them. We should also ask our people to pray for these concerns at home, at Mass, and at our chapels of perpetual adoration of the Eucharist.

You would not be attending this eighth National Black Catholic Congress unless the relationship between the Catholic Church and Black Americans was a matter of great importance to you. We pray together that the Holy Spirit will guide and inspire us. We can never limit the providential work of the divine Spirit. While we may not always see in what precise way the Spirit is moving in the work of evangelization, we can be confident that the Spirit, whom Christ himself breathed on the apostles, is never working against the authentic efforts of the church. It is that Spirit who fills us with genuine love for those we wish to call in the name of Christ and fills those who would be called with love for us in return.

My brothers, I have spoken to you forthrightly about the challenges that the Catholic Church must face if we are to examine honestly the questions raised by serious reflection on evangelizing African Americans effectively. If the analysis presented here is fundamentally correct, then we can expect no overnight change in the present situation. I firmly believe that we must decide to act in new ways. Otherwise, someone will be giving a similar address ten years from now, and the challenge will be greater because the situation will be worse: Why not act now?

Some of what I have said may be discouraging. Let us not be discouraged. When we are discouraged, let us recall the powerful, prophetic words of Pope Paul VI's landmark apostolic exhortation *Evangelii Nuntiandi:*

> Let us therefore preserve our fervor of spirit. Let us preserve the delightful and comforting joy of evangelizing even when it is in tears that we must sow. May it mean for us as it did for John the Baptist, for Peter and Paul, for the other

apostles and for a multitude of splendid evangelizers all through the church's history, an interior enthusiasm that no one and nothing can quench. May it be the great joy of our consecrated lives. And may the world of our time, which is searching, sometimes with anguish, sometimes with hope, be enabled to receive the Good News not from evangelizers who are dejected, discouraged, impatient, or anxious, but from ministers of the Gospel whose lives glow with fervor, who have first received the joy of Christ and who are willing to risk their lives so that the kingdom may be proclaimed and the church established in the midst of the world.

Mary, mother of Africa and mother of the church, pray for us!

8

Black Catholics in America

Where Do We Go from Here?

November 2, 1985

When the heroic Congressman John R. Lewis marched across the Edmund Pettus Bridge, he carried in his backpack his well-worn copy of New Seeds of Contemplation *by Thomas Merton, the Trappist monk, priest, and advocate for racial reconciliation and peace. President Barack Obama has famously said that were it not for John Lewis and his historic march across that bridge for the voting rights of African Americans, he might have never been elected president of the United States. I can almost say that were it not for John Lewis, I might have never become a Catholic priest. If I had not known of Mr. Lewis's interest in Thomas Merton, I might not have developed a lifelong interest in Merton's life and writings, which had a significant impact on my gradual discernment of my vocation to the priesthood. I find in Mr. Lewis's remarkable life and example a powerful model for African American Catholics, who are discerning the best way of helping the church to become more welcoming and more authentically "catholic."*

I followed Mr. Lewis's life story with interest after reading that he, like me, was deeply disturbed by the brutal murder of Emmett Till in Money, Mississippi, in 1955. My interest only intensified after he was elected chairman of the Student Nonviolent Coordinating Committee in the early 1960s. I was quite amazed that someone so young had such courage and commitment to nonviolent resistance and protest as the best way to confront racial oppres-

sion in the United States, embodying the examples of both Jesus Christ and Mahatma Gandhi.

Mr. Lewis often said that for the cause of freedom, justice, and social equality there was a need to engage in "good trouble, necessary trouble." This seminal idea shaped his entire life. As one of the original thirteen Freedom Riders, committed to travel with a racially integrated group from Washington, DC, to New Orleans, he said of these dangerous rides: "We were determined not to let any act of violence keep us from our goal. We knew our lives could be threatened, but we had made up our minds not to turn back." They were beaten and assaulted many times.

On March 7, 1965, on Bloody Sunday, Mr. Lewis led the first of three Selma to Montgomery marches across the Edmund Pettus Bridge. Alabama state troopers confronted the marchers at the end of the bridge ordering them to end the march. The marchers knelt down to pray, as the police turned tear gas on them. Troopers on horseback charged the demonstrators and beat them until many were seriously injured. To the end of his life, Mr. Lewis bore the marks of the skull fracture he endured.

This chapter provides an overview of some of the history of the Catholic Church's imperfect efforts to bridge the racial divide that exists in the church. It concludes with a number of suggestions, which, though written some time ago, have not lost their urgency.

I hope this overview will be very helpful to Catholics of all ages and racial backgrounds when they study Brothers and Sisters to Us *(1979) and* Open Wide Our Hearts: The Enduring Call to Love *(2018), the two landmark pastoral letters addressing the racial prejudice that endures in the Catholic Church. I hope they will be motivated to make the "good and necessary trouble" that John Lewis so eloquently advocated in his words and his deeds. In recommending Mr. Lewis as a valued companion to Catholics on the clearly unfinished journey down the long road to racial justice and reconciliation in the church, I am not suggesting that readers should embrace all of the political and legislative agendas endorsed by Mr. Lewis. Though he took inspiration from Thomas Merton, he was not a Catholic. As a progressive Democrat, he did not embrace Catholic moral teachings on marriage, family life, human sexuality, and the defense of developing human life in the womb. But this important caveat should not cause us to close our ears and our hearts* to a prophetic voice in areas consistent with the Good News of Jesus Christ. His bold vision can inspire Catholics of all backgrounds to search eagerly for the courage and the wisdom needed to fully embrace and welcome African American people into every aspect of a church that is "universal" and not exclusively "Eurocentric."

In an essay written for publication in The New York Times on the day of his funeral (July 30, 2020), Mr. Lewis revealed the deep interior motivation that energized his life. It is not difficult to translate the words that follow and apply them to the efforts to renew the church by African American Catholics and all those who want the church to be a more effective "field hospital."

> I was searching for a way out, or some might say a way in, and then I heard the voice of Dr. Martin Luther King Jr. on an old radio. He was talking about the philosophy and discipline of nonviolence. He said we are all complicit when we tolerate injustice. He said it is not enough to say it will get better by and by. He said each of us has a moral obligation to stand up, speak up, and speak out. When you see something that is not right, you must say something. You must do something. Democracy is not a state. It is an act, and each generation must do its part to help build what we called the Beloved Community, a nation and world society at peace with itself.
>
> Ordinary people with extraordinary vision can redeem the soul of America by getting in what I call good trouble, necessary trouble. Voting and participating in the democratic process are key. The vote is the most powerful nonviolent change agent you have in a democratic society. . . .
>
> I urge you to answer the highest calling of your heart and stand up for what you truly believe. In my life I have done all I can to demonstrate that the way of peace, the way of love and nonviolence is the more excellent way. Now it is your turn to let freedom ring. So, I say to you, walk with the wind, brothers and sisters, and let the spirit of peace and the power of everlasting love be your guide.

Those who are not sure of where we go from here in bridging the racial divide in the Catholic Church can take strength from Mr. Lewis's uncompromising words, "We have made up our minds not to turn back!"

Have you ever visited Black slave cemeteries in the South? They are filled with historical treasures. When slaves died, their fellow slaves never used headstones as markers. Instead, following a remnant of an African custom, they covered graves with the clothes and household utensils used by the lamented slave on the last day of his or her life. Often a Bible opened to the deceased's favorite scriptural passage was placed in the topsoil. Wooden grave markers were sometimes used, but they soon deteriorated. Thus, when a stone marker is found it is almost certainly the result of the slaveowner's decision to violate social custom and erect a permanent memorial of special devotion to the slave.

In a slave cemetery in a small town in Georgia, there is a large stone marker that is eloquently inscribed with these words:

> This tablet is erected by her surviving master to the memory of Sarah, a most excellent coloured servant, who died in 1838. From the age of 11, at which she became the personal attendant of her mistress, Sarah was never known to tell a falsehood, to take the most trifling articles which did not belong to her or for a moment lose sight of her habitual good temper. Always cheerful, affectionate, intelligent and industrious, she was the very model of a faithful servant. She enjoyed, as she deserved, the respect, confidence and affection of each member of the family to which she was devoted. She lived and died as a good Catholic, and we, who grieve, commend her gentle soul to the care of the Saints.

We learn many things from this stone. Sarah had no last name, no family identity, because she was a slave. She is identified simply as the property of her master, but the singular qualities on her tomb were a tribute to her African ancestors. She was a Catholic, and so too, in all likelihood, were her owners. They obviously cared for her. Yet they saw no conflict between their Catholic faith and the possession of slaves. We must remind ourselves that in 1838 few Christian churches were outspoken against the slave trade or active in the abolitionist movement. Indeed, there were Christian apologists for slavery who argued that Providence had brought the Africans from their "pagan" homelands to a Christian country, and that the physical chains of slavery were of little consequence when compared with the spiritual chains of sin from which their Christian baptism had freed them.

By the late 1880s, two decades after the Emancipation Proclamation, the condition of Black Catholics and the attitude of the church toward them were changing slowly. Between 1889 and 1894, five Congresses of Colored Catholics were held, inspired by Daniel A. Rudd of Cincinnati, Ohio, editor of the *American Catholic Tribune*, a paper published by and for Black Catholics. It is interesting to note that the 1889 Washington, DC, congress passed a resolution expressing sympathy for the plight of the people of Ireland, "our brethren of the Emerald Isle, who, like ourselves, are struggling for justice." In an "Address to Their Catholic Fellow Citizens," Black Catholics complained that "the sacred rights of justice and humanity are still sadly wounded." They pleaded for Black schools and societies, as well as for help in eliminating discrimination by labor unions, employers, landlords, and real estate agents. Four years later, the 1893 Chicago, Illinois, congress issued a questionnaire on racial discrimination. They sent it to all bishops and they asked that their concerns be forwarded to the pope himself.

Archbishop John Ireland of St. Paul, Minnesota, was enthusiastic about these lay congresses, but Cardinal James Gibbons of Baltimore, Maryland, was cautious. In 1892 he wrote to Archbishop Ireland: "We will try to kill the congress or, failing that, determine that this should be the last congress."

Charles H. Butler spoke on behalf of the Colored Catholic Congress at the Catholic Congress of 1896, in Chicago. He warned fellow Catholics that "the Negro has been a conspicuous figure in our body politic, like the ghost in Macbeth." In Butler's view, the future depended on "whether the proud Anglo-Saxon intended to dispossess himself of mere race prejudice and accord his black brother simple justice." He rejected discrimination and segregation in the churches and in society. He concluded with this plea: "I appeal to you, first as American citizens, second as loyal sons of our Holy Mother the Church, to assist us to strike down that hybrid monster, color prejudice, which is unworthy of this glorious republic. We ask it not only for charity's sake, but as a right that has been dearly paid for."

Despite Catholic congresses and Daniel Rudd's newspaper, Black Catholics remained a small proportion of Catholics and of Blacks. There were about seven million Black Americans in 1883, and an estimated hundred thousand were Catholics. Most church leaders were not outspoken in their zeal for Black evangelization and racial justice. Archbishop Ireland, in 1891, insisted that efforts be made to "blot out the color lines." He advocated for equal political rights, equal education, and equal opportunity for employment. Further, the urban nature of American Catholicism minimized its contact with the greater part of the Black population, still predominantly rural. Only eighty-five years ago, in 1900, Black people were only a tiny 2 percent of New York City. In the South, Black Catholics studied in segregated schools and prayed in segregated churches, or found themselves relegated to church galleries. They received Communion after whites and confessed their sins in segregated confessionals. Some of these external sins of racism were missing in the North. But in many cases, Black Catholic life there was actually worse.

In 1906, W. E. B. Du Bois, a Harvard-educated Black activist and leader of the Niagara Movement, declared:

> Never before in the modern age has a great and civilized folk threatened to adopt so cowardly a creed in the treatment of its fellow citizens born and bread on its soil. Stripped of verbiage and subterfuge and in its naked nastiness, the new American creed says: Fear to let black men even try to rise lest they become the equals of the white. And this is the land that professes to follow Jesus Christ. The blasphemy of such a course is only matched by its cowardice.

Despite the eloquence and passion of Du Bois's words, very few Catholic voices were raised in his support.

During the 1920s and 1930s, Black candidates for the priest-hood and the religious life were generally not accepted into American seminaries and convents. It was not until the late 1950s that communities of religious women and diocesan seminaries began to welcome Black candidates. Those policies of the past partly explain why today we have fewer than three hundred Black priests and fewer than eight hundred Black sisters.

In the 1930s and 1940s, Black Catholics in New York City's Harlem were very active. In 1943, Msgr. William R. McCann, the pastor of St. Aloysius Church, who had baptized six thousand converts in twelve years, could boast: "Ten years ago the Catholic Church in Harlem was sneeringly referred to as the 'white man's church.' Today it needs no advertisement, and it is known as a potent instrument of good in our Negro community." The Catholic Interracial Council, Baroness De Hueck's Friendship House, and Dorothy Day's Catholic Worker contributed to improved relations between Black and white Catholics. Archbishop Francis J. Spellman arrived from Boston, Massachusetts, in 1939, and at the dedication of a new Harlem school announced: "There are no schools for Negroes. There are no schools for whites. There are only schools for all children. This is a Catholic school which any Catholic child who is qualified may enter." Official policy was clear, and considerable efforts were made to implement it. But the complex nature of New York City made that very difficult.

In 1947, Archbishop Joseph E. Ritter boldly desegregated the Catholic schools of St. Louis, Missouri. Archbishop Patrick A. O'Boyle did the same in the northern part of the Washington Archdiocese between 1948 and 1952. The southern part, in Maryland, had been heavily Catholic since 1634, but it proved more difficult. There, desegregation was not introduced until 1956. One mission church was closed when the parishioners refused to give financial support to an integrated church. In 1953, Bishop Vincent S. Waters wrote to the people of the Raleigh Diocese in North Carolina: "There is no segregation of races to be tolerated in any Catholic church. The Church does not propose tolerance, which is negative, but love, which is positive. If Christ said, 'Love your enemies,' we certainly can love our friends. These are our friends and members of our own body."

As late as 1959, however, five years after the 1954 landmark school-desegregation ruling of the Supreme Court, *Jubilee* magazine could state that only two parochial schools were integrated out of a possible 745 in the hard-core racist states of the deep South. Archbishop Joseph Rummel of New Orleans, Louisiana, rightly considered racism and segregation to be moral issues. Yet he was frustrated in his attempts to eliminate them from Catholic institutions. Resistance to integration was deeply rooted in Louisiana's history and culture. In 1962, with the help of his coadjutor, Bishop John P. Cody (the future Cardinal Archbishop of Chicago), he finally succeeded after excommunicating three Catholic laypersons who opposed him.

As the civil rights revolution gained momentum, the American hierarchy published a pastoral letter in 1958 titled *Discrimination and Christian Conscience*. It stressed that the heart of the race question in America was moral and religious.

A few years later, Pope John XXIII and Vatican II offered a new outlook to Catholic thinking: "The joys and hopes, the griefs and the anxieties of the people of this age, especially those who are poor or in any way afflicted, are the joys and hopes, the griefs and anxieties of the followers of Christ. Indeed, nothing genuinely human fails to raise an echo in their hearts." These opening words of *Gaudium et Spes*, the council's pastoral constitution on the church in the modern world, were not intended to be mere rhetoric. They were born of Pope John XXIII's unrelenting commitment to the defense of the dignity of every human person. The constitution continues, "The council lays stress on respect for the human person: All should look upon their neighbor, without any exception, as another self, bearing in mind above all that person's life and the means necessary for living it in a dignified way, lest they follow the example of the rich man who ignored Lazarus, the poor man." Pope John Paul II echoed these same words in New York in 1979.

The council challenged Catholics to read the signs of the times and apply the Gospel of Christ directly to their historical situations. This is precisely what the bishops of the United States did on November 14, 1979, when they published a pastoral letter on racism titled *Brothers and Sisters to Us*.

The first words of *Brothers and Sisters to Us* are:

> Racism is an evil which endures in our society and in our church. Despite apparent advances and even significant changes in the last two decades, the reality of racism remains. In large part it is only the external appearances which have changed. How great is the sin of racism which weakens the church's witness as the universal sign of unity among all peoples? How great the scandal given, by racist Catholics who would make the Body of Christ, the church, a sign of racial oppression! Yet all too often the church in our country has been for many a "white church," a racist institution.

The pastoral declares that all of us as Catholics must acknowledge a share in the mistakes and sins of the past. We have been prisoners of fear and prejudice. We have preached the Gospel while closing our eyes to the racism it condemns, and we have allowed social pressures to prevent us from seeking social justice.

The pastoral concludes with several important specific recommendations. Three of these must be recalled, since they have not been fully accomplished.

Concerning vocations and seminaries:

> Particular care should be taken to foster vocations among minority groups. Training for the priesthood, the permanent diaconate and religious life should not entail an abandonment of culture and traditions or a loss of racial identity, but should seek ways in which such culture and traditions might contribute to that training. Special attention is required whenever it is necessary to correct racist attitudes or behavior among seminary staff and seminarians. Seminary education ought to include an awareness of the history and the contributions of minorities as well as an appreciation of the enrichment of

the liturgical expression, especially at the local parish level, which can be found in their respective cultures.

Concerning leadership in the church:

We recommend that leadership training programs be established on the local level in order to encourage effective leadership among racial minorities on all levels of the church, local as well as national. We see the value of fostering greater diversity of racial and minority group representation in the hierarchy. Furthermore, we call for the adoption of an effective affirmative action program in every diocese and religious institution.

Concerning church investments and racism:

We ask in particular that Catholic institutions such as schools, universities, social service agencies and hospitals, where members of racial minorities are often employed in large numbers, review their policies to see that they faithfully conform to the church's teaching on justice for workers and respect for their rights. We recommend that investment portfolios be examined in order to determine whether racist institutions and policies are inadvertently being supported; and that, wherever possible, the capital of religious groups be made available for new forms of alternative investment, such as cooperatives, land trusts and housing for the poor. We further recommend that Catholic institutions avoid the services of agencies and industries that refuse to take affirmative action to achieve equal opportunity and that the church itself be a model as an equal opportunity employer.

Some may be surprised at how strong these recommendations are, and may ask: "What more can the church say? Where do we go from here?" There is no need to *say* more. The need is to *do* what we have said. Are there dioceses where this letter has never been published, studied, preached, or implemented? How many have never heard of it? I fear many Black and white Catholics cannot go forward until they go back to the council documents and to this landmark pastoral letter and ponder their teachings. More and more Americans are rightly expressing their moral outrage over South Africa's unwillingness to bring an end to apartheid, but we must examine the record of our own country, our own church, and our own hearts before we judge others.

On September 9, 1984, on the feast of St. Peter Claver, *What We Have Seen and Heard* was published by the ten Black Catholic bishops of the United States. This letter builds directly on Pope Paul VI's apostolic exhortation on evangelization, *Evangelii Nuntiandi* (December 18, 1975). The pope stated:

> Evangelization is a question not only of preaching the Gospel in ever wider geographic areas or to even greater numbers of people, but also of affecting and as it were upsetting, through the power of the Gospel, mankind's criteria of judgment, determining values, lines of thought, sources of inspiration and models of life, which are in contrast with the Word of God and the plan of salvation.

Later, in addressing the church of Africa, he said: "You are now missionaries to yourselves. You must now give your gifts of blackness to the whole church."

What We Have Seen and Heard applied these words to Black Americans.

> We believe that these solemn words of our Holy Father were addressed not only to Africans today, but also to us, the children of the Africans of yesterday. We believe that the Holy Father has laid a challenge before us to share the gift of our blackness with the church in the United States. This is a challenge to be evangelizers.

The letter stresses that Black Catholics are in a position to counter the assumption that to become a Catholic is to abandon one's racial heritage. The Black presence within the Catholic Church in America is a precious witness to the universal character of Catholicism.

In August 1985 Pope John Paul II took it upon himself to offer a formal apology to Black Americans for the tragedy of the slave trade. Speaking in Cameroon, he said: "Unfortunately, in the course of history men belonging to Christian nations did not always act as Christians. And now we ask our African brothers and sisters, who have suffered so much because of the slave trade, for forgiveness. The Christians of the past and the present are imperfect, and they make mistakes." With his words, the Holy Father has built a bridge that links the words on Sarah's tomb to those of *What We Have Seen and Heard.* While some may find it difficult to forgive, it is significant that the leader of the church has asked for forgiveness and has done so on African soil.

Where do we go from here? This, of course, is the most difficult question of all. It is clear that there is no single strategy for the future of Black Catholics. All of us must reflect on our particular pastoral situations and draw our own conclusions concerning what we must do to strengthen the ministry of the church in the Black community. I single out seven points.

1.　We must review and deepen the church's dedication to evangelization in the Black community. Particular attention should be given to creative implementation of the Rites of Christian Initiation for Adults. Prudent catechetical, homiletic, liturgical, musical, and artistic adaptations should be made for Black evangelization wherever they are appropriate and in keeping with the norms of the church. The media, which have such a dramatic impact on our youth, must be creatively brought into the service of evangelization. Serious attention should be given to new pastoral structures that might make the Catholic faith more attractive in the Black community. White people who minister in the Black community should have adequate training in Black culture, values, and religion in order to be effective evangelists. It is estimated that there are 1.2 million Black Catholics in America today, out of a total Black population of nearly 25 million. In the light of the millions of Black Americans who are unchurched, is there any reason why we cannot seek to double the number of Black Catholics by the year

2000? Let us be attentive to the incredible growth of Catholicism in our sister churches in Africa and learn from them.

2.   We Catholics must work with the other Black Christians and the larger Black community to confront the serious problems that plague the Black community. One of the most pressing problems is that of the growing number of pregnancies outside of marriage. Recent figures suggest that 57 percent of all the Black children born in America are born to unwed fathers and mothers. Black Americans are justifiably proud that we have not accepted the abortion mentality that accompanies so many unwanted pregnancies in this country. We are facing another crisis, however. Our young people must be effectively taught the importance of growing to maturity, obtaining an education, securing employment, and getting married *before* they begin their families. The pattern of three generations of unwed mothers in a single family may be the single greatest internal obstacle to the emotional and economic stability of the Black family in America. Perhaps we can learn from the Black Christians who, as slaves, named their daughters Sarah, Ruth, Rebecca, and Naomi, and named their sons Benjamin, Joshua, Jeremiah, and Micah. With these names, they taught their children to make their own the virtues associated with those biblical personages. The children took them as examples in their daily lives. Are there effective ways of exploring the story of St. Charles Lwanga and the Uganda Martyrs (who died rather than yield to sexual advances at the royal court) in order to convey the fundamental importance of sexual responsibility?

3.   We must not abandon our commitment to education. Catholic schools have traditionally distinguished themselves, not only by their academic programs, but by their dedication to helping young people develop authentic human, Christian values. Such value formation is essential in the urban communities where most Black Americans live. The American bishops made this commitment in *Brothers and Sisters to Us*:

> We urgently recommend the continuation and expansion of
> Catholic schools in the inner cities and other disadvantaged
> areas. It would be tragic if today, in the face of acute need

and even near despair, the church, for centuries the teacher
and the guardian of civilization, should withdraw from this
work in our own society. No sacrifice can be so great as to
warrant the lessening of our commitment to Catholic education in minority neighborhoods.

4.   We must develop a greater spirit of cooperation. While
there are legitimate differences among Black Catholics, these
must not lead to attitudes of competition. Black sisters, bishops,
laypeople, deacons, brothers, and priests must pool their resources
for the good of the larger Black community. We should be grateful
for one another's successes and come to one another's aid when
we fail. This is no time for jealousy. If a program is successful
in Oakland, California, and can be adapted to meet the needs of
Brooklyn, New York, then we should rejoice and use it there too.
I believe that there is an urgent need for us Black Catholics to put
aside our past grievances so that we can develop effective structures
of pastoral cooperation at the local, regional, and national levels.

5.   We must make sure that church documents that pertain to
Black Catholics are available to our people and those who serve
them. Many Black Catholics know nothing of the social encyc-
licals of recent popes, the documents of Vatican II, and *Brothers
and Sisters to Us*. Indeed, many have never read *What We Have Seen
and Heard*, though it is a year old. The final draft of the pastoral
letter on Catholic social teaching and the economy will obviously
have a particular significance for Black Americans, who are disproportionately poor. If these documents are to be effective, they
must be read, studied, discussed, and implemented by the widest
circles of people at every level of our parishes and dioceses, and
not simply by our Offices for Black Catholics.

6.   Black Catholics should play an increasingly important role
in calling the church to a deeper awareness of its catholicity. There
is a sense in which the church is never fully Catholic. At every
juncture in history and in every cultural embodiment, the church
is ever in search of catholicity. Think of the great differences in
liturgy, theology, and piety among the churches in Eastern and

Western Europe, Latin America, Asia, and Africa. The church does not lose its catholicity when it respects and builds on the culture and traditions of a people; it finds its catholicity and deepens it. Among our great and powerful hopes for the future are qualified and dedicated Black Catholics contributing to every phase of American life and serving at the highest levels of leadership in the church.

7.   Finally, and perhaps most important of all, Black Catholics in America must not lose sight of the spiritual vision. We have many practical and political goals in the area of social justice, education, and employment that we share with the larger Black community. But we must never forget that we have come this far by faith. Our central motivation and inspiration is the Gospel of Jesus Christ. Thus, a genuine commitment to prayer, meditation, the reading of the Scriptures, and the celebration of the sacraments, especially the Eucharist and reconciliation, is essential to ensure that our efforts on behalf of our people are not merely pragmatic programs of social change. Valuable as they may be, they are not enough for us as Catholic Christians.

These are some of the things we have seen and heard and some of those that we hope to see and hear. The task before us, like that before those who preceded us, is formidable. But no matter how great the obstacles, how discouraging the frustrations, or how bitter the disappointments, we dare not lose heart.

> Courage, Brothers and Sisters! The battle for humanity is not lost or losing. All across the skies sit signs of promise. The Slav is rising in his might, the yellow millions are tasting liberty, the black Africans are writhing toward the lights and everywhere the laborer, with ballot in his hand, is voting open the gates of opportunity and peace. The morning breaks over bloodstained hills. We must not falter, we may not shrink. Above are the everlasting stars.
> —W. E. B. Du Bois, "The Niagara Manifesto," 1906

9

Father Augustus Tolton (1854-1897)

A Saint for Our Time

MARCH 8, 2011

The last chapter of this book introduces readers to the story of the Servant of God, now the Venerable Father Augustus Tolton, a formerly enslaved free human being, who we hope and pray will soon be canonized by the Catholic Church. Though his was an extraordinary life of heroic virtue and Christian service, he is less well known to Catholics than the Venerable Archbishop Fulton Sheen, who also has ties to Illinois and whose canonization is being considered.

The canonization of Father Tolton would be a great moment of spiritual renewal for the church in the United States, a recognition of the deep faith of African American Catholics, and a challenge to those American Catholics who continue to think of the church as almost exclusively constituted of descendants of people of European origins. But knowing the details of Father Tolton's life of selfless service to the poor and his unwillingness to speak ill of those members of the church who made him feel completely unwelcome, I chose to use this final introduction as a reminder to my readers that each one of us, by virtue of our baptism, has a vocation to become a saint.

As a bishop I would often make pastoral visits to our Catholic elementary and secondary schools. During autumn I often asked the students if they knew the origins of the word "Halloween." Most of them said they did not. Once in a while one of them would ask, "Doesn't it have something to do with All

Hallow's Eve?" This would lead to a discussion of the evening before *All Hallow's Day* or *All Saints' Day* and the way the name gradually, through a complex history, became Halloween, the secular day when children dress up in frightful costumes, sometimes evoking the dead (*All Souls' Day*), but more likely colorful characters from popular movies and comics. Then they all go through their neighborhoods "trick or treating," seeking to fill their baskets with delicious things to eat.

When I asked the children if they knew any saints, they almost always said that you must die before you can become a saint. But, they often added, you cannot really become a saint until the pope himself makes you a saint. And he cannot do that until you "perform" at least two miracles. They are always surprised when I explain that when the Holy Father officially canonizes a saint, he is not "making them a saint." He is confirming the sanctity of the lives that they have already lived and declaring them to be worthy of public recognition and imitation. They are even more surprised when I tell them that, while miracles are affirmation of saintly lives, they are not essential for sainthood. The children are usually amazed to learn that there are millions of saints who have never been formally canonized by the church, including the Gospel writers. I tell them that some of their relatives and friends who have died may well be saints in the Kingdom of Heaven. I reminded them that the saints are not figures in a church window, statues on pedestals, or pictures on holy cards. They are real people like them, redeemed sinners who lived complex, challenging lives during which they tried each day to love God with their whole being and made a sincere effort to love everyone else in the world as much as they loved themselves.

I encourage the children, their parents, and teachers to strive to be keenly aware of saints in their midst and to strive to become saints themselves. Then I tell them the story of Father Tolton and ask them to pray for his canonization during their lifetime. Inevitably, one of them asks, "What will Father Tolton be the patron saint of, if he is canonized?" I tell them that the church decides this at the time of canonization. But I emphasize the truth that saints are spiritual role models. They are examples for each of us to imitate as disciples of Jesus Christ. They do not primarily do things for us. They, like Father Tolton, inspire us to do things for others. Ordinarily, St. Cecilia will not make us better singers, if we can't sing, St. Isidore will not make us better farmers, if we have no knowledge of farming, and St.

Sebastian will not make us champion athletes, if we have no natural ability and we do not practice. Nor will saints necessarily help us find lost objects, earn good grades in school, or sell our homes. Saints primarily inspire us to do things for others and for the world. The church is considering canonizing Father Tolton because throughout his seemingly obscure and very brief life he gave us an outstanding example of what it means to learn our faith, love our faith, and live our faith!

Father Tolton, who was declared Venerable (the title that precedes beatification in the process of canonization) in June 2020, would be a saint for our time because he lived and died, faithful to the Gospel of Jesus Christ, amid the turbulence of a complex and conflict-filled era, not unlike our own. Like St. Thomas More, the Venerable Augustus Tolton tried each day to say none harm, do none harm, and think none harm. He provides us with the towering example we all need to help us heal the racial divide in our country and in our church.

On Thursday, February 24, 2011, I returned to my home in the Archdiocese of Chicago to participate in a unique event. I returned to the magnificent Chapel of St. James with its splendid copies of the windows of La Sainte-Chapelle, built in Paris by Saint Louis IX, King of France, to house a relic of the Crown of Thorns. I prayed many times each day in this chapel as a high school student at Quigley Preparatory Seminary. The building, no longer a seminary, now houses the Archbishop Quigley Center, the Chancery of the Archdiocese of Chicago. The chapel remains unchanged, the jewel of the center. I returned to this spiritual center of my youth to participate in mid-afternoon prayer during which His Eminence, Francis Cardinal George, Archbishop of Chicago presided over the Proclamation and First Session of the Canonical Trial examining the life, virtues, and reputation of holiness of Father August Tolton. This was the first public step in the Cause of his Beatification and Canonization.

It was unique because he is the first priest of the Archdiocese of Chicago to be proposed for canonization. It is also unique because Fr. Tolton was the first priest of African descent born in the United States and ordained to serve the church here. His canonization would be a milestone in the Catholic history of this country. Fr. Tolton's canonization would have a special significance for the Diocese of Belleville because he was ordained a priest of the Diocese of Alton, Illinois, a now suppressed diocese which once embraced the territory of the Diocese of Belleville.

The Proclamation and First Session consisted in part of a series of oaths and the formal signing of official documents by Cardinal George; Bishop Joseph N. Perry, auxiliary bishop of Chicago and Diocesan Postulator of the Cause; and members of historical and theological commissions. It was an impressive event which has rarely taken place in the United States. In attendance were descendants of Fr. Tolton's family members. With the formal opening of his Cause, Fr. Tolton receives the title "Servant of God." Once it has been established that his life was "Heroic in Virtue," the Holy See will give him the title "Venerable." Further study and investigation must follow before the church bestows the titles "Beatus" and "Sanctus" (Blessed and Saint). Ordinarily, these titles are not bestowed until there are signs of divine favor, a miracle indicating the power of Fr. Tolton's prayers of intercession. I invite you to save the prayer at the end of this article and pray it often. If you should receive what you believe to be a miraculous response to your prayer, you should document the event and report it to the office of Bishop Perry in the Archdiocese of Chicago. The summary of Fr. Tolton's life that follows is derived from the writings of the Most Reverend Joseph N. Perry, diocesan postulator for the Cause.

During Lent, which begins on Ash Wednesday, March 9, 2011, we are all called to go into the desert with the Lord Jesus Christ, to purify our hearts with prayer, fasting, almsgiving, and acts of repentance, and accompany our catechumens on their journey up to Jerusalem for the Easter Vigil Sacraments of Baptism, Confirmation, and Eucharist. By these sacraments new members are initiated into the Christian mysteries and into the Catholic Church. By this initiation we are all called to follow the path of "heroic virtue," the path to the holiness of life, the path to sainthood. As you ponder Fr. Tolton's life, which may be unknown to you and quite unlike your own, recall that his life of faith was fed by the same Word of God, the same Body and Blood of Christ as yours. His life was conformed to the image of Christ, the Suffering Servant. May his life, like that of Marie-Françoise-Thérèse Martin (Saint Thérèse of Lisieux, the Little Flower) teach us that the road to sanctity is marked by doing ordinary things in an extraordinary way out of love for God.

The Early Years

He was a man beset on all sides by racism and its tragic consequences. Yet, he dared to believe that no door can be kept closed against the movement of the Lord and the power of the Spirit.
—Fr. Eugene Kole, OFM, president of Quincy University, during the Centennial Observance of Fr. Tolton's death, July 12–13, 1997

Father Augustus Tolton (1854–1897) lived his brief life of forty-three years during a particularly troubled period in American history. This was the period of the Middle Passage when cargo ships from Europe made their way to west Africa and enslaved human beings, transporting them across the Atlantic Ocean in chains and stacked on top of one another by the thousands and "selling" them to plantation owners. The ships returned to Europe filled with tobacco and cotton cultivated by slave labor. Augustus was born a slave of slave parents who were all baptized Catholics by arrangement of the Catholic families who "owned" them and sadly did not see the contradiction between their faith in Christ the Liberator and their presuming to "buy and sell" other human beings. His father, Peter Tolton, left to fight for freedom with Union troops at the start of the Civil War. Much later it was discovered that he died in a hospital in St. Louis. Peter's wife, Martha Jane Tolton, having accomplished a harrowing escape from those who "owned" her and her children, found refuge in Quincy, Illinois, a station of the Underground Railroad that assisted escaping slaves reach freedom. There in Quincy, she raised her children, seeking out Catholic schools for them. Augustus's boyhood and youth had as a backdrop the period of Reconstruction and the nation's ambivalence about the plight of freed People of Color.

While a new government struggled to gain control, the subjugation of free African American men and women continued in the former Confederate states. They suffered at the hands of racist groups such as the Ku Klux Klan. Racial inequality and segregation were taken for granted even by the Catholic Church.

As a young boy, Augustus worked long hours in a tobacco factory. Several local priests and sisters took Tolton under their wing to tutor him in the catechism, languages, including Latin, and the necessary academic subjects that won him entry into Quincy College, which was conducted by the Franciscan Fathers.

He was mature for his age and he showed signs of a vocation to the priesthood. But it proved difficult finding a seminary in the United States that would take a Black student. After years of searching and petitioning only to receive letters of denial or no response at all, the Franciscan Fathers were able to prevail upon their Superior General in Rome to make contact with the cardinal in charge of the Propaganda Fide. Augustus Tolton was accepted and entered the college of the Propaganda and studied philosophy and theology for six years with seminarians from mission countries. He was ordained to the priesthood on April 24, 1886, at the Basilica of St. John Lateran, the cathedral church of the pope as Bishop of Rome.

The Priesthood

Fearing that Fr. Tolton's priesthood would be filled with suffering given the prevailing racial prejudice in the United States, his superiors thought he would serve as a missionary priest in Africa. However, his mentor, Giovanni Cardinal Simeoni, challenged the church in the United States to accept Fr. Tolton as its first African American priest. "America has been called the most enlightened nation in the world. We shall see if it deserves that honor." Father Tolton returned to his home Diocese of Alton, Illinois, which once embraced the Dioceses of Springfield and Belleville. After his First Mass in Quincy, he was assigned to St. Joseph Church, the "Negro Parish."

Many local priests counseled their parishioners to stay away from St. Joseph Church. When white parishioners went to Fr. Tolton's parish to receive sacraments and counsel from him, a neighboring Catholic pastor and dean of the area ordered him, in no uncertain terms, to restrict himself to serving the People of Color. He also complained several times to the local bishop, demanding that white parishioners be ordered to stay away from Fr. Tolton's parish. Many white people stopped attending the church while others remained steadfast in their support of Fr. Tolton and the Negro apostolate.

In the midst of this ferment, Fr. Tolton suffered under increasing isolation and feelings of apprehension, perpetrated by local clergy with whom he needed association, to say nothing of the town's lay Catholics. He became well known around the country as the first visible Black Catholic priest, renowned for his preaching and public speaking abilities and his sensitive ministry to everyone. He was often asked to speak at conventions and other gatherings of Catholics of both races.

At that time, a fledgling African American Catholic community needed organization in Chicago. Archbishop Patrick Feehan, aware of Fr. Tolton's painful experiences in the Alton Diocese, received him in Chicago in 1889. His bishop did not hesitate to give permission for the transfer, accusing the priest of creating an unacceptable situation by inviting fraternization between the races.

Fr. Tolton opened a storefront church in Chicago and later built a church for the growing African American Catholic community on the South Side at 36th and Dearborn, managing to complete the lower level where the community worshipped for some time while he raised funds for the church's completion. Katharine Drexel (now Saint Katharine), foundress of the Sisters of the Blessed Sacrament (for African American women excluded from other orders), contributed to the building of the church.

Fr. Tolton became renowned for attending to the needs of his people with tireless zeal and a holy joy. He was a familiar figure in the littered streets and dingy alleys, in the Negro shacks and tenement houses. Father Tolton had the pastoral sensitivity needed to bring hope and comfort to the sick and the dying, to bestow spiritual and material assistance, and to mitigate the suffering and sorrow of an oppressed people.

His biographers write that Fr. Tolton worked himself to exhaustion while dealing with the internalized stress that came with navigating the rough, cold waters of racial rejection. Like most poor People of Color, Fr. Tolton lacked adequate health care. The first week of July 1897, an unusual heat wave hit Chicago, during which a number of people died. Father Tolton suffered a heatstroke under the daily scourge of 105-degree heat and collapsed on the street. Doctors at Mercy Hospital worked frantically for four hours to save his life. But like St. Paul, Augustus had run the race, kept the faith, and fought the fight. He died at 8:30 in the evening of July 9, with his mother, his sister, a priest, and several nuns at his bedside. Funeral Masses were celebrated for him in Chicago and in Quincy, where he wanted to be buried. Large crowds of priests and laity participated, singing his favorite hymn, "Te Deum" ("Holy God We Praise Thy Name").

His Legacy of Faith and Service

In death as in life the community has held to the memory of Fr. Tolton's life of holiness and selfless service of others. His memory looms large for his genteelness, his indiscriminate pastoral care given to all people: Black and white, Catholics, those of other faiths, and those of no faith at all. Stories have been handed down about his exhausting ministry in the poorest neighborhoods of Chicago. He walked the streets and visited the tenement houses surrounding his parish, devoting himself to the desperate poor.

Despite his own sufferings, Father Tolton remained steadfast in his priesthood, faithful and serene. Despite the vile things said to him by racists in the community, he never dished back the prejudice that was thrown in his face. He returned no criticism, no resentment, and no unkind words to those who rejected and belittled him because of the color of his skin. He bore on his shoulders and in his heart a unique burden as the first and only African American priest in our nation. The Suffering-Servant Song of the prophet Isaiah must have had a special meaning for him.

Believing with all of his heart that the Catholic Church was the true church of Jesus Christ, Fr. Tolton was convinced that, despite rejection, the Gospel of Christ lived authentically could play a central role in the liberation and advancement of those whose ancestors had been brought to these shores in chains in direct violation of the Gospel imperative, "Love your neighbor as you love yourself." His correspondence with Saint Katharine Drexel and others brings to light a humble and devout man of remarkable faith. He proved an example of a true priest of Jesus Christ in an extraordinary time, when most Americans could not imagine that a son of Africa could make a significant contribution to society or to the church, not even one ordained and dedicated as *sacerdos in aeternum*. In a June 5, 1891, letter to Mother Katharine Drexel he wrote, "I shall work and pull at it as long as God gives me life, for I am beginning to see that I have powers and principalities to resist anywhere and everywhere I go."

Father Theodore Warning, a priest of the Archdiocese of Dubuque, spoke of living with Father Tolton and his mother in 1896 while he attended a summer session at the University of Chicago. He stopped at St. Monica's to seek a place to stay because it was close to the campus of the university. Father Warning wrote:

> They lived in a poorly furnished but very clean house. The meals were simple affairs. Father Tolton, his mother and I sat at a table having an oil cloth cover. A kerosene lamp stood in the middle. On the wall directly behind Father Tolton's place hung a large black rosary. As soon as the evening meal was over, Father Tolton would rise and take the beads from the nail. He kissed the large crucifix reverently. We all knelt on

the bare floor while the Negro priest, in a low voice, led the prayers with deliberate slowness and unmistakable fervor.

Several educational and ministerial ventures across the country carry Tolton's name. We have the Augustus Tolton Ministry Program at the Catholic Theological Union here in Chicago. Most recently, a high school has been named after him in the Diocese of Jefferson City, Missouri, the location of the farm at which the Toltons labored and from which they escaped the evil, sinful scourge of human slavery.

It is not unusual for African American Catholic parishes across the country to have a portrait of Fr. Tolton displayed. Most recently a scholarship program has been set up for elementary and high school students attending schools in the Archdiocese of Chicago.

People visit Fr. Tolton's grave in Quincy, Illinois, frequently as individuals and as groups of pilgrims. Fr. Tolton remains an uplifting sign of hope and promise not only for African American Catholics but also for all Catholics striving to live by the Good News, which brings salvation to all people. His love for the Catholic faith, his total commitment to the priesthood, his long suffering, and personal cheerfulness in face of oppression offer a true inspiration for religious brothers and sisters, seminarians, deacons, priests, and the Christian faithful in our time. Fr. Tolton's dream of a society in which the human dignity of all is respected remains "a dream deferred."

The life story of Fr. Tolton carries significance for the church in the United States. We have no recognized saints who survived the periods of slavery, Reconstruction, and the civil rights era in the United States. If this cause reaches positive outcomes, it would be a credit to the many people, Black and white, who suffered and died or were murdered for the cause of racial justice as well as a tribute to the church's prophetic witness displayed in those historical periods.

Fr. Tolton's life is a triumph of perseverance and faith. He is a model of enormous courage and dedication to the church, priestly zeal and fidelity in the face of the social hostilities endemic to that time. Society and the church threw "no's" at him consistently. We trust that the church will not say "no" this time when the church can benefit from reflection upon his suffering path. He is a model of holiness for anyone who wants to serve God and find grace through the suffering experiences of life. He is a model for priests and the sufferings priests are asked to bear in order to serve faithfully.

As an American born and raised up for heroically living the Christian life, Fr. Tolton is of our culture, and he battled to make American society authentically Christ-centered. Every one of us can participate and many others have participated in this battle with him. His story reminds us that the United States is a work in progress: White people participated in the Underground Railroad's rescue of fellow human beings who escaped from bondage. The Underground Railroad authenticated the radical human dignity of those who had been unjustly enslaved and revealed the radical human dignity of those rescuing their sisters and brothers. Priests of the church and men and women religious took Augustus Tolton by the hand and walked with him through the dark forest of the sin and heresy of racial prejudice. In doing so they revealed the face of Christ.

Prayer for the Canonization of Father Augustus Tolton

O God, we give you thanks for your servant and priest, Father Augustus Tolton, who labored among us in times of contradiction, times that were both beautiful and paradoxical. His ministry helped lay the foundation for a truly Catholic gathering in faith in our time. We stand in the shadow of his ministry. May his life continue to inspire us and imbue us with that confidence and hope that will forge a new evangelization for the church we love.

Father in Heaven, Father Tolton's suffering service sheds light upon our sorrows; we see them through the prism of your Son's passion and death. If it be your Will, O God, glorify your servant, Father Tolton, by granting the favor I now request through his intercession so that all may know the goodness of this priest whose memory looms large in the Church he loved.

Complete what you have begun in us that we might work for the fulfillment of your kingdom. Not to us the glory, but glory to you O God, through Jesus Christ, your Son and our Lord; Father, Son and Holy Spirit, you are our God, living and reigning forever and ever. Amen.

Acknowledgments

For some writers, the process of writing seems rather effortless. For others, it can be a slow and even painful process. For still others, the written text only emerges under the influence of what Ernest Hemingway called "grace under pressure." I began this book reluctantly five years ago when I had no thought that what I was writing "under pressure" would become part of a book. I wrote the first words, my 'early jottings,' on August 9, 2014, the day Michael Brown Jr. was shot and killed by a police officer in Ferguson, Missouri. I was very familiar with the neighborhood where Michael died from my years of service as Auxiliary Bishop of St. Louis. After watching the painful news coverage of this horrendous event, I made this notation in my journal. "The racial divide in this country is becoming more and more acute. Is there anything I can do or say that can contribute to bridging this tragic and dangerous divide?"

Therefore, I must begin by acknowledging that Michael Brown Jr.'s brief life and sad death were the initial catalyst for the writings that eventually became this book. Over the next five years I wrote several pastoral letters, reflections, homilies, and lectures that addressed different aspects of the racial divide. Though writing is ultimately a solitary process, the finished work is made better by many people who contribute in different ways to the writing process. I wish to acknowledge some of those contributors here. I have a group of friends (former seminary classmates, former students, former parishioners, and others whom I affectionately call "the Usual Suspects") to whom I regularly send drafts of my writings for their comments and constructive criticisms. I wish to mention some of them by name. Dr. Edward J. Mahoney, professor of Theology, St. Michael's College in Winooski Vermont; Mr. Julian C. D'Esposito, an attorney from Chicago; Dr. Chester L. Gillis, a professor of theology at Georgetown University; Dr. Geert Van Cleemput of Antwerp, Belgium, and former professor of philosophy at George Washington University; Dr Michael P. Ward, a psychologist from Los Angeles; Mr. Ross Kolby, an artist from Norway; Mr. Michael Schaeffer, a member of the Faculty of Theology at Gibault Catholic High School; Mr. Jonathan Bickham, an attorney from Houston; Mr. John Schwaig, a glass artist from St. Louis; Rev. Allen F. Corrigan, a priest of the Diocese of Cleveland; and Mr. and Mrs. Paul (Gail) L. Whiting Sr., lifelong friends from Tampa Florida all made helpful suggestions and raised hard questions that helped me to clarify my developing thoughts on difficult issues.

Mrs. Judy Hoffmann, my Administrative Assistant, typed and retyped the manuscript. Mr. Morris LeBleu, the Director of Communications of the Diocese of Lake Charles, Louisiana; Mrs. Sue Huett, Director of the Office of Worship, Diocese of Belleville; and Msgr. John T. Myler, S.T.D., Rector of the Cathedral of St. Peter, Diocese of Belleville generously read and reread drafts eliminating errors with their attentive eyes. My efforts benefitted from my frequent conversations about the issues addressed in this book with Mrs. Karen Siddall, who takes care of the Bishop's Residence. Her unique perspective as a Catholic wife, mother, and grandmother grounded my thinking. My sister, Patricia Braxton Wills, who has lived her entire life on the cutting edge of the racial divide, brought her valuable point of view to our discussion of the chapters.

I tested and refined parts of a number of chapters in the form of lectures at Georgetown University, the Catholic University of America, the University of Notre Dame, St. Louis University, John Carroll University, Purdue University, the Catholic Theological Union at the University of Chicago, Seattle University, DePaul University, and the Chautauqua Institution in New York. The penetrating questions from these audiences forced me to rethink some aspects of my exploration of the racial divide.

I led in-depth conversations on my pastoral letters "The Catholic Church and The Racial Divide in the United States," and "The Catholic Church and the Black Lives Matter Movement," and my essays "There Are No Minority Americans," "The Horizon of Possibilities: Old Wounds Revisited," and Rev. Dr. Martin Luther King Jr. with the students and faculties of Althoff Catholic High School, Gibault Catholic High School, and Mater Dei Catholic High School, with the members of "The Wisdom Community" (a group of Priests serving in the Diocese of Belleville), and the Permanent Deacons of the Diocese and their wives. Because of their different backgrounds and the different ways of seeing and understanding the racial divide, the participants in these dialogues raised pointed and challenging questions requiring refinements and clarifications in my thinking.

A crucial example of this is the fact that I do not use the word "racism" in the way some authors do. I distinguish bias, rash judgment, stereotype, and prejudice from racism. I am not inclined to agree with those who argue that "it's all racism." If that is true, almost everyone might be called a racist. My intense conversations with groups like those mentioned above, led me to express my perspective in this way: "Many people go about their daily lives with a degree of awareness that they harbor biases, prejudice, and stereotypes in their hearts about certain groups of people. They may even acknowledge that these attitudes are wrong and constitute a genuine moral flaw. But just as they never do anything to uproot these wrongful attitudes from their hearts, they never do or say anything that directly harms members of these groups. This moral flaw becomes racism, which is a moral evil and a grave sin, when someone allows these attitudes to lead them to think they are objectively superior to all members of the group in question. This denial of universal human dignity and worth can easily lead to the assumption of white privilege and the affirmation of white supremacy. This, in turn, may lead to a willingness and even a desire to harm (e.g., ostracize, oppress, enslave, or even kill!) those who are judged to be inferior and lack the right to "life, liberty, and the pursuit of happiness."

I appreciate those who insisted that I provide greater clarity to the nuances of my thoughts, which has caused me to use the word "racism" more guardedly and less frequently than others. This approach in no way blinds me to the widespread systemic and institutional racism in American society.

In a special way I wish to acknowledge Mr. Robert Ellsberg, my editor at Orbis Books. This book might not have been brought to completion without his encouragement and support. He nudged me to persevere in my writing and bring the work to completion when I was preoccupied by other matters and when writing was more difficult than usual. He has the unique ability to see when I was too close to the text making it difficult for me to be objective about various passages. Without Robert, this work might never have been finished.

I must acknowledge the life changing influence of Mr. Richard F. Morrisroe, a city planner from East Chicago, Indiana. When he was a young priest from Chicago, he was nearly killed by a shotgun blast to his back by an ardent segregationist on August 20, 1965, in Lowndes County, Alabama. He and Episcopal seminarian, Jonathan Daniels (who was slain in the attack) were in Alabama working to register African Americans to vote. Richard's selfless gospel witness, his guileless concern for the Black community, and his affection for me have shaped my life, my ministry, and my writings at the deepest level.

Finally, I must acknowledge remarkable priests from the Archdiocese of Chicago whose lives and ministry were dedicated to bridging the racial divide. They are Rev. Rollins Lambert, Rev. George Clements, Rev. Daniel Mallette, and Archbishop James P. Lyke, OFM. Though their lives in this world have ended, their powerful example and friendship helped to make me who I am.

When I was concentrating on writing this work, I felt as if I were on an island by myself, even though I was deeply engaged in my ministry as Bishop and Pastor of the Local Church of Belleville. Feelings of isolation, loneliness, and frustration are often part of the writing process. Happily, there are certain individuals, the dearest of the dear in my life (and they know who they are), who were always at hand to refocus my attention, to lift my spirits, and renew me with their love. Because of them, discouraging storm clouds notwithstanding, my island of solitude, was an island in the sun. I thank them from my heart!

Deo gratias!

About the Author

The Most Reverend Edward K. Braston, Ph. D., S.T. D., has become nationally and internationally known as a leading voice in the Catholic Church on the racial divide in the United States and in the Church. His pastoral letters and other writings on this subject have led to invitations to lecture at the University of Notre Dame, St. Louis University, The Catholic University of America, John Carroll University, Georgetown University, Seattle University, Purdue University, the Catholic Theological Union, Northwestern University, and at many national conferences addressing the racial divide. At the invitation of Peter Cardinal Turkson, Prefect of the Vatican Congregation for the Promotion of Integral Human Development, the Bishop participated in the Vatican's international conference marking the 50th anniversary of Pope Paul VI's encyclical *Populorum Progressio* (On the Development of Peoples) in April 2017.

A former member of the faculties of theology at Harvard Divinity School, the University of Notre Dame, the Catholic University of America, and Scholar in Residence at the North American College in Rome, the Bishop served for many years as the personal theologian to James Cardinal Hickey in the Archdiocese of Washington and as the Official Theological Consultant to William H. Sadlier, Inc., a leading Catholic publisher in the field of religious education.

He earned his doctorate in theology from the Catholic University of Louvain in Belgium and he is the author of *The Wisdom Community* and *The Faith Community* as well as many articles on Systematic and Pastoral theology. He has served as Auxiliary

Bishop of the Archdiocese of St. Louis, the Bishop of Lake Charles, Louisiana. After fifteen years of service as Bishop of the Diocese of Belleville, Illinois, he became Bishop Emeritus in July 2020.

Index